CHURCHES AND POLITICS IN LATIN AMERICA

SAGE FOCUS EDITIONS

Churches
and Politics
in Latin America

Edited by
Daniel H. Levine
Preface by JOHN P. HARRISON

 SAGE Publications   Beverly Hills   London

For information address:

SAGE Publications, Inc.
275 South Beverly Drive
Beverly Hills, California 90212

SAGE Publications Ltd
28 Banner Street
London EC1Y 8QE, England

Printed in the United States of America

Library of Congress Cataloging in Publication Data
Main entry under title:

Churches and politics in Latin America.

  (Sage focus editions ; 14)
  Bibliography: p.
  1. Church and state in Latin America—Addresses, essays, lectures. 2. Christianity and politics—Addresses, essays, lectures. 3. Latin America-Politics and government—Addresses, essays, lectures. 4. Catholic Church in Latin America—History—Addresses, essays, lectures. 5. Latin America—Church history—Addresses, essays, lectures. I. Levine, Daniel H. II. Series.
BR600.C46   322'.1'098   79-23827

ISBN 0-8039-1298-6
ISBN 0-8039-1299-4 pbk.

FIRST PRINTING

CONTENTS

PREFACE

The religious as a professional group have done more than any other sector of society in the past two decades to publicize the disparities of wealth in Latin America and what this means for the people who live there. In this most Catholic of the major world areas, groups within the Church have actively engaged in politicizing the mass of the previously inert and disorganized poor and in so doing have either consciously or inadvertently challenged the dominant social structure which the Church traditionally has championed as the binding element needed for the political stability in which the institutional Church best functioned. This challenge to the existing social order by "career religious"— Evangelical Protestants as well as Catholics—is peculiar to Latin America in the scale of action and in the degree of intensity and explicitness of expression. It has resulted in a continuing dialogue—and in some instances working political alliances—between heretofore conflicting ideologies. It has even given birth to a regional theology for a regional Church. Not all of this has been integrated institutionally, as has been made abundantly clear in the areawide meetings of the hierarchy. The political implications of this process of socialization at the "grass-roots" level has brought the Church into conflict with existing governments, particularly those under military control, where the doctrine of national security not only has emasculated human rights, including those of nuns and priests, but has even threatened the integrity of the institutional Church.

It is this significant new social orientation of the interrelationship of religion and politics in Latin America that is examined with authority and detail in this volume of essays. They place the participation of the Catholic Church and, to a lesser extent, the Evangelical Protestant sects, in the context of both religious and political responses to the ferment that permeates present-day Latin American society. The introductory essay by the editor, Daniel Levine, together with his brief statements prefacing the three sections into which the articles are organized, provides the conceptual structure within which the individual contributions fit and supplement each other. In their totality the articles provide an analysis of the extensive evangelizing and new social role of religion among the "Pilgrim People of God" as they exist within the context of the contemporary matrix of life in Latin America.

The new social and pastoral programs have precipitated serious conflict between Church and national governments, within local formal and informal power structures, and within the respective churches. The extent that the announced identification of the Catholic Church with the plight of the poor extends to the promotion of structural changes in society, as they may be required for effective observance of human rights in their social as well as individual sense, is both a delicate and fundamental question fervently debated by the bishops at Puebla, with no firm line of action being agreed upon. (The intricacies of the political and intellectual maneuvering that accompanied these discussions is given here a structured presentation imbued with moral fervor.)

A basic assumption of this book is that the interaction of politics and religion is a natural condition and yet is not necessarily a situation where religion has to be supportive of the status quo. The extent to which the present intensive pastoral activity of the religious community among the urban and rural poor, described and analyzed in this book, is a new and in certain respects revolutionary situation requiring a unique accommodation by both the Church and the national governments can, perhaps, be most dramatically indicated in historical terms. Not since the Christianizing efforts carried out by missionaries in cooperation with the Spanish Crown during the early sixteenth century have the religious directed their efforts to so massive a target population. Today, as in the sixteenth century, the pastoral effort is essentially being carried out by the regular clergy, while the translation of this effort into political action by the state once again seems ultimately to revert to the institutionally organized secular hierarchy with its closer ties to the decision-making mechanisms of the political process.

The sense of dissatisfaction with which the more vocal—and perhaps more informed—sectors of Latin American society have viewed their relative position in the world economy has given rise, since the end of World War II, to the creation of a number of regionwide organizations that have attempted to improve the conditions within the several nation-states through an analysis of shared conditions in what may be viewed as an ongoing endemic crisis. The existence of these organizations has given Latin America, if not coherence, a much greater internal sense of self-identification as a distinctive major world area than existed heretofore. All these regional organizations make this identification explicit by including "Latin America" in their formal institutional name. This is a phenomenon of the past three decades and is in itself an indication of the profound nature of the process of change that continues to evolve.

An important product of these recently created organizations is the fact that their membership is acutely aware of what is taking place domestically within every nation in the region. They are scarcely reluctant about sharing their knowledge, not only with their fellow professionals or their home governments but with the world at large, whenever they believe the socioeconomic goals they see may be served by such publicity.

Covert actions do not today remain covert for long in Latin America, in large part as a result of the communications network these regional organizations have created. It is also notable that the combination of intellects involved in these group activities has resulted in two major theoretical or ideological products that have had a worldwide resonance if not acceptance: dependency theory resulting from the confluence of economics and sociology at CEPAL (the Economic Community for Latin America); and liberation theology that gestated during the preparations for the second meeting of CELAM (the Latin American Council of Bishops) in Medellín, Colombia, in 1968, where the presence of Pope Paul VI made the sessions an auspicious launching platform for this activist-oriented theology.

There is a direct relationship between liberation theology—the position held by those religious most fundamentally opposed to the socioeconomic status quo—and dependency theory that is inherent to but not specifically dealt with in the discussions in this book. The conditions resulting from the extreme maldistribution of wealth in Latin America were readily apparent to the religious in their expanded pastoral programs. In seeking an explanation as to how this, for them, manifestly unjust social structure came into being and continued to function, they drew upon dependency theory, where the cause was found to be the expansion of liberal capitalism into Latin America in the form of multinational corporations which, in turn, allied themselves with the merchant-landowning, dominant sector of domestic society whose members monopolized the residual benefits.

The above statement may be a caricature of the several strands of dependency theory, but in its simplicity it closely resembles the basic socioeconomic message that enters into the nonreligious instructional aspects of the ongoing dialogue in the intimate ambience of the *Comunidades Eclesiales de Base* (CEBs), the extent and purpose of which are fully examined in an essay focused on Brazil and are an integral consideration in several other articles. The acceptance of this explanation of conditions that are depressingly observable to the religious activists is what has brought most of them to the acceptance of many precepts of Marxist thought, prominent among which is total opposition to "imperialist capitalism."

A central problem for the socially activist, radicalized clergy, or liberation theologians—all of which are classifications used for the more socially conscious religious in the chapters that follow—is their general unfamiliarity with economic thought and, indeed, the processes through which dependency theory has moved in its attempt to design a frame of reference best suited for the complicated decision-making process needed for the improvement of the Latin American economy, including a more equitable distribution of income. No means of testing the economic implications of socially oriented decisions are available to them. The economic bases for social policy are accepted on faith rather than understanding. In this lack of comprehension of economic policy decisions, the activists are scarcely distinguishable from the more conservative members of the hierarchy.

The situation, then, is that a considerable mass of the population is being politicized by more privileged members of society, who are sympathetic to improving their economic lot without providing them with an observable self-generating mechanism for transferring into political realization their natural desires for a better life economically and a concomitant fuller spiritual existence. If one recent development in the Latin American churches can be singled out as being the most significant, these essays seem to indicate that it is the growth of the CEBs. To paraphrase Bruneau, one wonders if they have a sufficient internal dynamism for the expression of their members' sociopolitical welfare after the existing dimensions of repression become less pressing. One may also question the extent that the economic and social claims of the CEBs will be supported by the hierarchy when the oppression of national security and other forms of authoritarianism makes it impossible for the institutional Church to operate with its traditional autonomy in the spiritual realm.

This book provides any interested and thoughtful reader with a good basis for making his or her own projection as to the probabilities of what can be expected from the new directions in the Catholic Church and the Evangelical Protestant Churches upon the political activities of the faithful and institutions in which they worship. As the various ranges of the Andean cordillera unite occasionally in a single massif before again spreading out in separate strands, this book provides the same binding function for the interaction of religion and politics in Latin America at a time immediately subsequent to the 1979 CELAM meetings in Puebla and that of the more disparate Protestant sects, also in Mexico, the previous year. To this extent is is also a landmark.

—John P. Harrison

ACKNOWLEDGMENTS

Many institutions and individuals helped make this book possible. A number of the articles published here first appeared in a special issue of the *Journal of Interamerican Studies and World Affairs*. I am deeply indebted to John P. Harrison, Editor, for his sustained encouragement, enthusiasm, and backing. I also want to thank Gerry Machovec, Editorial Assistant, for her skill, efficiency, and great good humor. Several of the articles in this volume (along with other papers) were presented and discussed at a Workshop on Religion and Politics in Latin America sponsored by the Latin American Program of the Woodrow Wilson International Center for Scholars of the Smithsonian Institution. I am grateful to Abraham Lowenthal and Alexander Wilde for making so stimulating and memorable a get-together possible. Penetrating commentary and friendly, useful criticisms have been offered along the way by (among others) Hugo Assmann, Douglas Chalmers, Harvey Cox, Ralph Della Cava, Cornelia Flora, Paolo Krischke, Renato Poblete, Paul Sigmund, Alexander Wilde, and William Wipfler. Finally, I want to thank the authors themselves for their insight, patience, commitment, and good humor.

—D.H.L.

Part I

BACKGROUND AND GENERAL ISSUES

Introduction

Over the past several decades, Latin American churches have moved from being unquestioned allies of the established order to positions which increasingly bring them into conflict with the powers that be in the economy, society, and politics of many nations in the region. These have been years of intense self-examination, conflict, and innovation for Latin American Christians, and the chapters in this book provide an opportunity to assess the sources and nature of the transformations under way, the current state of affairs in key areas, and the likely future relations of religion and politics in the region.

Given the historical and contemporary predominance of Catholicism in Latin America, it is appropriate to begin any discussion of religion and politics in the area with a few words on the Roman Catholic Church. The accumulated drives for change and reorientation which burst to the surface at the Second General Conference of Latin American Bishops, held in Medellín, Colombia, in 1968, have since found expression in the development of new theologies, new organizational structures, new religious and social practices, and a heightened sensitivity to social and political problems. As Catholics of different orientations have gradually worked out the implications of Medellín in their individual and institutional lives, they have been increasingly drawn into the political arena. Both "push" and "pull" factors are important in this process, for as the chapters presented here demonstrate, the dynamic relations between religion and politics in Latin America today are founded on notable factors of change in each. The sense of commitment and activism felt by many Catholics thus has its roots both in a transformed notion of the requirements of an authentic religious faith and in the pressures of the restrictive political environments so characteristic of Latin America today which often make even the most innocent act a matter of "national security" and a target of repression—and, hence, political.

Speaking of "conflict" in the churches, then, it is important to direct attention both to disputes within the ecclesiastical institution and to clashes involving the churches and their members with political authority. Both kinds of conflicts are salient in Latin America today. Thus, the tensions and conflicts between church and state so visible in nations like El Salvador, Chile, or Brazil are the result not only of changes in religion, but also of transformations in society and politics. As military-authoritarian regimes throughout the region seek to tighten their grip, tensions with religious institutions have grown apace. Military leaders call on their old allies in the churches, but now they find relatively few supporters, as religious leaders, on the whole, have cut their traditional ties and identifications with the old order. Indeed, in this regard it is worth pointing out that church leaders (bishops, for example) often lag far behind rank and file elements whose demands for an active commitment to change are compelling precisely because they combine a call for transformation within the churches with a drive for change in the nation at large.

The chapters in Part I provide a basis for approaching and understanding these issues. Levine looks at the origins and recent development of the major currents of change in Latin American Catholicism. The need to keep religion and politics in a dynamic, dialectical balance is stressed, as the sources of new Catholic involvements in questions of social and political change are explored. This is a uniquely appropriate moment to assess changes in Latin American Catholicism, for in 1979 the Third General Conference of Latin American Bishops was held in Puebla, Mexico. At Puebla, the bishops sought to evaluate the years since Medellín while charting a viable and independent course for the future of the Church. In many ways, Puebla reflects all the ambiguities, tensions, and hopes for the future so visible among Latin America's Catholics. Writing during the preparations for Puebla, Renato Poblete, S. J., analyzes the process of change leading up to Puebla. He notes important elements of continuity and change in this process, while shedding useful light on the sources and implications of intrachurch conflict. He is optimistic as he explores the way in which church leaders are seeking a creative and politically autonomous line of thought and action. Writing on Puebla itself, Phillip Berryman takes a different perspective. Berryman is concerned, above all, with the impact of Puebla (both as an event and as a set of guidelines for the future) on the situation of committed radical Christians in Latin America today. Considering Puebla as an event means looking at the forces involved and at the effective degree of openness and participation which marked the conference. Considering Puebla as a set of guidelines for the future, Berryman's discussion highlights the central place which issues of politics, poverty, conflict, and structural inequality had in the bishops' deliberations. He notes that considerable ambiguity is visible on key points, as the bishops' desire to satisfy many groups, and to avoid potentially damaging political ties, led them to treat many central issues in such general terms that it is often difficult to derive clear guidelines for action.

Discussions of religion, society, and politics in Latin America often begin and end with the Roman Catholic Church. But despite the continued predominance of Catholicism, it is important to realize that Protestant churches are vigorously growing and changing throughout the region. Moreover, Protestant representatives from all over Latin America recently held a general meeting at Oaxtepec, Mexico, in which many of the issues debated at Puebla played a central role. T. S. Montgomery examines the process of change in Latin American Protestanism, noting some important parallels to the recent experience of Catholics in the area.

1

RELIGION AND POLITICS,
POLITICS AND RELIGION
An Introduction

DANIEL H. LEVINE

Religion and politics have depended on and influenced one another since the origins of what we know as Latin America. Their relation is both mutual and multifaceted; mutual because religion and politics have evolved together over the years, taking material and symbolic support from one another, and multifaceted because it embraces interinstitutional conflict and accommodation (e.g., the "church-state" relations which dominated earlier scholarship) as well as more subtle and elusive exchanges whereby religious and political orders gave legitimacy and moral authority to one another. In this process, religious notions of hierarchy, authority, and obedience reflected and reinforced the pattern of existing social and political arrangements to such an extent that the two orders often seemed indistinguishable.

Historically it is true that the weight of Catholic influence (both material and symbolic) has gone to reinforce existing social arrangements in Latin America. *But this is not a necessary relation.* For it is not religion per se which produces conservative effects, but rather a particular set of historically determined concepts, traditions, and organizational commitments. As these change, we may expect new models of social and political action to arise in association with them. In the same measure, change in the political order, leading to new concepts and forms of action, will necessarily alter the impact of politics on religion, providing new pressures, problems, and models for action.

These potentialities are now being realized throughout Latin America, as both religion and politics undergo profound and far-reaching changes. These parallel and often explicitly related processes give voice to a general sense of crisis and uncertainty which has stimulated a search for new ideals, understandings, and forms of action. This convergence of change in a traditionally dominant church with societies themselves undergoing rapid marches and counter-marches has produced a setting uniquely geared to conflict, innovation, and self-questioning.

Such is the setting of our inquiry. Now, as in the past, religion and politics are closely related in Latin America. Indeed, a great deal of the conflict so visible in Latin American Catholicism in recent years has centered precisely over a struggle to redefine the meaning of religious symbols, and in this way redirect the social and political thrust of the Church as an institution and of Catholicism as a set of religious beliefs, practices, and motivations.[1] The intense interest in and concern for politics which lies at the heart of this process has in fact made the relation of religion and politics, if anything, closer and more dynamic in recent years than ever before.

The articles presented here all touch on one or another aspect of this process. In introducing them to the reader, I want to stress the importance of keeping religion and politics in a dynamic and dialectical balance, giving full and equal weight to each in our analysis.[2] Both religion and politics must be taken seriously as sources of motivation and guiding ideas. In this relation, action and meaning cannot be simply deduced from either side of the equation. Rather, these are empirical questions. Therefore, it is necessary to trace out the sociological linkages between religious and political themes in particular contexts and problems, for the transformation of religious ideas poses new problems and dilemmas for politics, while at the same time the pattern of political change raises new problems and dilemmas for religion.

Religion and politics are thus both analytically and empirically related—*the two cannot and should not be separated.* This position differs considerably from that taken in much recent work on "development," "modernization," and the role of religion in these processes.[3] In general, such writings see increasing functional specialization and institutional differentiation as both inevitable and good. In this view, no single institution can embrace all human activity or provide valid frameworks for its significance. Rather, spheres of competence are marked off and the whole is best represented by the metaphor of a marketplace—an arena in which different interests interact and work out changing codes of mutual coexistence.

This is a view of society with deep roots in the Protestant Reformation and its aftermath in Liberal and Utilitarian thought. The insistence on increasing secularization and differentiation common to much of this work often leads to a stance which strips religious institutions and leaders of most activities and functions not "explicitly religious," (e.g., concerned with cult, ritual, or salvation) turning these over to other institutions. To put it crudely, in this view preachers should preach, leaving politics and the care of the social order in general to the "experts."

Elsewhere I have argued that this perspective is a poor guide to the study of religion and politics in general (Levine, 1978; Levine and Wilde, 1977). In the specific case of Latin America, these authors totally failed to anticipate and understand the dramatic reemergence of political themes in Catholicism, especially (although not only) on the "Left." By arguing for a neat separation of spheres of action, their approach assumes that a parallel separation is possible in the minds of the actors themselves. But if religion really *is* a source of powerful motivations and lasting orientations in many areas of life, then the problem for analysis is to trace out the real links between religion and those actions—not simply to seek a dividing line.

In any case, the line which separates religion and politics is not as clear and sharp as these theories would have us believe. It all depends on what is meant by the terms. So far, I have used both "religion" and "politics" in a conventional way, with no attempt at more precise definition. "Religion" has referred to those activities surrounding church institutions (centered on cult and ritual), while "politics" has been identified implicitly with government or actions affecting government in some way. But these conventional usages are not sufficient, for, as I suggested earlier, an important part of the dynamic relation between religion and politics in contemporary Latin America rests on the expanded and altered meaning of the terms themselves. Consider, then, the potential scope of each.

For our puroses, a working definition of religion should help isolate a set of beliefs and motivations and shed light on the way they generate regular patterns of action. Thus, we need a concept linking beliefs to action. For Catholicism, "pastoral action" provides such a concept. The idea of pastoral action, of course, derives from the biblical metaphor of a shepherd caring for his flock. Traditionally this "care" has been centered on charity, moral suasion, and tending to the needs of the sick and lonely. But pastoral action can mean many things, and in Latin America today it is an open question as to just how far, and in what direction, it extends. Is it limited to the provision of comfort, solace, and charity? May it encompass testimony, bearing witness to and sharing the conditions of peoples' lives as a sign of human solidarity? Need it include denunciation of those social conditions which make a fully human and moral life impossible, such as extreme poverty and oppression? Or must it be developed further to provide a basis for action to change society, making religious communion a part of social and political reconstruction? These issues are all alive in the Church today.

In much of Latin America, the Catholic hierarchy's response to pressures for greater political involvement has been to emphasize what the bishops see as "pastoral" (and hence, "non-political") actions.[4] But if the scope of the "pastoral" is expanded along the lines suggested above, it is hard to see how such actions can be kept out of politics. This becomes particularly difficult as the meaning of politics itself is stretched beyond the confines of government or partisan conflict, for, like pastoral action, "politics" can also be broadened to include denunciations of injustice. This brings new issues to the agenda of national life, or massive community action, such as land invasions, which seek to redress grievances and change the structure of power and opportunity in daily life. Such activities, while not political in a narrowly partisan or official sense, are nevertheless essentially political, as they raise basic issues of power, authority, legitimacy, and distribution.[5]

If both pastoral action and politics are expanded in this way, they flow easily together, and the distinction of religious from political roles and functions loses much of its presumed sharpness. Moreover, when these evolving concepts are tied to institutions, the potential for new and complex forms of action is enormous. This is particularly so in Catholicism, whose extraordinary development of hierarchical structures linking local, national, and international actors and resources provides a uniquely dense and complex context for action. Here, actions undertaken out of pastoral motives at the local level may be funded by international agencies working through the structures of the Church, with considerable repercussions on the national political scene. This process is particularly visible where, in the face of growing authoritarian rule, the Catholic Church has become, for all practical purposes, the only public voice of opposition (Smith, this issue).

While religion has long been considered a problem for politics, it is important to note that politics presents no less a problem for religion. Traditionally, the problems religion poses to the political order in Latin America have been seen in terms of "church-state" conflicts, centering e control of schools, the regulation of marriage and divorce, birth control, and the like. The traditional problems politics has posed for religion in Latin America are the mirror image of these—the threat of growing secularization and the expansion of the state into areas previously left to religious guidance and control.

Although this kind of conflict persists in many areas, I would argue that it is no longer of central importance, especially in Latin America. Rather, with the changes noted above, religion now poses a problem for politics above all as a source of motivation for radical action and as an institutional shield for dissent from authoritarian rule. This new stance implies that politics and social life in general bring new problems to religion. The following section explores three basic aspects of this situation: (1) changing images of the Church and their impact on the way religious faith leads to social and political activism; (2) new perspectives on change and transformation (as opposed to static models) for understanding the world; and (3) in this context, the meaning of power, force, and violence, and the related issue of the church's stance on social division and class conflict in general.

These issues take form in the development of a series of groups and positions concerned with the proper relation of the Church and of religion in general to social and political change in Latin America. Three broad positions, on Left, Right, and Center will be discussed below:[6] first, on the "Left," the example of Camilo Torres and the development of Liberation Theology, combining new theological positions with a commitment to social and political revolution; second, on the "Right," the emergence of groups like the Societies for the Defense of Tradition, Family, and Property now spreading throughout the region, which combine an extremely traditional religious stance with reactionary social and political positions closely tied to the ideologies of national security being elaborated by military regimes in the area; and finally, in the "Center," a growing group of bishops and key Catholic institutions striving to maintain the unity of the Church against fierce pressures from Right and Left alike, while still hoping to respond in some creative way to the demands of contemporary social and political life.

Basic Issues

Much of the motive force of recent changes in the Latin American Catholic Church has come in the gradual working out of the impact of the Second Vatican Council (Vatican II) and the subsequent Second General Conference of Latin American Bishops held in Medellín, Colombia, in 1968 (Medellín). A fresh look at those key events is particularly appropriate now, for while the articles in this issue were being prepared (early and mid-1978), preparations were underway for a Third General Conference of Latin American Bishops to be held in Puebla, Mexico, in late 1978. The Puebla meeting was organized to review and evaluate the decade since Medellín, while charting a course for the future (Poblete, this issue). Such a review brings out the enormous stimulus to change in the Latin American Church which came from Vatican II and Medellín. Let us consider, then, the content, direction, and impact of the changes begun there.

Vatican II marked a major attempt to rethink the nature of the Church, the world, and the proper relation between the two. Alongside the traditional model of the Church as an institution, which had stressed eternal, unchanging aspects of belief, structure, and hierarchy, the Council elaborated a vision of the Church as a "Pilgrim People of God"—a living, changing community of the faithful making its way through history. Viewing the Church as a "Pilgrim People of God" thus means, in a very basic sense, accepting the importance of historical change, both as a *fact* and as a powerful source of changing values.[7] This acceptance of change, as opposed to more traditional insistence on stasis and permanence, has had far-reaching and (one suspects) unanticipated consequences for the Church. Let me suggest several.

If situations and institutions are historically determined, then no particular social form is necessary—all change with time and new conditions. From this perspective, it is then no longer possible to be certain about the proper relation of individuals and groups within society, or even within the Church. Moreover, attention to the historical sources of change leads quite readily to a concern for understanding how societies developed as they did. Once this step is taken, the Church is decisively freed (at least in potential) from its previous identification with conservative forces and existing structures. Societies change as a matter of course, and they can be changed by human will, and not simply endured in hopes of a better life to come.

The Council's emphasis on the Church as a Pilgrim People of God also had profound impact on the structure and meaning of authority in the Church—the kinds of authority, activity, and obedience seen as necessary and legitimate. By laying such great stress on the historical experience of change, this model helped move emphasis within the

Church away from a predominant concern with roles, rank, and juridically defined hierarchy, and towards testimony and witness (in the biblical sense of solidarity through shared experience) as sources of authority and models for action (Levine, 1978). This new emphasis is of central importance, for if authority is grounded in testimony and witness, then the holders of authority (bishops, for example) are moved to action and expected to act as a necessary expression of their religious roles.

The link of authority to action also has had a major impact on the scope and meaning of obedience within the Church. The expectation of relatively automatic obedience has been called into question increasingly by priests, nuns, and laity alike who feel that for authority to have a legitimate claim to obedience, its holders must act to promote social justice. Moreover, the stress on action and shared experience, by putting the bases of authority and obedience on a more egalitarian, community-oriented footing, has contributed to important pressures for making collegiality and power-sharing a reality within the ecclesiastical institution itself. The often glacial pace of movements on this dimension has led to great frustration among key groups in the Church, particularly religious women (sisters), whose implications for the future are still uncertain (Gilfeather, this volume).

This renewed emphasis on shared experience, solidarity, and action draws heavily on biblical (especially Old Testament) images which stress the role of God as an active presence in the world. In this view, belief and authentic faith are seen as most completely expressed in actions to promote social justice (Miguez Bonino, 1976; Miranda, 1974). Moreover, activism itself has a different focus, because with the pervasive emphasis on historical experience, it is no longer a simple matter of applying known doctrine to the case at hand. Rather, as we shall see, the process begins with social analysis, searching in society for the "signs of the times"—events and situations which stimulate and enrich religious reflection.

These new perspectives were amplified by the Council's more general reevaluation of the meaning of social action, which gave it new autonomy and status in the Catholic scheme of things. Several dimensions are central to this process, most notably: (1) an opening to secular disciplines, particularly in the social sciences, as sources of valid knowledge about the world; and (2) related to this, a recognition of the autonomous validity of temporal values and of the possibility of drawing religious lessons and meaning from the problems and experiences of daily life. Let me review these briefly.

Vatican II stimulated the incorporation of many ideas and categories of analysis from contemporary social science into Catholic thinking about society. This began in a mild way, with general sociological analysis and a broad concern for "development." But, as we shall see, this small opening quickly expanded, above all in Latin America, to encompass new ideas about violence, "structural change," and essentially Marxist notions of economic dependency, praxis, and revolution. The possibility of drawing valid values from the world is related, for it implies a basic reorientation of Catholic activism. While earlier approaches (traditional, Catholic Action, and Christian Democratic alike) all in some measure sought to transform the world in accord with the principles of a known body of Christian doctrine, these new perspectives lead in a different direction.

The starting point here is social, not religious. Thus, rather than form specifically or exclusively "Christian" groups, those inspired by religious faith, in this view, join with others sharing their social goals, be they Christian or not. In Latin America, this perspective led quickly to the development of extensive and often controversial Christian-Marxist alliances—alliances whose goals were derived not from authorized expressions of Catholic social doctrine, but rather from a searching look at society, a look increasingly taken in the light of Marxist categories of analysis.

Of course, the Council's impact did not reach so far all at once. The first fruits of these changes came rather in a flurry of interest for "development" and a series of development projects of Christian inspiration. This orientation peaked in the early years of Christian Democratic rule in Chile, when it seemed as if that party might indeed make development a reality within this framework. But by the time of Medellín, this optimism had all but disappeared, and the appeal of Christian Democracy had soured in a rash of divisions, conflicts, and disappointments. At Medellín, the bishops took quite a new tack, and their conclusions (Council of Latin American Bishops, 1970) mark without a doubt the single most important milestone in the recent development of Latin American Catholicism.

Like Vatican II, Medellín provided a broad reconsideration of all aspects of religious life, locating them with specific reference to the contemporary transformation of Latin America. For our purposes, Medellín is particularly important for its treatment of the key issues of force and violence, and the related question of social division and class conflict.

The matter of violence was put in perspective at Medellín by Pope Paul's comments during his visit to Colombia condemning violence as antievangelical and un-Christian. While supporting efforts at social change, the Pope thus ruled out violence as a legitimate tool of social transformation. The bishops differed, arguing, basically, that many kinds of violence exist. Thus, violence cannot be identified with only individual or even collective acts of aggression, but must be recognized as well in the day-to-day operations of unequal, unjust, and oppressive social structures. This was defined as "institutionalized violence." The distinction of "institutionalized violence" from more overt forms of aggression was a major step, for it opened the way to justifying counter-violence—violent acts intended to undo the inherent, institutionalized violence of the established order, replacing it with a more just society.

This social analysis was placed in a broader context of religious belief by the bishops' discussion of sin. Conventionally considered to refer to personal situations and individual morality, sin was extended here to characterize entire social systems whose injustice, oppression, and institutionalized violence were sinful, because they imposed social conditions which made a fully moral and decent life impossible. Once this kind of connection is made, it is clearly a short and relatively easy step to argue that if oppressive social, economic, and political structures are sinful, and hence prevent the full realization of human potential, then religious liberation, which involves freedom from sin, is in some measure tied to change in these structures—by revolution if necessary.

Finally, the Church's attention was focused once again, at Vatican II and at Medellín, on the poor, and more generally on the sources and meaning of poverty.[8] Of course, the Catholic Church has long paid considerable attention to the poor. But in social terms, most of this concern was expressed in welfare programs—aid to the poor within the bounds of existing social, economic, and political arrangements. Moreover, poverty was largely seen as a result of individual failings: hence, charity and job training were stressed. With the new orientations just described, however, poverty can be seen in a new light, as a structural (not an individual) problem. From this perspective, the misery of poverty and the injustice which causes it can never be resolved through individual charity alone. Rather, the structures which cause poverty must be changed—and this is a matter of power and political action.

More is at stake here than the simple reorientation of polic programs, for a large part of the post-Medellín debates in the Latin American Church has involved attempts to reinterpret the symbolic meaning of poverty as well. For proponents of change, poverty need no longer be simply endured in the hopes of greater rewards in Heaven. Action and change are necessary and legitimate. Indeed, the phrase "the poor shall inherit the earth" is often taken in a much more direct and literal sense than has hitherto been the case. Moreover, the "poor" of the Gospels have often been transformed, among radical Catholics, into the working class or proletariat, and action to promote the coming of the Kingdom of God identified for all practical purposes with revolutionary struggle.

This renewed and transformed concern with poverty has also been expressed in a growing movement by priests and especially religious women to share the life and experiences of the poor—living with them, working with them, joining with them in the goals, frustrations, and general activities of daily life. As Dodson and Gilfeather note in their contributions here, this experience has often had a profound effect on the individuals involved. By bringing them into direct contact with the full misery and injustice of the life of the poor, it has made them more aware of the need for change, and served in this way as a spur to the organization of movements for social and political change by priests in several countries.

The impact on religious women has been particularly profound. As Gilfeather points out, because of a general scarcity of clergy, sisters in Chile (and elsewhere) increasingly have taken on duties and responsibilities hitherto reserved for priests. The experience of these responsibilities, coupled with the impact of living with the poor, has led to a profound transformation in religious values and a high degree of radicalization in and frustration with the structures of the Church. The sisters are restive within the institutional structures of the Church, which, while giving them greater burdens and responsibilities, nevertheless clings to a tradition of male-dominated authority structures which drastically restrict the recognition and rewards available to the sisters for their labors. In this case, new models of the Church, transformed authority structures, and the symbolic struggle over the meaning of poverty come together in a fascinating and potentially explosive mixture.

This brief sketch of the impact of Vatican II and Medellín indicates the depth and extent of change. A predominant concern with stasis was replaced by an emphasis on change. Social conflict and division were openly recognized, and a beginning made towards a full and open commitment to the poor. Finally, at least tentative steps were taken towards the legitimation of violence.[9] How have these ideas and initiatives been expressed in Latin America? No single, unified response is visible. Instead, several alternatives stand out, and the next section examines these in closer detail.

Cases: Left, Right, and Center

The case of Camilo Torres is a good place to begin, for in many ways Torres was a precursor, exemplifying in his own brief career all of the elements of change just discussed.[10] Torres entered the priesthood under the influence of French social Catholicism as espoused by Dominican priests then living in Colombia. His vocation was thus strongly influenced by a particular dedication to social reform through Christian action. This orientation was reinforced by his advanced clerical education, which took him to Louvain University in Belgium. In the mid-1950's, Louvain was a center for reform-minded Latin American Catholics and a source of much Christian Democratic thinking. Thus, when he returned to Colombia in late 1958, Torres came inspired by ideas of development through Christian action.

But he soon grew frustrated with elite persuasion, reformist methods, and with the very assumption that some uniquely Christian solution to social problems existed. His career evolved rapidly, and in 1965 he founded a movement, the United Front, intended to bring together all progressive forces in the pursuit of political change. These activities led to conflict with the ecclesiastical heirarchy, which ended with Torres' voluntary "reduction" to lay status to devote himself full time to politics. Events moved swiftly: the United Front was formed in May, 1965; Torres left the priesthood in June; he entered a guerrilla front in October; and he was killed in early 1966 in a skirmish with an army patrol.

This brief but spectacular career raises at least three issues for Latin American Catholicism, all of which were taken up and treated more systematically in later years: first, the relation of religious faith to action in the world; second, the status of power, force, and violence; and third, the proper relation between Catholics and other (specifically Marxist) groups in the promotion of change.

Camilo Torres clearly believed that authentic religious faith required action to transform an unjust world. Religion was not simply "spiritual," a disembodied faith brought out only on Sundays. Rather, it was an integral part of life. Hence, genuine faith could only achieve full expression in a just and equitable society. In his words, "When circumstances impede men from devoting themselves to Christ, the priest's proper duty is to combat these circumstances . . . the revolutionary struggle is a Christian and priestly struggle" (1972: 264-265).

It is important to be clear about this issue. Torres did not oppose politics in religion, or somehow put politics before religion. Rather, he saw the two as intimately and necessarily joined, and looked for the way religious commitments required action to make them effective. In his view, a true Christian was obliged to be political, for only in this way could love of neighbor, the key Christian precept, be made effective. Individual acts of kindness and charity were negated by the unjust structures of society. And since these structures were founded on power, only power (not appeals to conscience or good will alone) could change them. The rapid turn to politics and guerrilla action flowed directly from these understandings. Once one recognized the fact of social division, and became aware of the full implications of phrases like "love thy neighbor," then the use of power and even violence as means to a more just society was legitimate.

Finally, Torres anticipated the extraordinary development of Marxist-Christian dialogue and cooperation, for as he moved away from Christian (and Christian Democratic) reformism and its concern for building church-related programs, he came logically to value alliances with any and all groups dedicated to the cause of revolution.

The career of Camilo Torres is important, for it was not a fluke or a chance aberration, but rather responded to many growing pressures for change in church and society alike. These pressures and new perspectives have been developed most systematically in Latin America in what has come to be known as Liberation Theology. A brief look at Liberation Theology will thus round out our view of the Left's response to change in church and society. As the name implies, Liberation Theology is concerned with the meaning of religion for social and political liberation, and vice versa. It has evolved in recent years as a distinctively and self-consciously Latin American approach to the relation of religion and politics.

The Latin American focus of these writings is significant in itself, for it reflects a deliberate effort to root the understanding of religious faith in the particular experiences of contemporary Latin America. Theology is thus placed in the context of real social experience, and this once cloistered and abstract discipline is transformed into a reflection on concrete historical situations and struggles.[11] In this way, the methodology of Liberation Theology begins with a look at concrete social problems, drawing themes and imperatives for action from this analysis. The central problem for religion is thus no longer atheism, indifference, or even hostility to religion per se, but rather social and political transformation. Gutiérrez, a leading Peruvian theologian, states the issue sharply:

> Much contemporary theology seems to start from the challenge of the *non-believer*. He questions our *religious world* and faces it with a demand for profound purification and renewal. . . . This challenge in a continent like Latin America does not come primarily from the man who does not believe, but from the *man who is not a man,* who is not recognized as such by the existing social order: he is in the ranks of the poor, the exploited; he is the man who is systematically and legally despoiled of his being as a man, who scarcely knows that he *is* a man. His challenge is not aimed first at our religious world, but at our *economic, social, political and cultural world;* therefore it is an appeal for the revolutionary transformation of the very bases of a dehumanizing society. The question is not therefore how to speak of God in an adult world, but how to proclaim him as a Father in a world that is not human [1974: 69].

Liberation Theology faces the issues of power, force, and violence quite directly, building them into its analysis of the nature of authentic religious commitment. Like Camilo Torres, Gutiérrez argues that Christians must look at society realistically, giving full weight to the struggle and conflict so visible everywhere. Traditional Catholic positions which oppose class struggle in the name of an ideal of Christian love and unity are rejected. Real Christian love, Gutiérrez argues, is founded on commitment to a more just society and action to bring it about (1973: 278).

The influence of contemporary social science, and particularly of Marxist thought,[12] is notable in the adoption of a perspective of continuous change, the identification of the working class as the motor of this change, and a deep concern with the fusion of theory and action in an authentic revolutionary *praxis*. Let me review these briefly.

The recognition of change is central to Liberation Theology, and fits well with a view of the Church as Pilgrim People of God. From this perspective, writers like Assmann (1971), Dussel (1976), Gutiérrez (1973), or Segundo (1973, 1976) illuminate the kinds of problems faced by religious people as they seek social and political change. Above all, they want to avoid any rigid identification with the present, and thus keep Catholic thought and action open to change. Assmann says it well:

> The transcendence of God rests on the fact that he is always before us, on the frontiers of the future. God is pro-vocative, that is, he calls us ahead, and can only be met as one who moves forward with his people in a continuous dismantling of structures [1971: 21].

For Liberation Theology, change is both permanent and ultimately rooted in social conflict. This point of view stems in large measure from the disillusionment already noted with "development" as practiced in Latin America. "Development" was originally seen as a non-revolutionary path to progress and broad social benefits through economic growth and industrialization in a capitalist framework. But for radical Catholics, such "development" has masked a reality of increasing poverty, misery, and inequality. Rejecting "development," these writers have turned for orientation to the theories of "dependency" which have emerged in Latin America in recent years.[13]

From dependency theory, Liberation Theology acquired an explanation of the Latin American situation and a set of categories which strengthened and gave focus to the social and economic concerns so central to its religious analysis. Even a minimal glance at the vast body of writings on dependency suggests the reasons for their attractiveness to radical Catholics. To dependency theory, the inequality and misery associated with capitalist development in Latin America are not accidental, but rather are a necessary consequence of the subordination of Latin American societies and economies to the interests of dominant world capitalist powers. *Their* development depends on the continued exploitation of Latin America and other "underdeveloped" regions. Moreover, their policies and programs are implemented by local allies in control of social, cultural, economic, and political institutions. The solution, for dependency theory and Liberation Theology alike, lies not in more of the same (that is, more "development") but in the construction of a new social order.

What finally is "liberation"? Basically, liberation involves freedom from bondage of all kinds—the bondage of ignorance, alienation, poverty, and oppression. Such liberation is neither wholly spiritual nor wholly material. Rather, it is the fusion of the two which gives this perspective its unique and compelling force. Religious and political liberation go together: "purely religious" actions, limited to the institutional Church, are rejected as a false consciousness; while "pure politics" lack meaning in the cosmic scheme of things. In this view, the key role of religious action is to join the two planes, removing traditional religious legitimation of the social order while channeling religious energies and motivations toward its transformation.

Religion is linked to politics through the emphasis on *praxis* which runs through these writings. Praxis refers to a course of action so theoretically informed and self-aware that the activity itself expresses consciously the insights which logical study and reflection provide. Liberation Theology stresses both individual and collective praxis of this kind, making action, in effect, a necessary consequence of authentic faith—a kind of validation of the reality of that faith. This concern for conscious, self-aware action has received two notable expressions in recent years: first, in the work of Paolo Freire, the Brazilian educator; and second, in programs for cooperation and joint action with Marxists. Consider Freire first.

Paolo Freire (1968, 1974) has had an enormous influence on Latin American Catholicism. He argues that education must do more than impart skills. Each student must acquire an active role in creating his own awareness of the surrounding world. This process (*concientización* in Spanish) is intended to develop in each person a critical awareness of society as a human, and therefore changeable, product. To Freire, the first and most basic step in change is liberating people from the oppressors they have internalized, for he argues that the dominated absorb the dominators' vision of them. Thus, the poor believe themselves to be "lazy" and "stupid." Only when the social order is demythologized, through the development of critical consciousness, can people proceed to liberate themselves. In this process, the transformation of religious concepts plays a major role. If religious symbols can also be demythologized and freed of their ties to the existing social order, then a major step toward psychological and cultural liberation will have been taken.

A more directly political path has been followed by Catholic radicals pursuing dialogue, cooperation, and open political alliances with Marxists. These initiatives have appeared all over Latin America since

Medellín, evolving furthest in Chile during the Allende regime. The evolution of Christians for Socialism in Chile is important, for it raised in practical terms most of the issues under consideration here. Thus, questions of activism, power, the meaning of politics for religious action, and the proper role for Christians (particularly priests and religious) in politics all came to the surface in sharp and controversial forms (Eagleson, 1975). Shortly before the overthrow of Allende, the movement was condemned by Chile's bishops, who feared that Christianity's central religious message was being swamped in an overwhelming political commitment. To the bishops, Christians for Socialism made bad policy and poor theology as well: bad policy by aggravating political divisions within the Church and commiting its survival to the fortunes of the socialist regime; and poor theology by reducing the Church's dynamic plane to an exclusively political one. If the Church were to become political, the mission of salvation might be lost:

> The Church is meant to be the salt of the earth. "And if salt becomes tasteless, how is its saltiness to be restored?" (Mt. 5:15) If the Church is turned into a political or temporal faction, who will save us? [Eagleson, 1975: 224]

With the fall of socialism in Chile, many in the Church have drawn back from full political commitment. The reaction of Chile's bishops has been echoed broadly in the region (Conferencia Episcopal de Colombia, 1976). But in dealing with the issues of politics and political commitment raised so sharply by Liberation Theology and Christians for Socialism, leaders of the Latin American Church are in a difficult situation, for they face concerted and often bitter opposition from all sides.

Considerable attention has been given here to the evolution of what is generally called the Christian Left. It is important to realize, however, that other equally vigorous positions exist. Indeed, as radical Catholics moved to more open political commitments, their activism has been matched, if not exceeded, on the Right, most notably by the Societies for the Defense of Tradition, Family, and Property (TFP) which have emerged in many countries.[14] Moreover, the weight of these groups on the Right has been reinforced in several key Latin American military establishments by the development of attitudes deeply hostile to the Church, rooted in the armed forces' views on "national security."

TFP and the military both reject the postconciliar and especially the post-Medellín changes in the Church as a betrayal of the religion they were brought up to honor, revere, and defend. The basic TFP world view combines very traditional forms of Catholic religious practice (the Latin mass, continued veneration of discarded saints, the ostentatious display of lachrymose religious images, and the like) with a strong commitment to reactionary social, economic, and political positions. TFP members see themselves as part of a general counterrevolutionary offensive, and explicitly attribute most of the ills of the modern world to the aftereffects of the French Revolution (Corrêa de Oliveira, 1970). The most notable aspect of their social doctrine is a belief in the absolute sanctity of private property (De Castro Mayer et al, 1971) combined with an appreciation of the healthy virtues of social inequality. Naturally enough, they reject any dialogue with non-Catholic groups as the opening wedge of communist infiltration—a clever tactic for weakening the defenses of western, Christian civilization (Corrêa de Oliveira, 1971).

The reaction of the military is less specifically religious in tone and inspiration, but also reveals a deep hostility toward the contemporary Latin American Church. The military's views are grounded in their doctrine of "national security," according to which there is no real distinction between war and peace (Comblin, 1976, and Calvo, this volume). Because the natures of war and conflict have changed, *all* times are now times of war. As a result, national security itself can no longer be confined to the external defense of secure frontiers, but now requires *internal* unity and discipline to counter the social conflict and subversion which impede national progress. Since unity must be enforced and subversion combatted at every turn, the role of the state and especially of its security apparatus is greatly enhanced, while traditional civil liberties and representative institutions are eliminated.

The military see their struggle as part of the general defense of western, Christian civilization against communism. Hence, no contradiction is perceived between their position and "Christian principles," and extensive use is made of Christian images, symbols, and alliances wherever possible. But given the developments in the Church already described, and the ambiguities of "pastoral action" which have been noted here, the generals are continuously faced with "Christian" actions, which in their eyes amount to simple subversion. Moreover, the problem is not limited to "radicals," for as Calvo and Smith will point out later, the very leaders of the institutional Church, the bishops, instead of supporting the military's defense of "Christian values," have gradually moved into opposition over issues of human rights, social justice, and in the simple attempt to defend priests, nuns, and lay people engaged in pastoral action who are arrested as subversives. The net result has been growing tension and strain between the Church and the military regimes which now hold power in many countries.

The central institutions of the Church, led by the bishops, are caught in the middle. Since the late 1950s, their general goal has been withdrawal from partisan politics and concentration of energies on internal renewal and pastoral action. But, as we have seen, this position is full of ambiguities. Quite apart from its inherent difficulties, however, it is also under attack from many sides. The Left rejects it as hypocritical and unrealistic, while the Right calls the bishops to decisive action against communism. Caught in the center, the bishops are trying to hold the Church and the Catholic community together in the face of enormous divisive pressures, while retaining maximum possible autonomy from governments and political groups alike.

In many cases, this central position has been reached after a series of ups and downs concerning politics and political action. The enthusiasm of the late 1960s for development, social action, and internal Church reform was quickly tempered by reaction to what a number of bishops saw as the excesses of Liberation Theology and Christian-Marxist alliances. But in the shadow of the growing wave of authoritarian, "national security" regimes (most notably in the Southern Cone countries of Brazil, Argentina, Chile, and Uruguay), many Church leaders have been forced to take a new look at the issues as politics, this time in the form of the military, intrudes once again on the life of the Church.

The evolving position of the Chilean bishops is a good example of this process, for although Chile is an extreme case, it nevertheless encapsulates and concentrates many of the issues seen in fragmented form elsewhere. As we have seen, the hierarchy originally condemned Christians for Socialism in Chile because they feared (1) a relativization of the Christian message and its subordination to political goals, (2) the implications of any political division of the Church whereby different groups would each claim the mantle of Church authority for their positions, and (3) the reduction of transcendental commitments to the level of political ideologies. Thus they argued it is not true that everything is ultimately political, or that politics need be a primary form of commitment. Limits and distinctions were required. The Gospel does not depend on

political action for its effectiveness, the Church in any case takes no
particular political model as its own (transcending all), and finally,
Church action is basically different *in kind* from political action, as
force and power (so central to politics) are set aside (Eagleson, 1975:
179-228).

But by 1977 the tables had been turned. The Allende regime was no
more. Gone with it were not only the activists on the Left (in Church
and society alike), but also the entire apparatus of Chile's civil society
and juridical, republican traditions. In 1973, a number of bishops were
willing to legitimize the military regime, seeing it at the least as a respite
from turmoil and constant conflict. But by 1977 the conflict had not
gone away. Rather, the "internal" war continued, with the Church itself
now coming under attack (Sanders and Smith, 1976). The Church's
response has taken many forms. On the public scene, in 1977 the bishops
issued a collective pastoral entitled *Our Life as a Nation* which explicitly
took issue with the doctrine of national security, reaffirming the values
of democracy, pluralism, and openness. They rejected the regime's
attempt to cast itself as the defender of Christian values, noting that

> we do well to recall the teaching of the Church. She strongly up-
> holds legitimate pluralism in the realm of ideas and socio-political
> groups, while also pointing out the need for national unity and the
> proper way to obtain it.
>
> The road to peace and unity cannot be reached through imposi-
> tion. Unity, like truth (including religious truth), cannot be im-
> posed by force. It must be proposed to people so that it can be
> accepted on the basis of inner conviction and a personal decision
> [Chilean Episcopal Conference, 1977: 8-9].

In Chile, as elsewhere in Latin America, the bishops are groping for
ways to preserve the unity[15] and autonomy of the Church while maintaining its ability to contribute creatively to the welfare of the community through social and pastoral action. In this regard, as Smith
shows in this volume, the Church's great organizational flexibility has
been of crucial importance. While it cannot change authoritarian regimes on its own, nevertheless the Church has managed to organize and
finance institutions to help the victims of oppression while keeping alive
the hope for a different kind of future. In many cases, church organizations (particularly at the local level) have in effect become surrogates
for the social and political participation and interchange no longer per-

mitted in society at large. The real potential for serving as an institutional shield, a shelter for activities prohibited by the government, makes the hierarchy's deep concern for preserving the unity of the institution or the Church all the more understandable. The full impact of these developments on the life of the Church is still unclear, but it seems inevitable that this growing, direct involvement *with* the poor and weak *against* the power of the state, which finds the Church itself becoming a victim in many cases, will affect the institution's future stance toward the issues and choices we have thus far considered.

Conclusions

Throughout the course of events considered here, the ecclesiastical hierarchy has generally resisted attempts to push it along exclusively political tracks.[16] In this regard, it is important to note that both Christians for Socialism and the TFP-military position emphasize political action as legitimate and necessary for the Church. Each wants to harness the moral authority of Catholicism to its own image of the good social and political order. Each defends a different image of the Church, and calls it to combat in a different cause.

The bishops resist "politics" as such, but politics clearly lies at the core of all these disputes. In a basic sense, politics is a crucial field of action for controlling, delimiting, and defining the activities of the institutional Church and its agents. More generally, politics is a crucial field of action as it is the arena in which individual moral choices are brought together with collective consequences. Finally, politics is a crucial field of action because of its close, dialectical relation with religion. Believers feel compelled to political action as an expression of their religious faith, and their actions manifest a general kind of commitment within which it is difficult to disentangle religion from politics at all.

Their mutual centrality is not surprising. Politics, after all, deals at the most general level with the organizing principles and symbols of the entire society. Religion, in turn, provides values which give meaning to human life, placing any given set of social or political events in a broader framework of significance. In Latin America today, religion is a problem for politics, and politics no less a problem for religion, as each gropes for new understandings of itself and of its relation to the other.

Finally, politics is a crucial field of action, for while the churches and the faithful act in and on politics, at the same time political forces impinge powerfully on them, shaping the challenges they face and the constraints and opportunities within which they must work. Thus, the problems and possibilities of the Catholic Church in Chile, Brazil, Argentina, or El Salvador now differ sharply from those of earlier years, just as the Chilean situation at any of these times is far removed from the context of contemporary Honduras, Colombia, or Cuba.

NOTES

1. Good reviews of recent Latin American developments include Smith, 1975, and Comblin, 1977.

2. This point is more fully developed in Levine, 1978.

3. Two quite different examples of this tendency, among many, are Vallier, 1970, and Silvert, 1967.

4. In this vein, Msgr. Alfonso López Trujillo, as Secretary General of CELAM argued that political neutrality is an essential precondition for the Church's pastoral independence. He refers, above all, to neutrality to partisan politics (1975).

5. See Levine and Wilde, 1977, for a full discussion of the various meanings of pastoral action and of politics.

6. Since they are derived from political alignments, terms like Left, Right, and Center often fail to capture the dimensions of religious orientation which underly positions taken. I am using the terms here in accord with conventional understandings, with full awareness of their ambiguous and sometimes misleading character. The text should make the meaning of these terms clear in each particular case. There is a long-standing tendency in Catholicism to search for a "third position," opposing both Left (communism) and Right (capitalism). This stance is severely criticized in Dussel, 1978.

7. For a fuller account of Vatican II, see Hebblethwaite, 1975 or O'Dea, 1968. The implications of new models of the Church in Latin America are discussed more fully in Levine, 1978 and Smith and Sanks, 1977. As both Smith and Gilfeather point out in their contributions to this volume, the emergence of new models of the Church can also be seen on a different, though related dimension. Traditionally, Catholicism has taken a very broad view of its membership. As a universal *church*, it was open to all who met only minimal requirements for entry. Thus, Catholicism traditionally rejected the (Protestant) model of *sects*, which looks to an elite core of members, highly motivated, aware, and knowledgeable. There is considerable evidence in Latin America now that many Catholics are moving to a view of the Church which stresses greater knowledge, more conscious commitment, and high levels of participation, all sect-like qualities, with important

implications for the authority structure of the Church and for the relations of groups within it.

8. Turner (1974, 265-267) suggests that a concern for the meaning of poverty is typical of periods of intense cultural crisis and reorientation, what he calls "liminal periods." His analysis fits the current Latin American scene well.

9. For a complete discussion of the difficulties the Church faces in legitimizing violence in the specific case of Colombia, see Levine and Wilde, 1977.

10. On Torres, see particularly Broderick, 1975.

11. As Dussel states (1976: 145), the text for theological reflection is not a set of abstract categories, but rather a social situation.

12. The great attraction of Marxist thought to Latin American Catholic radicals has been criticized sharply by the North American Jesuit, Coleman, in these terms: "As a social scientist, I have often been puzzled, if not irritated, by the almost religious importance many Latin American theologians of liberation give to the writings and analysis of Karl Marx. At times, Marxist thought (albeit with a revisionary attempt to extrapolate a 'scientific' Marx from Marx the materialist, atheistic philosopher) is identified *tout court* with social scientific analysis. Such an approach does not accord with the anti-dogmatic stance of a social science" (1976: 133).

13. The literature on dependency is enormous. Kahl (1976) provides a good introduction to the issues and a useful discussion of their development in Latin America.

14. The first TFP nuclei were founded in Brazil in the years preceding the military coup of 1964. TFP militants played a major role in organizing public opposition to the Goulart regime. Later, in Chile, TFP was active in the opposition to Allende, often forming the core of such right-wing groups as *Patria y Libertad*.

15. They hope to maintain the unity of the Catholic community around the Church's central ecclesiastical institutions. Hence, they reject those who, like Torres or Liberation Theology writers, argue that the Church's unity requires the construction of a new social order (López Trujillo, 1975).

16. The bureaucratic politics of this process are yet to be studied in full. There have been important struggles over the control and orientation of CELAM, and attempts to curtail Liberation Theology through restrictions on funding by international, particularly German, Church agencies (Metz et al., 1978).

REFERENCES

ASSMANN, H. (1971) Opresión-Liberación Desafío a los Cristianos. Montevideo: Tierra Nueva.

BRODERICK, W. J. (1975) Camilo Torres. Garden City, NY: Doubleday.

CELAM [Council of Latin American Bishops] (1970) The Church in the Present Day Transformation of Latin America in the Light of the Council. Bogotá: CELAM.

COMBLIN, J. (1977) "The Church in Latin America after Vatican II," LADOC 7 (January-February): 1-18.

———— (1976) "Theology of captivity: Christianity and the national security system." Harvard University. (unpublished)

CHILEAN EPISCOPAL CONFERENCE (1977) "Our life as a nation." LADOC 7 (July-August): 1-14.

COLEMAN, J. (1976) "Civil religion and liberation theology in North America," pp. 113-138 in S. Torres and J. Eagleson [eds.] Theology in the Americas. Maryknoll, NY: Orbis.

CONFERENCIA EPISCOPAL DE COLOMBIA (1976) Identidad Cristiana en la Acción Por la Justicia. Bogotá: SPFC.

CORRÊA DE OLIVEIRA, P. (1971) Trasbordo Ideologico Inadvertido y Dialogo. Madrid: C.I.O.

———— (1970) Revolución y Contra-Revolución. Buenos Aires: Tradición, Familia, y Propiedad.

DE CASTRO MAYER, A., G. DE PROENÇA SIGAUD, P. CORRÊA DE OLIVEIRA, and L. MENDONÇA DE FREITAS (1971) Reforma Agraria, Cuestión de Conciencia. Bogotá: Asociación Colombiana Para la Defensa del Derecho Natural.

DUSSEL, E. (1978) "El tercerismo eclesial (Táctica Política y Mecanismo Ideológico)," in E. Tamez and S. Trinidad [eds.] Capitalismo y Anti-Vida La Opresión de Las Mayorías y la Domesticación de los Dioses, Tomo I. San José, Costa Rica: EDUCA.

———— (1976) History and the Theology of Liberation: A Latin American Perspective. Maryknoll, NY: Orbis.

EAGLESON, J. [ed.] (1975) Christians and Socialism: Documentation of the Christians for Socialism Movements in Latin America. Maryknoll, NY: Orbis.

FREIRE, P. (1974) Las Iglesias, la Educación, y el Proceso de Liberación Humana en la Historia. Buenos Aires: Asociación Editorial La Aurora.

——— (1968) Pedagogy of the Oppressed. New York: Seabury.

GUTIERREZ, G. (1974) "Liberation, theology, and proclamation," pp. 57-77 in C. Geffré and G. Gutiérrez [eds.] The Mystical and Political Dimensions of the Christian Faith. New York: Herder & Herder.

——— (1973) A Theology of Liberation History, Politics, and Salvation. Maryknoll, NY: Orbis.

HEBBLETHWAITE, P. (1975) The Runaway Church Post Conciliar Growth or Decline. New York: Seabury.

KAHL, J. (1976) Modernization, Exploitation, and Dependency in Latin America. New Brunswick, NJ: Transaction Books.

LEVINE, D. (1978) "Authority in Church and society: Latin American models." Comparative Studies in Society and History 20: 4.

——— and A. WILDE (1977) "The Catholic Church, 'politics,' and violence: the Colombian case." Review of Politics 39 (April): 220-239.

LOPEZ TRUJILLO, A. (1975) "El Compromiso Político del Sacerdote." Tierra Nueva (Bogotá) 14 (July): 17-53.

METZ, J. B., et al. (1978) "Memorandum de Teologos de la República Federal Alemana Sobre La Campaña Contra la Teología de la Liberación." Diálogo (Guatemala) 38 (March): 31-35.

MIGUEZ BONINO, J. (1976) Christians and Marxists: The Mutual Challenge to Revolution. Grand Rapids: Eerdmans.

MIRANDA, J. (1974) Marx and the Bible: A Critique of the Philosophy of Repression. Maryknoll, NY: Orbis.

O'DEA, T. (1968) The Catholic Crisis. Boston: Beacon.

SANDERS, T. and B. SMITH (1976) "The Chilean Catholic Church during the Allende and Pinochet regimes." American Universities Field Staff Reports, West Coast South America Series 23: 1.

SEGUNDO, J. L. (1976) The Liberation of Theology. Maryknoll, NY: Orbis.

——— (1973) The Community Called Church. A Theology for Artisans of a New Humanity. Maryknoll, NY: Orbis.

SILVERT, K. H. [ed.] (1967) Churches and States: The Religious Institution and Modernization. New York: American Universities Field Staff.

SMITH, B. (1975) "Religion and social change: classical theories and new formulations in the context of recent developments in Latin America." Latin American Research Rev. 10 (Summer): 3-34.

——— and T. SANKS (1977) "Liberation ecclesiology: praxis, theory, and praxis." Theological Studies 38 (March): 3-38.

TORRES, C. (1972) Father Camilo Torres Revolutionary Writings. New York: Harper Colophon.

TURNER, V. (1974) Dramas, Fields, and Metaphors: Symbolic Action in Human Society. Ithaca, NY: Cornell Univ. Press.

VALLIER, I. (1970) Catholicism, Social Control, and Modernization in Latin America. Englewood Cliffs, NJ: Prentice-Hall.

2

FROM MEDELLIN TO PUEBLA

RENATO POBLETTE, S.J.

Ten years ago the Latin American Catholic Bishops held their Second General Conference in Medellín, Colombia. The conference had a great influence not only within the Catholic Church, but also on the formation of socioeconomic and political issues in Latin American countries. At the time of this writing, we are in the midst of preparations for the Third General Conference taking place in Puebla, Mexico, in October 1978. Therefore, this seems a good opportunity to reflect on the general processes of change in the Church leading to Puebla and their implications for the future.

Medellín and Puebla constitute two privileged moments in the life of the Latin American Church. History will consider them as two expressions of ecclesial discernment in which not only the bishops take part, but all people of God in Latin America. Both events mark the culmination of a process of intraecclesial maturation concerning the nature of the Church's evangelizing task in the different areas in which she carries out her mission.

But while both events can be considered as end points, they can also be seen as beginnings. In effect, Medellín is the product of the life of the Latin American Church. One cannot understand it without reference to that life, which marks it with a dynamic characteristic to be analyzed later in this paper.

Ten years after Medellín, Puebla has been called upon to perform a similar function. The Church ponders over its rightful mission, which has a permanent and universal character but which must also be considered in certain historical, economic, social, political, and cultural contexts. Therefore, from the standpoint of the Faith, temporal realities are analyzed so that the Church's mission will respond more fully to its proper identity and its own being, simultaneously resulting in greater service to the people of Latin America.

When discussing Latin America, consideration must be given to its dual dimension of unity and diversity. Different economic, political, social, cultural, ethnic, and religious conditions make it difficult to issue valid general judgments. Latin America is, and must be considered, a complex and differentiated unit. Each local church has its own characteristics derived from the richness of its particular history and varied local challenges. Consequently, our reflection must never ignore this dual character—the union of history and destiny, and the diversity and complexity arising from local conditions. Neither must we forget that other problems exist, such as arms races and the juridical solution of existing conflicts, which must be approached and understood in common. The Latin American episcopate's announcements on these matters will undoubtedly have a greater impact than those from individual churches alone.

In the following reflections we are specifically interested in considering the maturation process of the Church concerning the exigencies of its evangelizing mission in the face of temporal facts. Medellín and Puebla are approached with this perspective in mind—as two moments in the process of doctrinal clarification and renewed commitments on the part of the Church—in the face of challenges to Christian conscience and action presented by the social, economic, and political characteristics of Latin America.

The Latin American Church
Before Medellín

It is a mistake to assume that the social action of the Latin American Church started in Medellín. Awareness of the social projection of the gospel and the Church's commitment to the demands of the gospel is older. This is made evident not only by statements from the various episcopates, but also by important actions undertaken in the fields of social and political work carried on by Catholic laymen.

Documents issued by diverse hierarchies reveal that with each succeeding occasion, the bishops have become increasingly certain that the social relations peculiar to the different aspects of life must be ruled by "Justice" as a *sine qua non* of the righteous practice of charity. In this manner, the mentality which looked to "charity" and "resignation" as a solution for social injustice is finally overcome. Two examples are found in the documents of the Chilean Episcopal Conference, "The Church and Chilean Peasant," issued in 1962, and "The Social and Political Duties of Catholics in the Present Time," issued in 1964. Another example is found on the Latin American level, when in 1966 CELAM (Council of Latin American Bishops) prepared the declaration of the Latin American episcopate gathered at Mar del Plata on "The Church and Latin American Intregration." These are eloquent examples of the decided good will of the Church in contributing to the temporal liberation of all men and countries as part of its evangelizing task.

Prior to Medellín and with the wisdom of the Universal Church, the Second Vatican Council, through publication of the Conciliar Constitution *Gaudium et Spes* and Paul VI's 1967 *Enciclica Populorum Progressio,* contributed to the enlightenment of the doctrinal reflection and action already undertaken by the Latin American Church.

Pre-Medellín documents insist not only on the practice of charity or welfare, which has always been part of the Church's work, but also on progressively making the church take into account the need for structural reforms to overcome injustice. It is no longer enough to provide immediate solutions of social assistance (always necessary) or to appeal only to the conversion of the heart of man, but rather it is necessary to uproot the profound causes of social evil through the promotion of structural reforms. These reforms, which are means and not ends in themselves, must lead to the integral development of the whole man and all men.

In accordance with the above, many national churches—those of Brazil, Chile, Venezuela, Colombia, Ecuador and Costa Rica—have supported the creation of movements of Christian inspiration such as cooperatives, trade unions, and projects for human promotion. The Church also helped create political parties of Christian inspiration.

Structural reforms, particularly agrarian reform, received decisive help from churches such as those in Chile and Ecuador which symbolically and actually contributed to the accelaration of the process by surrendering their own lands. The Church has also provided technical aid to the peasants through, for example, the Institute of Agrarian Promotion (INPROA).

It was precisely in the field of the promotion of structural reforms that the first serious disagreements arose within the social and political movements of Christian inspiration. Sharing the profound conviction of the need for structural change to pass from unjust situations to more just ones, disagreements developed regarding the proper speed of change and the best strategy to promote it effectively. The divisions which arose undoubtedly were more at the level of the "thinking elite" and leaders rather than that of the *"comunidad de base,"*[1] but the impact of these splits and the loss of energy they signified seriously damaged the effectiveness of what would have been a joint and sustained action on the part of Christians.

The impact of the Cuban revolution in its first period, together with the personality and activity of its principal leaders, attracted the sympathy of many Christian groups. In fact, during the 1960s and 1970s a number of Christians, disillusioned with reformism, started to speak about revolution. They adopted Marxist categories and methods of analysis, Marxist thought, and finally adopted Marxist strategy.

Until approximately 1965 the social doctrine of the Church constituted the fount of inspiration for the social and political actions of Christians. They not only searched for ethical orientation as such, but even thought that a finished model of a new society could be offered. This model, obtained through a series of social reforms, was to be an alternative to the intrinsic contradictions of liberal capitalism.

To a certain extent the Conciliar Constitution *Gaudium et Spes* frustrated the expectations of more committed groups in Latin America. It emphasized the autonomy of the temporal, proposed more of an anthropology than a model, and insisted that the mission of the Church be strictly religious. Thanks to the intervention of certain Latin American bishops, an addendum was made in No. 42: "But, from that precisely religious mission, functions, lights and energies are generated which can serve to establish the human community as per Divine Law."

It is perhaps during that decade that secular ideologies began to replace the Church's social doctrine. They rejected the mediation function of the social doctrine between faith and the social and political compromise, and attempted to subordinate faith to ideology and political commitments.

Critical groups within the Church reacted, charging that the social doctrine of the Church was abstract, ahistorical, static, and identified with a particular political and social movement—Christian Democracy. From their point of view, Christian Democracy had shown itself incapable of promoting a real revolution and a definitive break with liberal capitalism and imperialism. Other Christian groups more receptive to the Church's social thinking were so busy with tasks emanating from their urgent political responsibilities that they neglected doctrinal formation. They perceived, not without disillusion, that the Church was neither proposing models nor identifying herself with any of them, even though they were Christian-inspired. Consequently, the Church's social doctrine was eventually forgotten by some of these groups.

Medellín marked the beginning of a reevaluation of the Church's social doctrine. With the conference acting parallel to the consolidation of Liberation Theology, vast Catholic sectors supported more strongly the alternative position outlined previously.

The Significance of Medellín

From the standpoint of its immediate significance in the life of the Church, the 1968 meeting of the Latin American episcopate in Medellín deeply affected the living forces of the Church. It helped consolidate the bishops' consideration of the temporal dimension of the Church's evangelizing task and guaranteed its commitment in the fight for justice. It also gave Christian legitimization to many changes begun a decade ago, when it was thought that all structural changes emanated from Marxist groups. The Christian sectors realized the value of ecclesial ratification of their just aspirations. In addition, Medellín deeply and thoroughly analyzed the reality of Latin America and, from the standpoint of faith and with the moral authority belonging to the Church, denounced injustices in extremely vigorous language.

Together with the legitimation of the change process, this denunciation morally compelled many Latin American episcopates to take a more positive stand and renew their commitments in evangelizing and promoting justice and peace in Latin America.

The doctrinal horizon of the deliberations and conclusions of Medellín is based on the *Enciclical Populorum Progressio,* the Conciliar Constitution *Gaudium et Spes,* and Paul VI's 1968 speech in Bogotá. Its doctrinal scope must be understood in the frame of reference provided by these documents.

The meeting was structured around three fundamental topics: human promotion by the reaffirmation of justice and peace; evangelization and growth in faith; and finally, reflection on the visible Church and its structures.

A notable characteristic of the Medellín documents is the urgency of the call to immediate action. The document on "Justice" tells us that "It is necessary to work. It has not ceased to be the hour of speech but it has come to be, with an even more dramatic *urgency,* the hour for *action"* (CELAM, 1970: Justice 1, 3).[2] The same urgency was expressed in the document on "Peace" which states that the "static vision of the situation becomes even more intolerable when projected into the future," for a multiplication of problems and tensions is foreseen (Peace 2, 7).

The principles emphasized in these documents include *concientización;* that is, the awakening of the masses to consciousness so that through their participation in the realization of change and in the common effort to create a new society, they may become the true agents of their own liberation. This process of making the masses conscious is, in fact, an effort to enable them to assume their responsibilities in civic and political life. *Conscientización* is, then, a means of achieving *liberation.*

The word liberation is very frequently used in the Medellín texts to indicate the process of helping man free himself from the oppressiveness in which the majority of Latin Americans find themselves. "Our peoples desire their liberation and growth in humanness . . . they are filled with longing for total emancipation, liberation from all slavery, for personal maturity, and collective integration." The documents state that the laity is faced with the challenge of a liberating and humanizing commitment: to "liberate men from cultural, social, economic, and political slavery, all of which oppose our development" (Justice 1, 4, 7).

Another key concept in the documents is *participation.* The document on "Peace" states "that men should be the agents of their own history" (Peace 2, 14a), and declares that "justice, and therefore peace, are won through the dynamic action of the awakening and organization of the popular sectors of society which are capable of pressing action by public officials who are often impotent in the carrying out of their social projects without popular support" (Peace 2, 18).

Some of the central ideas which will cause greater repercussions in the future are the concepts of the liberation of man from all servitude, and the denunciation of established violence in structures of sin.

The reforms proposed by Medellín specifically reject approval of violent revolution and the violent activities of some groups, for in the majority of cases they only engender a spiral of more violence, repressive violence, kidnapping, torture, and terrorism.

The Latin American Church
After Medellín

Medellín signified a revitalization of ecclesial conscience and behavior in the face of social commitment required by the gospel, with the majority of episcopates writing pastoral letters on the theme of Medellín. Here the hierarchy increasingly exercised social criticism—the denunciation of injustice in all its forms.

As the Church is simultaneously universal and local, transcendental and historical, the general orientation of her preaching and activity responds to the most serious problems presented at any given moment. In the period before Medellín, stress was placed on seeking justice in human relations and gradually on the urgency of structural reforms. Since then, the changes taking place in the political order, with a proliferation of military regimes and economic models which imply a high social cost, have matured the ecclesial conscience, to the point of awareness that the greatest threat to justice lies in the increasing violation of human rights, the negation of many fundamental public liberties, recourse to torture as generalized practice, delay of the just aspirations of the most needy, and denial of any right to participate in politics—all well-known instances of this process.

The Church is not an opportunist in its fight for human rights: Pius XII focused his maximum concern and interest on this subject, and in John XXIII's 1963 encyclical *Pacem in Terris,* he asserts that if human rights are not respected, there is no possibility of peace for humanity.

In ecclesial reflection since Medellín, human rights comprise the basic requirement of an integral *development* of all men as the goal of economic activity. What is needed is civic coexistence based on majority consensus expressed in juridical, organizational, and governmental structures which are genuinely *democratic.* It may even be said that in the Church's view, there is no respect for human rights without integral development in the economic sphere and democracy in the political sphere. Denunciation of violations of human rights must accompany denunciations of violence in all its forms: terrorism, kidnapping, torture, extortion, and so on.

The Church's revitalization following Medellín signified a renewal of its commitment to the fight for justice, but also led to growing divisions among Christians concerning the pace of change and the most effective strategies to promote it. A new element surfaced to make this debate more disagreeable: the possibility of resorting to subversive violence as the only means to end the "institutionalized violence" which had been condemned in such hard terms at Medellín. Many impatient groups felt the condemnation of institutionalized violence and structures of sin expressed at Medellín justified returning to subversive violence or exclusively accepting those social processes which could result in a total change in the forms of human coexistence. Thus, many members of groups such as the Montoneros and Tupamaros have been formed in Catholic circles. At least originally, they seek in the Medellín declarations inspiration and orientation for their activities.

Added to this concern with violence was the effort to reduce the liberation praised by Medellín to a purely economic and political dimension. Economically, this meant the rupture of dependence; politically, it meant the abolition of all political power considered oppressive in nature.

The more general views of reality were also affected by this tendency and led many Christians to equivocal positions in social action to reduce the Church or people of God to the level of the social and economic poor. The massive presence of extreme poverty in Latin America exacerbated this position.

As a result of the increasing intraecclesial tension arising from different perceptions of the Church's temporal task and current historical commitment, at least three Catholic trends have emerged with distinct doctrinal and pastoral conceptions and divergent political positions. They are: (1) Catholic *integralism* of the political right wing; (2) Catholic progressivism, inspired by the official Papal documents and by those of the Latin American hierarchy; and (3) a current created around the Theology of Liberation, one manifestation being the movement called "Christians for Socialism." In addition to these three categories, there is a great variety of common Christians indifferent to a more sophisticated reflection, who practice a traditional Catholicism expressed in popular religion and who have been but superficially touched by the debate taking place among the more enlightened elite.

The Theology of Liberation is strengthened as a method of analysis and as a language capable of striking at the consciences of Christians to the extent that it is presented with biblical images. This gives it an evangelical character and a more directly religious tone than that of the social teaching of the Church. At the same time, it takes reality and historical practice as a privileged place from which thought must emanate in the light of faith, life, and destiny of man in general and the people of Latin America in particular.

To explain the causes of the socioeconomic prostration of Latin America, some branches of Liberation Theology use the theory of dependency to identify it as the cause of all evils in Latin America. This relates it to the Marxist diagnosis, in vogue for over a decade, and leads to consensus over the necessary strategy for breaking the chain of dependency from the capitalist system and in creating conditions for the liberation of men from all servitude. For them, this road can be offered only by socialism. However, they neglect to mention which form of socialism is offered, or what the real possibilities are for its establishment. Here, the answers are not clear. Meanwhile, this internal division continues to weaken the Church's task and its pledge for justice in Latin America.

It is important to point out a major fact in the life of the Church, especially for its lay members: the diminishing influence of the social and political groups of Christian inspiration in Latin America. Paradoxically, however, these same groups have again started to value doctrinal formation and appreciate the potential contribution of the social teaching of the Church. Dialogue with them, which for historical reasons became tense or impossible, has now been reestablished.

Neither the Church itself nor these groups now expect a model of organization of human coexistence to come from the social teaching. Both have learned that the value of this discipline and its special contribution to everyday life will have to be found in the explication of values and principles which must be respected in any model or system which seeks to order social relations. Lay Christians can elaborate their own model. The Church, as such, has none, but does have something to say to each of the models. In this measure social teaching becomes a fount of inspiration, an inducement, and sometimes even a utopia.

Finally, the Church has lost considerable influence in economic and political processes. Elites cannot ignore the presence and activity of the Church, but they have closed their ears to her word. The denunciation of injustice, whose most cruel expression is the violation of human rights, constitutes the primordial task of the Church in present historical circumstances. She has assumed this task with all the gravity that is required, exposing herself to the consequences. Thus, with the Church interpreting the feelings of vast majorities in Latin America, her moral prestige has grown in a sustained manner and she has truly become "the voice of those who have no voice." She finds herself, as never before, in the best situation for fulfilling her evangelizing task.

The Pre Document of Puebla

The main points of the Medellín documents dealing with the relation of the Church and society have been presented. Judging from the tone of the Pre Document,[3] we shall now attempt to demonstrate that the meeting in Puebla will follow the same course as that of Medellín.

The Pre Document of Puebla cannot be compared with that of Medellín. It is a working document to be criticized, modified, or even rejected. Of course, it is not an episcopal document of prophetic style, as was Medellín. This Pre Document for Puebla is partly the result of suggestions made during the four regional meetings of the various Latin American episcopates which took place during July and August 1977. Documentation covered over 300 pages. Minutes and suggestions reflecting the ongoing concerns of the bishops were compiled and later put in order.

On the topic of concern to us here, the relation of the Church to social problems, the Pre Document makes a social, economic, and political diagnosis while listing important points on the Church's social thinking. The diagnosis attempts to avoid comprehensive theories on the problems of underdevelopment and prostration in Latin America. Since the injustices are so evident in themselves and with different theories still not proven, the bishops did not want to set forth any one theory. Primarily, the Pre Document recognized that not only on the continent as a whole, but also in each country, there has been considerable *economic* progress over the last ten years (CELAM, 1978: para. 135). The central point repeated throughout the document (para. 135, 153) is that in spite of economic progress, the gap between rich and poor has widened in all countries (para. 140, 141) and the problem of *extreme poverty* remains one of the most important challenges (para. 142, 145).

These two facts present the greatest challenge to evangelization and to the true meaning of being a Christian. Although there is more poverty in Africa and Asia, these are non-Christian continents. To what extent can Latin America be considered Christian when justice and solidarity are not present and when life is not lived in a more fraternal society (para. 146)?

In the Pre Document this diagnosis binds the theme of extreme poverty with the problem of unemployment (para. 150) and other conditions of life which illustrate the great state of prostration. On the other hand, the possibilities of popular organization and mobility reportedly are weak, trade unionism is hampered, and the violation of union rights continues (para. 159). Furthermore, necessary structural reforms such as tax, agrarian, and judicial reform have not been carried out or are easily flouted (para. 162, 169). The political scene is characterized by a proliferation of military regimes to the detriment of civil participation (para. 173).

The concept of authority and the high concentration of power which are characteristic of regimes inspired by the ideology of national security have caused a wave of violation of human rights. This phenomenon is part of the rise of violence made more acute in relation to political order: subversion and countersubversion, insurrection and counter-insurrection, terrorism and kidnapping, repression and torture (para. 176).

Instead of leading to coexistence, political behavior is no longer integrated and becomes exclusionist without seeking political consensus, negotiation, or arbitration (para. 177). Pressure groups (para. 178) are then analyzed; the military sector, university students, trade unions, and so on. Among these groups, those with economic power stand out, their influence in government having increased during recent years. In accruing major advantages from national economic progress and foreign investments, they have become separated from the rest of the population. They also frequently control the social communication media.

One point of dispute in this Pre Document involves the causes of the state of prostration which affect great masses (para. 187). The causes are multiple, since numerous factors converge: historical, ethnic, cultural, economic, and political. Some are related to the problem of international justice, but it is difficult to solve them within Latin America unless there is greater integration of the countries or greater powers of negotiation. Economic dependence is pointed out as one of the most serious factors (para. 189), but not the only one. Others are imbalances in commerce, foreign debt, overdeveloped laws on the part of developed countries, and high royalties. In short, technological and scientific dependence are also important. All through history economic development of the developed countries has been accomplished through exploitation of the underdeveloped (para. 192). This dependence is also a cause of underdevelopment, tax evasion, and the flight of profits. Great emphasis is also placed on the grave problem of arms races, and military expenditure in general (para. 193).

The document implies the need for a real cultural revolution, as most Latin American problems are related to a cultural ethos in which work, honesty, austerity, and saving are considered of little value (para. 196). Perhaps not enough emphasis has been placed on the need for solidarity. Many problems are due to corruption, venality, and public and private immorality which not only disintegrate social relations, but also comprise unjust means of acquiring riches.

The other part of the Pre Document is related to several doctrinal problems. The social teachings of the Church insist on the theme of the community of goods and proper use of wealth for the common good (para. 723): "Property in its essential social projection cannot be a fount of privilege or of oppression, but of freedom and fraternity."

The theme of integral liberation which embraces the diverse dimensions of human existence is presented (para. 732). Liberation must lead everyone to participate in the same condition and enjoy the same rights and liberties, as well as favor fraternal communion with other men and with God (para. 734).

It defends the mission of the Church, which cannot be confined to a religious field alone, but also must be interested in temporal problems (para. 737). Among the doctrinal orientations, it insists that evangelization, integrally conceived, must be a fount of animation for the social presence of the Church (para. 745). Action for justice is thus a constitutive element or, better yet, an integral part of evangelization.

Some ideologies which have special standing in Latin America are analyzed, among them liberalism and various forms of socialism. There is criticism of the individualistic ideology of capitalism, inspired by the interests of a social class (the bourgeoisie) which applies the principle of freedom with serious contradictions, makes property an absolute right, and accepts social legislation only with great difficulty. Its fundamental motive is profit (para. 763). The document defines different socialisms and states that if a type of socialism respecting liberty, guaranteeing human rights, and ensuring a fraternal and truly democratic coexistence were fostered in Latin America, there would be no contradiction with Christianity.

In its criticism of Marxism, the Pre Document asserts that Marxist analysis cannot be disassociated from dialectical materialism. Capitalism, like collectivism, is a form of the sin of riches. Both systems, limiting their horizon to the economic, produce similar effects, generating forms of oppression and repression which spring from idolatry—an idolatry of material goods. Each in its own way is materialistic and atheistic, practically or theoretically (para. 787).

The Pre Document criticizes the theory of National Security and its connection with totalitarian theories and the submission of all human activity to the aims of the state. The document condemns not only rightist integralism, which instrumentalizes the faith and social teaching of the Church to restore old systems, but also leftist integralism, which instrumentalizes the faith in order to establish a revolutionary system, normally of the Marxist type.

The Pre Document suggests certain goals in the construction of a new society: (1) mechanisms to give voice to those who have no voice and to give form to desires which cannot be expressed (one has to act through them so that no one is marginal in the new society, and one must be able to work with those who are the most needy (para. 824); (2) formation of a community of goods for a society without privilege in which sufficient property gives everyone a necessary space for autonomy (para. 826), with emphasis on the social dimension of property, the common destiny of possession (para. 830), and the destruction of all "social domination" (para. 829); and (3) the construction of a true democracy.

Division of power is stressed, contrary to the practice of totalitarian regimes which tend to accumulate all power within the state. Democracy must be political, juridical, economical, and social—simultaneously. All intermediate groups are important and democracy should learn to live with them fully (para. 834-842).

Finally, the doctrinal portion describes as a necessary goal the discovery of a new way of life not limited to the possibilities available within the present model alone, but further implying austerity, especially on the part of those who own more, so that everyone's basic needs can be satisfied.

The Pre Document has had an extremely wide circulation, having been reprinted and discussed in almost all Latin American nations. During April and May 1978, each National Conference of Bishops prepared comments and sent them to the Council of Latin American Bishops. At CELAM a group of bishops representing the four regions into which Latin America had been divided, for practical reasons, together with a small group of experts, analyzed all contributions. Bearing in mind the most important points emphasized by the bishops, they then wrote the Basic Document of the Puebla meeting.

The Basic Document, shorter than the Pre Document, corrects some deficiencies of the older document and serves as the working paper for

Puebla. It contains the same concerns, and its socioeconomic and political analyses are similar to those of the Pre Documents.

Judging from the amount of preparation and analysis of the desires of all bishops attending the Latin American Conference of Bishops, one can certainly forecast that the Third Assembly of Puebla will be a step forward from the meeting held at Medellín.

NOTES

1. The popular level activities of the *comunidades de bases* are dealt with more fully in the Gilfeather and Smith articles in this volume.

2. While there is a 1973 English version of the Medellín document (CELAM) published by the U.S. Catholic Conference entitled "The Church in the Present-Day Transformation of Latin America in the Light of the Council," quotations in this article are English translations by the author from the Spanish original. The first number in these citations refers to the general category, and the second number refers to the numbered sections in that category.

3. The full title is "La Evangelizacion en el presente y en el futuro de America Latina . . . Documento de consulta a las Conferencias Episcopales."

REFERENCES

CELAM [Consejo Episcopal Latino americano] (1978) La Evangelización en el presente y en el futuro de América Latina. Puebla, Mexico, 1978. Preparación. Documento de consulta a las Conferencias Episcopales. III Conferencia General del Episcopado Latinamericano. Bogotá: General Secretariat of CELAM.

——— (1970) "The Church in the present day transformation of Latin America in the light of the Council." Second General Conference of Latin American Bishops. Bogotá: General Secretariat of CELAM.

3

WHAT HAPPENED AT PUEBLA

PHILLIP BERRYMAN

Bishop's meetings are usually not newsworthy. Most American Catholics are probably ignorant of the fact that their bishops meet semi-annually, let alone of their agenda. How explain, then, the presence of 2000 journalists at Puebla (McGrath, 1979: 5)? Certainly part of the explanation was the new Pope's visit to Mexico, but the press also sensed drama and conflict in the bishops' meeting: How would the issue of increasing Church-government conflict be treated? Would "liberation theology" be condemned? According to press reports, even the U.S. Senate, the CIA, and the Pentagon were concerned, apparently wondering whether there were any mitred ayatollahs.[1]

Allowing for journalistic oversimplification, I would argue that the intuition was essentially correct: Puebla was a clash—or better, the manifestation of an ongoing clash—within the Catholic Church in Latin America, a theological and pastoral conflict with political significance. While some (Sanders, 1979) would hold that the Puebla documents should be interpreted from their inner unity, I would hold that only when the conflicting positions are clearly understood can such unity as exists be appreciated.

Here I propose to examine the Puebla documents from the viewpoint of radicalized Catholics, i.e., those who see working for "liberation" (including deep structural change) as central to being a Christian in Latin America today. I will begin with some general remarks about the nature of the Puebla meeting, the various tendencies in the Latin American episcopate, and the events leading up to Puebla.

The formal title of the Puebla meeting was the Third General Conference of the Latin American Episcopate. Bishops' meetings have precedents going back to the early Church councils. A meeting such as CELAM III derives its importance partly from the doctrinal notion of bishops as "successors of the Apostles" and also from their weight in

Latin American society, where they are symbolically somewhat on a par with high civil authorities. Although strictly speaking, the Puebla meeting does not have any power and cannot enforce its decisions, since each bishop is sovereign in his own diocese, it is important for the tone it sets and as a voice of the Church on the continental level.

Since I will be insisting that Puebla is best understood as the result of a clash, I should attempt a description of the contending groups. This description is based on accounts of participants in the Puebla process, including bishops. (Note that the bishops themselves recognized that "we cannot deny that there are different viewpoints among us and divergent ways of looking at the present reality" [CELAM, 1979a].[2] Given the hierarchy's usual practice of maintaining a politburolike posture of public unity, this remark is revealing.)

Schematically, we can distinguish three groups or tendencies among the bishops (conservatives, liberationists, and center) on the basis of their agenda for internal Church issues and for the Church's presence in the world.

> *Conservatives:* Their image of the Church emphasizes the hierarchy and cultic and doctrinal elements. They would like to correct what they see as doctrinal errors and an attempt to set up a teaching authority in rivalry to the bishops on the part of liberation theologians and members of religious orders ("parallel magisterium"). They have typically been silent in the face of repression, whether through fear of conflict with governments or out of anticommunist sentiment.

> *Liberationists:* This group's vision of the Church is centered on the poor and on *communidades de base* (CEBs), and the hierarchy is seen in a serving role. Emphasis is placed on the ethical elements of Christianity. Liberationists tend to criticize not simply "abuses" such as torture, but current development models themselves, and to call for systemic change. Social programs are focused on leadership training and organization.

> *Center:* This group occupies a middle ground and is most concerned about the unity of the Church. With the conservatives it emphasizes hierarchical authority and with the liberationists it sees the need to defend human rights, at least in extreme situations. Its theological views tend to reflect Vatican Council II, e.g., stressing the distinction of the roles of clergy and laity. Its view of social change is (implicitly at least) more reformist than revolutionary, e.g., promoting development projects.[3]

Such a typology immediately demands a number of qualifications. These tendencies were identifiable in groups in the Puebla meeting, but it should be noted that bishops' positions may also be seen as a continuum. Although I am unapologetically sympathetic with the liberationists, I will try to maintain some objectivity.

Some would like to see the conservative group as more "religious" and the liberationist group as more "political," but I would hold that it is not a question of religion vs. politics but of how both faith and politics are seen and lived.

It is legitimate, then, to use conventional categories of right and left, although the "right" in this case tends to reflect the language of Christian Democracy, i.e., somewhat to the left of the Democratic party in the United States. There were no open advocates of Friedman economics or Pinochet politics at Puebla. Undoubtedly there are bishops whose sympathies lie in such directions, but their views were not enshrined in the documents. Similarly, it is impossible to imagine a serene discussion of Marxism or even Hayden-Fonda socialism at a meeting of the U.S. Catholic bishops.

By the same token, the "radicals" are such in a relative sense. There are probably no true Marxists among them, i.e., no bishops whose basic social vision is a coherent, structured Marxism. They defend the legitimacy of Christian-Marxist dialogue and collaboration, and some utilize Marxist ideas eclectically. Most of them strongly advocate nonviolent means of action, although they would not put the violence of those who struggle for liberation on the same plane as repressive violence.

I would argue that the liberationist bishops tend to be those who have had more direct experience with the poor and in many cases have experienced conflict with the power structure firsthand, while the contacts of the conservatives tend to be with the clerical world and with the upper classes and civil authorities (for a similar judgment, see Boff, 1979: 17). Of course some bishops in their dioceses might act paternalistically or autocratically, or impede things out of timidity, in spite of their professed progressive views. And others of conservative theological views might instinctively react to situations in a progressive way or at least allow some innovation and risk. For our purposes here, however, what matters is what positions the bishops were willing to endorse at Puebla.

Bishops are generally not chosen for their intellectual achievements, and many have no real positions. One bishop participant said that many of his colleagues *"estaban en la luna."* In such cases personal friendships or Church politics might outweigh intellectual cogency.

Medellín and Sucre: The Sides Line Up

Having begun *in medias res,* I would like to flash back to review some of the events preceding Puebla in order to understand how the issues were framed.

It could be said that the main effect of Vatican Council II (1962-1965) was that the Catholic Church reconciled itself to the Protestant Reform (Bible reading, vernacular worship) and the modern world (religious freedom, acceptance of the autonomy of the secular). CELAM II took place during the high-water mark of the "revolutionary" 1960s but the Catholic Church in Europe and the United States was still focused largely on internal Church issues—e.g., death-of-God theology, birth control. When the Latin American bishops decided to make social analysis, rather than doctrinal formulations, their starting point, they were entering uncharted territory.

One little noticed but highly important aspect was the key role of the *peritos* ("experts"), including the emerging Latin American theologians, such as Gustavo Gutierrez. It seems that much or even most of the writing was done by the peritos. The bishops signed the documents—hence, their weight—but the experts left their mark in the direct style, inner coherence, and forward stance.

By taking social reality as its starting point, the Medellín conference broke away from European "ecclesiocentrism" and began to see the Church in function of the whole society rather than as a self-contained end in itself. In so doing it opened the way for the Latin American Church to express its own identity. Medellín's language is a mixture of conventional terminology on underdevelopment and marginalization and the dependence theory of Latin American social scientists, but its call for "urgent, bold, thorough, and profoundly renewing transformations" (CELAM, 1969: 72) could be read as support for revolution, and in its typology of conservative, developmentalist, and revolutionary mentalities, it showed most sympathy for the latter.

Many priests and sisters, encouraged by Medellín, sought to identify with the poor (Gilfeather, this volume) and consequently found themselves often pushed into conflictive situations where they came to take sides. This experience suddenly made the Marxist notion of class struggle seem reasonable. Their initial ethical decision to share the life of the people became a political position, an option for liberation, basic systemic change, socialism. What I would emphasize is that as significant groups found themselves moving beyond the explicit positions of Medellín, they felt they were being faithful to its spirit and inner logic. This movement was catalyzed by the formation of national priests' groups (Dodson, this volume) proliferating international conferences, and the establishment of communication networks. Soon explicit liberation theology emerged (Berryman, 1973; Oliveros, 1977) and 450 delegates from all over Latin America gathered in Santiago, Chile, in 1972 for the first meeting of Christians for Socialism.

The bulk of the 650 or so bishops in Latin America was not really in agreement with the progressive thrust of Medellín, and particularly not with these latter extensions of its spirit. But they could hardly attack their own episcopal text, approved by Rome. They needed an alternative intellectual position, one which could use Medellín and other Church documents to rein in what they saw as abuses.

This position was eventually elaborated by Roger Vekemans, a Belgian Jesuit, in close association with Bishop Alfonso López Trujillo, at that time an auxiliary bishop of Bogotá. Since in journalistic accounts these two were cast as the villains who set out to undo Medellín, I would urge that if they did not exist they would have had to be invented; that is, they represented a move on the part of the bulk of the hierarchy to reassert itself after a period of two or three years in which the progressives had made great advances, even using official Church institutions to advance their ideas and programs.

López, Vekemans, and the team they assembled accomplished two important objectives: (1) They articulated an intellectual platform in the review *Tierra Nueva* and other publications. Their criticism of liberation theology and Christians for Socialism maintains a scholarly tone. (2) They successfully politicked to acquire power in the Church so as to implant their alternative viewpoint. Bishop López Trujillo was elected general secretary of CELAM at the bishops' meeting in Sucre, Bolivia, in November 1972.

López was thus put in charge of the day-to-day management of CELAM institutions. During these years CELAM training institutes had been giving intensive courses to hundreds of priests, sisters, and laypeople a year. Since the Medellín peritos were the professors, these institutes were platforms for progressive tendencies. López collapsed them down to one institute in Colombia, which could be closely monitored, and the list of professors was almost completely changed. CELAM publications began to expound the *Tierra Nueva* line. If Medellín could not be repealed, at least its official interpretations could be controlled.

To reiterate, such a development was almost inevitable inasmuch as the Vekemans-López position is more in line with the thinking of the bishops (and the Vatican) than that of liberation theologians. What might be questioned is the effort to systematically exclude the liberationist position, even as a minority voice.

Since the topic here is the Puebla meeting, I will omit any account of the larger developments which make up its context: worsening conditions for the poor majorities in Latin America, transnationalization of the economies, proliferating military regimes, increasing repression, violence, torture, and assassination. In spite of repressive violence there is an upsurge in "popular organizations," partly due to people's perceptions that traditional organizations such as political parties offer no possibility for significant change. Frequently the clergy and hierarchy have found themselves in conflict with "national security regimes": One study documented the cases of 36 priests killed, 46 tortured, 245 exiled or expelled, and 485 arrested or imprisoned during 1968-1978 (Dial, 1979). For the progressives, the post-Medellín years have made it evident that "liberation" will involve a long, painful—and violent—struggle.

The Puebla Process

Official CELAM III was held to mark the tenth anniversary of Medellín. As the previous conference applied Vatican II to Latin America, the Puebla meeting was to apply Paul VI's apostolic exhortation *Evangelii Nuntiandi*, which came out of the 1974 Roman synod of bishops on evangelization.

It seems that López Trujillo and others (including Vatican authorities) saw the conference as an opportunity to give more status to the positions they were propagating. They hoped to insist on certain "clarifications" of Medellín and delegitimize certain interpretations of the liberationists, by presenting the official position of the Church and setting limits on how much pluralism would be tolerated in doctrine and practice. With equal determination others would struggle to prevent the dynamism of Medellín from being checked.

"Evangelization in the Present and the Future of Latin America" was the chosen title. Curiously, evangelization is a very new topic for the Catholic Church. At Puebla the bishops state that the Church "exists to evangelize" (CELAM, 1979b: para. 348; this citation will henceforth be referred to with paragraph numbers). But none of them learned this in the seminary, where they were taught rather to see the Church as the depository of the "means of salvation" rather fundamentalistically. Vatican II gave official status to a "Copernican revolution" in Catholic theology: God's saving grace is at work *throughout humanity* (not simply in the Church), and the Church is to be a *sign* of this universal call to salvation. However, even at Vatican II, "evangelization" was still related to the missions, i.e., "evangelizing" non-Christians. Medellín spoke of the "reevangelization of the baptized" but did not develop the idea. Only with the 1974 synod of bishops and *Evangelii Nuntiandi* did it become common to see evangelization presented as the central mission of the Church.

Presumably this development involves a radical reorientation of the raison d'être of the Church: The Church exists to communicate a message, a call to conversion, rather than to act as the dispenser of the means of salvation. This is either a radical new departure—or it is simply using new terminology for what has always been done. One has the impression that the bishops have not really internalized this development. Evangelization does not seem to be the real subject of Puebla—the topic itself created little controversy—but rather functions as a hatrack on which to hang other agenda items. It further has the advantage of appearing more "religious" than the topic of Medellín, which was the Church's presence in the "transformation" of Latin America.

Puebla was preceded by almost two years of preparation. In late 1977 the CELAM secretariat produced a preparatory document (1978a) ostensibly the result of a process of consultation among the bishops in their national conferences and regional meetings, although some bishops complained that their contributions were unrecognizable and that the document really emanated from López Trujillo's team. Another round of discussions and consultations followed, whose results were collated (this time by a group of bishops) into a working document (CELAM, 1978c), which in its outline and language foreshadows much of what emerged in Puebla.

It will be noted that the consultation took place primarily among the bishops rather than in the whole Church as such. The observations of other sectors fed into the process only to the degree to which each national episcopal conference saw fit to incorporate them. The process did, however, occasion innumerable meetings of documents, some officially convoked and some marginal to the Church structure, and it unleashed a deluge of hundreds of articles (extensive bibliography in Crie, 1979b; examples in Anonymous, 1978c; CRT, 1978; Delgado, 1978; Gutierrez, 1978a). Among all these documents two elaborated by a group which met in Venezuela in early 1978 (Anonymous, 1978a, 1978b) stand out as the most deliberate attempt to elaborate a liberationist position as an alternative to that being proposed by the CELAM secretariate.

Since the issues reappear in the Puebla documents, I will here omit any detailed discussion of the earlier documents. However, I cannot resist quoting a paragraph from the Brazilian theologian Clodovigis Boff, who attempts to cut through to the heart of the working document. When the Church speaks of a "new Christian civilization," its implicit model of society is a "new Christendom."[4] The Church's mission is seen as one of helping the transition from an agrarian-rural to an industrial-urban society, and the chief pastoral problem is defined as "secularism," i.e., the exclusion of God from the world. Boff counters that the secularization process is irreversible and that

> the knot of the question is not preaching but practice. Therefore the issue that should interest the Church in Latin America is not cultural—whether or not society continues to define itself as religious, as the document wants it to be. The decisive question for the Church should be social, especially on economic and political levels—whether society will be egalitarian and libertarian or not. It is not enough to say that it is open to transcendence. The decisive thing is to organize a just society so that it will live transcendently [1978: 15].

Puebla was delayed several months by the death of two popes, and thus there was another round of discussion, particularly among grass-roots groups. Finally in late January the delegates and hundreds of others gathered in Puebla, a city known for its conservatism. There were 184 voting participants (all bishops) and 140 nonvoting participants. Of the bishops, 168 were directly chosen by national episcopal conferences and seem to have been a fairly representative cross section of the Latin American episcopate. Four bishops were ex officio delegates, and Rome appointed 12, virtually all conservative. There was considerable criticism of the fact that almost all the 140 nonvoting delegates (priests, religious, and laypeople) were hand picked by the López group. Although sisters make up well over half the Church's full time personnel, only about 4% of the delegates were women. Of the 20 peritos only one could be considered sympathetic to the liberationist cause. Some unusual guests included European ecclesiastics known for their anticommunism and two representatives of the right-wing De Rance Foundation, which was later alleged to have been a major financier of the Puebla meeting.[5] While only bishops could vote, the other delegates could certainly contribute ideas and help set the tone (Sep, 1978: 16-24).

The radicals also rallied to Puebla. From Latin America, Europe, and North America arrived hundreds of people identified with the liberation cause. Some had ad hoc press credentials while others represented interest groups: Latin America exiles, human rights groups, women's groups, Chicanos, etc., and during the bishop's meetings there were press conferences, panel discussions, and other events reflecting their diverse agendas. Over 30 theologians and social scientists met daily a few blocks from the seminary where the bishops were enclosed, to serve as an unofficial resource group for a bloc of about 40 bishops. There was a deliberate effort to avoid creating a parallel conference or "counter-Puebla."

Enter Karol Wojtyla, Pope John Paul II, still an unknown quantity. Some hoped that a humanistic and cultured non-Italian pope, who had lived most of his adult life in a socialist society, might open some surprising doors. They were disappointed when his speeches sounded like they had been drafted by the López group (a definite possibility through Vatican contacts such as Cardinal Baggio). He pointedly told priests and religious to avoid "sociopolitical radicalisms" and cautioned about "incorrect" interpretations of Medellín. In a more general sense, he did not at first seem to be encouraging the bishops to take bold stands. Yet a closer reading of his speeches in Mexico reveals that he mentioned liberation 30 times and emphasized the defense of human rights, the links between the gospel and human promotion, and the rights of workers and peasants to organize (Wojtyla, 1979).

López Trujillo suffered a setback around the beginning of the meeting when copies of a letter he had written to a conservative Brazilian archbishop were circulated. This letter put the spotlight on his use of power and his contempt for bishops of other tendencies.[6] His role in the process being momentarily weakened, the way was open for more "centrist" figures to assume leadership.

Other events at the outset of the meeting were favorable to the liberationists. CELAM President Cardinal Aloisio Lorscheider of Brazil strongly emphasized human rights in his opening address. A motion from some conservatives not to put the social analysis first— which would have been tantamount to reversing the Medellín methodology—was rejected. A special commission chosen to coordinate the small working groups was made up of progressive or centrist figures.

This group made positive suggestions to the commissions and sought to give an overall tone to the documents. It is largely due to their effort that the "option for the poor" emerged as a leitmotif of the meeting.

Twenty-one working groups were formed to elaborate documents following an agreed-upon outline.[7] There was considerable shifting around among commissions as conservatives and radicals attempted to use their resources to best advantage—some joked that they were playing "man to man," as in soccer. The theologians and social scientists "outside the walls" formed parallel commissions to study and critique the documents in process and send their suggestions into the meeting (for a collection of their contributions, see Gorostiaga, 1979). They began with a "positive exegesis" of the Pope's inaugural address to CELAM III (Christus, 1969: 106-108).

Once the meeting was under way, there was little news of what was happening inside the tightly guarded seminary, to the annoyance of the press. The documents went through four drafts, passing from commissions to general sessions and back to commissions. It seems that the schedule was designed to keep the bishops in small commissions as much as possible so as to reduce the possibility of the overall thrust of things being changed. Changes could be made only in the form of additions or elimination of specific points, or in phrasing and emphasis. Still the documents seem to have progressed notably from the earliest drafts which were bland to the point of irrelevance (for an account, see Dussel and Espinosa, 1979; Cencos, 1979; Crie, 1979b, daily bulletins during the conference on Mexican press coverage and extensive documentation).

The Puebla Documents

What finally counts is what the bishops wrote and approved at Puebla.

The voice speaking at Puebla is emphatically *episcopal* as distinguished from *ecclesial:* The bishops are speaking as bishops vis-a-vis the Church as a whole. Certainly Medellín was a bishops' meeting, but at the time many Christians heard their own concerns expressed there and felt it was a meeting of the Church being given voice through the bishops. Since the tone of Medellín came largely through the peritos, López Trujillo maintained a careful control over their selection for Puebla. One indication of the "episcopal" nature of the documents is the strong emphasis on the hierarchical aspect of the Church. Many will probably take a more distant and critical view than they did of Medellín: Puebla is not the last word, but part of a dialogue.

As the meeting was closing, I asked one theologian what he thought of the final documents. "Quite good," he said. "We could compile a 'Little Red Book' of good quotations." He paused. "Of course *they* could put together their own 'Little Black Book'."

On virtually every page, and sometimes in the same paragraph or sentence, there are diverse categories and languages which reflect divergent—ultimately contradictory—visions of Church and society. For example, there is a conscious and somewhat forced attempt to make the phrase "communion and participation" a common thread throughout the documents. Its constant repetition tends to play down any element of conflict. But the repeated mention of "liberation" cannot but evoke the image of struggle.

The two languages and visions are not on an equal footing. The basic framework was set up by the conservative group and could only be modified by adding some elements and diminishing others. The conservatives laid down the basic harmony and melody, to which the liberationists could add some dissonances and counterpoint melodies, which at some moments became the main theme.

Is there a single meassage, a summary, a leitmotif, in the Puebla documents on which all can agree? I think not, and the initial post-Puebla commentaries confirm this estimate. Each attempt to summarize the documents reflects the angle of vision of the summarizer.

The 21 documents are grouped into five "nuclei" (see note 7 for more detail). The first nucleus, "Pastoral Vision," takes up the historical background, a social analysis of Latin American society, and a description of the situation of the Church. There follows a doctrinal section (Jesus Christ, the Church, Man and Human Dignity).[8] The third nucleus, on evangelization, takes up the most controverted topics, particularly the meaning of liberation, and ideology and politics. A fourth nucleus deals with groups in the Church (family, CEBs, clergy, laity, and the like) and the Church's activities (worship, education, and so on). The last nucleus, which represents largely the agenda of the progressives (especially the option for the poor, and the defense of human rights), was tacked onto the original outline, already discernible in the working document.

Puebla did not step back from Medellín, particularly in its denunciation of injustice, inequality, dependence, and repression.

From deep within the different countries of Latin America, there is a cry rising to heaven, ever louder and more striking. It is the shout of a people suffering and demanding justice, freedom, respect for the basic rights of man and peoples. . . .

The cry may have been weak then [Medellín]. Now it is clear, increasing, impetuous, and sometimes threatening [87, 89].

In the light of faith, we see the increasing gap between rich and poor as a scandal and a contradiction to the essence of Christianity. . . . The wealth of a few becomes an insult to the misery of the great masses. . . . In this anguish and pain the Church discerns a situation of social sin, all the more serious in countries calling themselves Catholic, and which are capable of changing [28].

[The] vast majority of our brothers continue to live in a situation of poverty and even misery which has gotten worse; they lack the most elementary material goods, in contrast to the accumulation of wealth in the hands of a minority, often at the cost of the poverty of the many. The poor not only lack material goods but also on the level of human dignity they do not have a full social and political participation. In this category are mainly our indians, peasants, workers, marginal people of the city, and especially the woman in these social sectors because of her doubly oppressed and marginalized condition [1135; see also 29].

This last sentence takes on added importance in light of the conservatives' insistence on seeing Christian poverty as being "poor in spirit," which weakens any treatment of poverty as a class phenomenon. Elsewhere the document eloquently speaks of the "faces" of poverty:

very concrete faces in which we should recognize the suffering features of Christ our Lord, who questions and challenges us:

—faces of indians and frequently also of Afro-Americans who, living marginalized and under inhuman conditions, may be considered the poor among the poor;

—faces of peasants who, as a social group, are shoved aside almost everywhere in the continent, without land, dependent internally and externally, subject to marketing systems which exploit them.

There are similar descriptions of the "faces" of workers, shantytown dwellers, the unemployed, youth, children, and the aged.[9]

Since access to goods and services as well as to political decision making is impeded, attacks on freedom of thought, religious freedom and physical integrity become worse. Assassinations, disappearances, arbitrary jailing, acts of terrorism, kidnappings, and continent-wide torture, not only show a complete disrespect for the dignity of the human person, but also attempt to justify themselves as national security needs [1262; see also 42 and 314; the last is a description of the national security state].

The free market economy . . . has increased the distance between rich and poor by making capital prevail over labor and the economic over the social [47].

A cold technocracy applies development models which demand a truly inhuman social cost from the poorer sectors, which is so much more unjust in that it is not shared by all [50].

Especially where there are regimes of force, the organization of workers, peasants, and other popular sectors is suspect, and repressive measures are taken to prevent it. This kind of control and limitation is not applied to businessmen's organizations which can exert all their power to assure their interests [44].

In speaking of dependence the bishops denounce

the presence of multinational conglomerates which often seek their own interests at the cost of the host country's welfare; [and the] declining value of our raw materials in relation to the prices of the manufactured goods we buy [66].

Examples of such denunciation are numerous, and one senses that they were not regarded as too controversial and were approved by consensus. What is much less clear is the *causality* of these evils, for an attempt at explanation involves the use, at least implicit, of some social science framework. In Latin America one must choose between conventional (developmental) and radical (dependence) frameworks. The former assume that development can take place in continuity and within present economic and political systems in an evolutionary manner, while the latter insist that genuine development for the majorities is systematically excluded in the present systems and that only a radical break (revolution, in some sense) can make it possible.

One particularly illustrative example of juxtaposed social visions appears in the document on the "Evangelization of Culture." The overall tone is "developmentalistic" and optimistic about the "coming universal culture." "In the transition from agrarian to urban industrial culture, the city becomes the moving force of the new industrial civilization" (429). Secularism is a threat to the faith of Latin American peoples. Hence the Church must update its evangelization so that the people may take on the values of the new urban-industrial civilization in a living synthesis whose foundation will continue to be faith in God and not atheism which is the logical consequence of the secularizing movement [436; see 434-435].

Obviously in this view the "urban-industrial civilization" is a given and the Church's concern is not to critique the society but to preserve the faith.

Yet there is a strong counterpoint melody. This urban-industrial culture is said to bring about "proletarization" and is controlled by the great powers who possess science and technology (417). People are being forced to enter this pretendedly universal culture, e.g., indians, when their land and labor are desired for "development" (422).

[But the Church] obviously questions that universality which is synonymous with leveling and uniformity, which does not respect different cultures, weakening, absorbing, and eliminating them. Even more, the Church does not accept that instrumentalization of universality which is equivalent to a unification of humanity by way of an unjust and injurious supremacy and domination by some peoples and social sectors over other peoples and sectors [302].

This qualification amounts to an emphatically alternative judgment on what the "coming universal culture" means.

But are not these complementary aspects of a single vision? The best evidence comes from the preparatory document (CELAM, 1978a, summarized 1978b), which presumably represents the thought of the López group in its purest form. There what is happening in Latin America is described as the "transition from agrarian-urban to urban-industrial society." The Church lost its chance during the similar transsition in Europe because of its opposition to secularism which was taken to mean opposition to modernity, but in Latin America it *"can be the animator* of the new process of the formation of urban industrial society" (Agudelo, 1978: 11).

The preparatory document was widely criticized for attempting to replace the struggle for justice with collaboration in the building of a new (Christian) civilization (Gutierrez, 1978b; Delgado, 1978; Boff, 1978). The López vision was considerably attenuated in the working document, and it ends up in Puebla in uneasy coexistence with a more critical vision.

Nowhere is the juxtaposition of social visions more evident than in the one explicit attempt to indicate the "deep roots" of Latin America's problems. The bishops list (a) the lack of structural reforms in agriculture, (b) the arms race, (c) the lack of regional integration, (d) economic systems which do not put man at their center and do not bring about the changes needed for a just society, (e) economic, technological, political, and cultural dependence, (f) crisis of moral values, and (g) the mystery of sin (63-70). It is true that the bishops make a disclaimer: As pastors they do not intend to "determine the technical nature of these roots" (70), but the resulting catalogue offers something for everyone and seems equally susceptible to interpretation from developmentalistic as from radical viewpoints.

There are at least two places where injustice and poverty are seen to be the result of social structures.

Upon analyzing more deeply this situation, we discover that this poverty is *not a transitory state:* but it is the product of economic, social and political situations and *structures* (30, italics added).

This statement amounts to a rejection of "stages of growth" developmentalism. Elsewhere the bishops speak of "two clear tendencies" at work in Latin America, one toward modernization, economic growth, urbanization, and technical advance, and another toward pauperization and increasing exclusion of the majority of Latin Americans from productive life.

These contradictory tendencies favor a privileged minority's appropriation of a great part of the wealth and of the benefits created by science and culture but on the other hand, generate the poverty of the great majority.

Thus there arises a grave structural conflict [1207-1209].

This is the clearest statement that the accumulation of wealth by some *causes* the poverty of others. One may suspect that "grave structural conflict" may become a catchphrase as did Medellín's "institutionalized violence."[10]

In sum, while Puebla's denunciation of injustice is fairly vigorous, its analysis is more a juxtaposition of various kinds of explanation. This ambiguity is a reflection of the coexistence of various visions within the Church. Some of these considerations will be amplified when we consider the bishops' indications for action and their model of society (if any).

While at first glance the doctrinal expositions on Jesus Christ and the Church would not seem relevant to our purpose, these topics are more "political" than might appear. The document on Jesus Christ passes over the work of recent Latin American theology, whose main insight has been the theological dimension of conflict in Jesus' life and death. Traditionally Jesus' death was presented as a "sacrifice" for humanity. The concrete circumstances might be moralized upon—e.g., Pilate washing his hands—but were not considered theologically important. Recent work, especially that of Sobrino (1977), highlights the fact that His death came as the result of a conflictive message and a struggle with religious and political authorities. His message led to His death and His resurrection vindicates His (conflictive) message. This does not mean that Jesus was a revolutionary in the modern sense—which would be an anachronism—but that the element of conflict is not an accidental cicumstance but is essential for understanding His message and life. There is moreover an affinity between the struggle of people for justice today and Jesus' struggle for the Kingdom. The Puebla document, by contrast, presents a static image of Christ, mainly in glory. Such an emphasis must be intentional.

Puebla's observations on the Church are found both in the document on the "People of God" and throughout all the documents. There are two kinds of images reflected: one more traditional "from above," which emphasizes hierarchical authority, and one "from below," which sees the local community, particularly the CEB, as the key element.

Several times it is repeated that the Church must be "independent of the powers of the world" so that it can fulfill its mission (144).

In the year or two prior to Puebla there was considerable discussion of the "popular Church." While the term is not utterly precise, it emphasizes that the Church's center of gravity should be in the *pueblo,* understood as the popular classes. For the Church to be genuinely the Church, it must be born in the poor, and indeed, in the struggle of the poor (see essays in CRT, 1978). The bishops seem to be countering this notion when they imply that the Church is congruent with Latin American society. They say that there is a "radical Catholic substratum" in Latin American culture (1) and see a kind of identification between the natural pueblo and the *Pueblo de Dios* which accompanies it in its history and which has been a unifying factor in the culture (234). Such an idea marks off the continent as Catholic turf. To radical critics, however, this will undoubtedly seem to be "ecclesiastical populism" and reflect an undialectical notion of the "people." For the liberationists the "new Church" is being born in the struggle of the popular classes.

While it does not condemn the term "popular Church" Puebla questions it.

> The term seems unfortunate. The "popular Church" seems to be different from "another" which is identified as the "official" or "institutional" Church, which is accused of being "alienating". This would imply a division in the bosom of the Church and an unacceptable negation of the hierarchy's function. Such positions, according to John Paul II could be inspired by well known ideological conditionings [263].

Note that this attack on the "popular Church" invokes both hierarchical authority and anti-communism, two key points of the conservative agenda as mentioned above.

Although a good part of the ferment in the Latin American Church comes from CEBs it seems that hardly anyone in the commission which dealt with this topic had any direct experience of them. The resulting document praises CEBs but ignores their political significance (for human rights, see Smith, this volume). For example, in some places it has frequently happened that a lay leader of a CEB is also a leader in one of the popular organizations. One wonders whether this kind of issue was brought up, or whether people feared either premature condemnations or preferred not to risk legitimating any political role for CEBs (for this whole question, see UCA Editores, 1979).

Another significant doctrinal point is the definition of what "salvation" and "liberation" mean. What is the relationship between otherworldly and this-worldly salvation? What are we to be liberated from and what for?

> Ths salvation offered by Christ gives meaning to all human aspirations and accomplishments but it always questions them and infinitely goes beyond them.

> This same salvation, the center of the Good News, "is a liberation from everything which oppresses man but above all liberation from sin and the evil one."

> But it has "very strong ties" with human promotion in its aspects of development and liberation . . . which are an integral part of evangelization [353-355].

Liberation has

> two complementary and inseparable elements: liberation from all servitudes, from personal and social sin, from everything that tears

man and society apart, and which has its origin in selfishness, in the mystery of iniquity. And liberation for progressive growth in being, through communion with God and man which culminates in perfect communion in heaven where God is all in all and there will be no more tears.

It is a liberation which is being worked out in history, the history of our peoples and our personal history which embraces the different dimensions of life: the social, the political, the economic, the cultural and all their interrelationships [482-483].

Such a balancing act can be read with satisfaction from different angles: Conservatives can emphasize the aspect of transcendence which they see threatened by "horizontalism," while progressives can point to the affirmation that development and liberation on this earth are intrinsic to Christian salvation.

What does Puebla propose in the way of action? I would find that its general orientations are more significant than whatever specific recommendations it may make. We now turn to some of these considerations.

Some will make Puebla's call to a "preferential option for the poor" the key for interpreting all the documents. The document so titled is the most vigorous and straightforward of all and the idea is mentioned in a number of other documents (382, 707, 711, 733, 769, 1217). The document itself begins with one of Puebla's more eloquent denunciations of the effects of poverty in Latin America and notes that the commitment of bishops, priests, religious, and laity to the poor has led the Church to denounce "profound injustices which derive from oppressive mechanisms" and that consequently the Church has suffered persecution (1136, 1138). The poor on their part "encouraged by the Church have begun to organize to live their faith in an integral way and therefore to claim their rights" (1137). To me this text subtly links popular organizations and CEBs: By alluding to them in the same breath it insinuates that they have a common root inspiration.[11]

The bishops sketch a theological basis for this option. The Church's commitment must be like that of Christ who "committed himself to the most needy" and whose death was the "greatest expression of poverty." The poor deserve preferential attention, apart from their moral or personal condition. Because the image of God in them is shadowed or disfigured "God takes up their defense and loves them." They are the prime objects of evangelization, and the evangelization of the poor is the sigh of Jesus' mission (1141-1142). Approaching the poor person in service, we do what Jesus showed us in "becoming our poor brother like us"

(1145). CEBs have helped the Church to "discover the evangelizing potential of the poor, insofar as they challenge it and call it to conversion and insofar as many of them live out the gospel values of solidarity, service, simplicity, and readiness to receive God's gift" (1147). The bishops call Christians to simplicity of life. Such a witness from the Church "may evangelize the rich whose hearts are tied to wealth, converting them and liberating them from this slavery and from their selfishness" (1156).

Concluding, the document says that CELAM condemns the extreme poverty of Latin America as antievangelical; makes an effort to get to know and denounce the mechanisms which generate this poverty; unites its efforts with other churches and with people of good will to eliminate this poverty and create a more just and fraternal world; supports the aspirations of workers to be treated as free and responsible and to participate in decisions which concern their lives; and defends their right to create their own organizations (1159-1163).

In the eyes of the liberationists this document will undoubtedly be considered the one that most unambiguously embodies what they stand for. Not for the least of its merits is its theological grounding of what some from the outside see as simply a political option.

A related development is the repeated idea that the defense of human rights is an essential part of the Church's mission. Parallel to documents on Jesus Christ and the Church is one called "Man and Human Dignity," which provides a doctrinal basis for these activities. In one document we read:

> [The] Church, as expert in humanity, has to be the voice of those who have no voice (of the person, of the community vis-à-vis the society, of weak nations vis-à-vis powerful ones). Its proper activity is that of teaching, denunciation and service.
>
> Declaring the fundamental rights of the human person, today and in the future, is, and will be, an indispensable part of its evangelizing mission [1268, 1270; see also 146, 338, 1304].

There follows a catalogue of human rights.[12]

Prior to Puebla there was considerable discussion of human rights, and particularly a critique of "bourgeois" conceptions, centered on political and civil rights, which ignore the structural mechanisms that keep the majorities from access to work and basic necessities (see two collections of essays: Assmann [1978] and Tamez and Trinidad [1978]).

Critics said that the Church could fall into the trap of simply defending human rights after the manner of the Carter government and thus lend its political weight to a move toward "restricted democracy" (civilian regimes replacing direct military government) which would in no way produce the structural changes necessary for the poor to enjoy basic rights. The radicalized sector speaks of the "rights of the poor," while the center tendency tends to see the defense of human rights more in the bourgeois sense. It seems that Puebla can again be read both ways on this issue.

A clear goal scored by the conservatives (soccer terminology again) is "Evangelization, Ideologies, and Politics." This document begins by recognizing that the Church has a right and duty to be present in the field of politics "because Christianity should evangelize the whole of human existence" (515). The Church's mission, however, is religious, and it has no political, economic, or social purpose in entering this field (519).

There follows a key distinction: *politics in the broad sense,* the pursuit of the common good, which involves the whole community, as distinct from *party politics,* whereby groups of citizens attempt to acquire power according to their own criteria and ideologies, which may differ. The Church is involved in the former in its witness, teaching, and pastoral work, but the latter is the proper field of the laity alone. Priests and bishops as "ministers of unity" and "men of the absolute" should refrain from party politics (except in very exceptional circumstances and with permission). Religious should also resist this temptation "so as not to cause the confusion of gospel values with a particular ideology." The bishops remind priests and religious of the Pope's warning not "to give in to socio-political radicalisms." There is a one-line warning to lay-people involved in pastoral activity not to use their authority in favor of parties or ideologies (521-530).

At first glance the text appears to be a clear prohibition of political activity on the part of leftist priests and religious. (Note, however, that the logic applies equally to the right—e.g., military chaplains or bishops and nuncios who appear in ecclesiastical regalia alongside generals in dress uniform at ceremonial occasions and thus lend their symbolism to regimes in power.) The clarity disappears when one looks closer. The description of party politics tends to connote a situation in which there is basic consensus in society and in which parties contend on an equal plane for public support. It is not so clear whether it is so applicable to a situation where society is organized in favor of a privileged minor-ity, where the poor are put down by violence, and where political parties have a largely ornamental function, or serve as vehicles for contending upper-class groups to dispute secondary issues. Furthermore, the case of priests active in political parties is rare today, although it was common during the Popular Unity period in Chile. The more usual case today is that of the popular organizations which Puebla in general supports. Does this document intend to prohibit participation in these movements by priests and religious? Since my remarks here may be read as tendentious I would simply say that the apparent clarity disappears the closer one gets to the reality of Latin America today and that the issue remains somewhat open. Archbishop Romero of El Salvador has published a pastoral letter on the Church and pastoral popular organizations wherein he lays down more specific guidelines (UCA Editores, 1979: 13-40).

Similar treatment is given to ideology which is defined as

a conception which offers a vision of different aspects of life from the angle of a particular group in society. Ideology manifests this group's aspirations, calls for a certain solidarity and combativity, and bases its legitimation on specific values. Every ideology is partial, since no particular group can pretend to identify its aspirations with those of society as a whole [535].

Ideologies tend to absolutize their interests, vision, and strategy and become "lay religions." The gospel and the Church's social teaching are not ideologies, but, on the contrary, they question the limits and ambiguities of ideologies. Three ideologies in Latin America are described:

liberal capitalism—Profit is what moves economic activity, and private property has a limitless right to the means of production. The results are scandalous contrasts, dependence, and oppression, both nationally and internationally. The document recognizes that capitalism has encouraged freedom and progress and that its negative effects have been limited by social legislation in some countries.

Marxist collectivism—Class struggle is its moving force as it attempts to establish a classless society by means of a dictatorship of the proletariat, generally actually a dictatorship of the party. All its historical expressions have been totalitarian. Those who think it possible to separate Marxist analysis from its philosophy are reminded of the unity of Marxism.

national security—It is tied to a particular economic-political model, elitist and top-down, which suppresses the people's participation in political decisions and carries out a "permanent war" of repression, justifying itself as a defender of Western Christian civilization (542-549).

Throughout Puebla capitalism and Marxism are treated in tandem (312-313, 418, 437, 495, 497): Both are materialistic, both are atheistic (one in practice and the other militantly) both are idolatrous (one of individual wealth and the other of collective wealth). Only once or twice is there any hint that the evils of capitalism are *present* in Latin America while those of Marxism are *hypothetical* dangers.

> Fear of Marxism keeps many from facing the oppressive reality of liberal capitalism. It can be said that, faced with the danger of one system of sin, they forget to denounce and combat the established reality of another system of sin [92].

The treatment of Marxism seems strong, but liberationists still have their toe in the door. As L. Boff insists (1979: 33), a warning about risks does not mean condemnation. Puebla also recognizes that historical movements may be distinguished from the philosophical theories which inspired them and that Christians who participate in them should practice "ecclesial discernment," fortify their own identity, and be aware of the difficulties (554-557). Presumably these observations are made with Marxist-inspired movements in mind.

Puebla insists that the Church does not need ideologies since its message is enough for it to "love, defend, and collaborate in liberation" (55, quoting the Pope). The impression given is that the Church, and specifically the hierarchy, considers itself above ideologies. In this connection the prize *bon mot* of Puebla must surely be that of Bishop German Schmitz of Peru, who said in one plenary session: "Let him who is without ideology throw the first stone" (Dussel, 1979: 31).

Liberation theorists have already sketched a critique of this position (Anonymous, 1978b). They note three meanings of the term "ideology": (1) a cover or justification for the dominant interests of the existing social system; (2) a total philosophy or world vision; (3) a system of means and ends for facing a particular historical period, trying to lead it to goals which are partial and subject to revision. Church documents have almost always treated ideology in the second sense, unfortunately thus ignoring how faith is conditioned by surrounding social reality, and even more seriously how religion has served to cover dominant interests (meaning 1). They urge that ideology be taken in meaning 3, which obviously gives it a more provisional and less total character.

They insist that since there are various ways of organizing society, the Church cannot be indifferent about whether systems favor the welfare of the many or of the few, encourage solidarity or individualism, or stimulate or repress freedom. In these questions of life or death, Christians must be "partial" with the partiality of the God who takes the side of the poor and the oppressed. "Faith therefore ... not only can but must be ideologized and take sides, and thus take flesh and commit itself to concrete human history" (Anonymous, 1978b: 229).

Puebla's treatment of violence is another balancing act.

We want to make a clear pronouncement on the deplorable reality of violence in Latin America. Physical and psychological torture, kidnappings, the persecution of political dissidents and suspects and their exclusion from public life for their ideas, are always worthy of condemnation. If such crimes are carried out by authorities in charge of watching over the common good they debase those who practice them, whatever the reasons they allege.

With equal decisiveness the Church rejects terrorist and guerrilla violence, which is cruel and uncontrollable when unleashed. In no way is crime justifiable as a road to liberation. Violence inexorably generates new forms of oppression and slavery, ordinarily more serious than those from which people wish to liberate themselves. Above all it is an attack on life which depends on the Creator alone. We should also emphasize that when an ideology appeals to violence it thereby recognizes its own insufficiency and weakness [531-532].

The next paragraph recommends nonviolent means and can be read as an endorsement for active mass nonviolence.

None of the Latin American bishops has publicly advocated or defended armed struggle, although in Nicaragua Archbishop Obando has pointedly refused to condemn the Frente Sandinista. A number of the most progressive bishops have clearly advocated active nonviolence and over ten years ago Helder Camara proposed a continental nonviolent movement along the lines of Gandhi and King. However, these progressives would undoubtedly disagree with the apparent "even-handedness" of this treatment which equates the violence of armed leftist groups with that of repressive regimes. The latter have killed many more than the former, almost always the poor who themselves have committed no violence.[13] Puebla tends to reinforce the notion that violence comes from ideology as though people went to the guerrillas after reading books. But the spiral of violence as experienced is: institutionalized violence→nonviolent action→violent repression, including murder and massacre. Those who take up arms do so only after having suffered violence repeatedly, and sometimes directly in self-defense. In short, a more differentiated treatment of violence would have been both sociologically more accurate and pastorally more relevant.

Do the bishops have a model of society or a social system in mind? Explicitly they state that the Church "does not attribute to itself competence to propose alternative models" (1211). Puebla frequently speaks of a "civilization of love" (Paul VI), largely in moral terms, and of a "new humanism" in which the economy will be planned for people and not vice versa, as occurs in both forms of materialism, individual and collectivist. The logic of such a position seems to imply some "Third Way," neither capitalist nor socialist. But if these are defined in terms of the ownership of the chief means of production (private or social), it is hard to imagine a third possibility, although there are degrees of each. The text states that the evil effects of capitalism have been attenuated in some countries (542, see also 47), presumably with the welfare state in mind, but of Marxism it can only grudgingly concede partially good intentions ("Although [it was] born of a positive critique of commodity fetishism and of the non-recognition of the human value of work" [543]). The inner logic of Puebla seems to point toward an ameliorated capitalism. That such a logic contradicts the explicit statement quoted above is not the only internal incoherence in the documents.

Puebla and the Future

What happened, then, at Puebla?

"*Empate en cancha ajena,*" one wit put it: "The visiting team managed a tie." Although the conservatives controlled the ecclesiastical machinery, the liberationists were able to blunt an attempt to delegitimize their existence in the Church.

As they stand, the Puebla documents do not signal any fundamental change in the stance of the official Church. Conservatives, radicals, and centrists undoubtedly all feel vindicated by the Puebla conclusions —and all are right.

Conservatives can feel satisfied by the frequent criticism of Marxism and of ideological understandings of Christianity as well as the condemnation of violence as a method for change. The hierarchy's authority has been upheld, questionable teachings have been criticised, leftist political activity of priests has been rebuked, and there is a new ecclesiastical language which can be used to weaken the liberation thrust of the last ten years.

For their part, the liberationists can be grateful that the worst was avoided: No one was condemned, and neither the ideas nor the dynamic of Medellín have been reversed. The coexistence of fundamentally different stances, already present at Medellín, could not be ignored, nor could the liberation position simply be voted down. They can point to the adoption of a number of their agenda points at Puebla: a denunciation of injustice and inequality which is stronger and more specific than that of Medellín with at least some indications of their structural causes, encouragement of CEBs, a strong emphasis on the Church's option for the poor, and an endorsement of human rights work as essential to evangelization.

The center group probably feels even more satisfied than either left or right and can more readily endorse all statements in the documents. The conference tended toward "moderate" positions precisely because of the force of the two extremes and the reconciling (or "brokering") role of this group. The Church's "religious" role was emphasized, and Church unity was maintained despite strong tensions, and its role in defending human rights in extreme situations was upheld.

The struggle made manifest in Puebla has continued unabated. After his momentary setback at the conference itself Bishop López Trujillo was elected CELAM president in March 1979 (CELAM, 1979c: 9). The electors were the presidents of national episcopal conferences plus one delegate from each country and were more conservative than the Latin American average. A whole conservative slate emerged in bloc voting, which was considered rough play by the normal standards of Church politics.[14]

López has lost no time in working to assure that his group's interpretation becomes the official one. The same meeting that elected him president issued a plan of action including courses, conferences, and publications, and made recommdations, such as:

The soul of CELAM's General Plan ought to be evangelization in the light of the Puebla Document in its spirit of communion and participation, in the Church and in the world.

> CELAM should make a study of Medellín and Puebla so that just as the mystique of liberation began in Medellín, the mystique of communion and participation should be extended on the basis of Puebla [CELAM, 1979c: 7].

Although this text does not categorically say that "communion and participation" are to replace "liberation," such is the emphasis in López' thought. In an editorial replete with the new language he makes the following description:

> Communion with our peoples, among groups, classes, factions. Communion which in Latin America has the task of *integration,* which may bring an end to threats, wars, and rifts, so that there may be a peace which really puts our peoples in motion toward their liberation [CELAM, 1979c: 6].

The clear implication is that people can be "integrated" without changing the structures which pit some against others (according to Puebla's own analysis).

Evèn the editing of the definitive Puebla text offered the López group an opportunity to use its power. Von Rechnitz (1979) places in parallel columns dozens of examples of changes in the text, almost always weakening the original.[15]

In a move evidently intended to show their independence of López, the Brazilian bishops elected one of their most progressive members, Luciano Mendez de Almeida, as their general secretary, along with other progressive officers. At their meeting, there was frank criticism of CELAM, which one bishop said was turning into a "second Roman Curia" (Carvalho, 1979). Since they are two-fifths of the Latin American episcopate and have their own structures and organization, they may all but ignore CELAM during the next four years and maintain purely formal relations with Bogotá.

Archbishop Marcos McGrath (Panama) one of the main leaders of the center group at Puebla, offers the following summary of the document:

> Its simplest expression is: EVANGELIZATION FOR COMMUNION AND PARTICIPATION. . . . Evangelization which first liberates from sin, both personal (conversion) and social (transformation of structures) toward communion and participation, first in the Church (Body of Christ, People of God) and then in our human communities and societies at every level through the presence of Christians in pluralistic society [McGrath, 1979: 20].

While recognizing the possibility of differing interpretations, McGrath insists on the unity and pastoral purpose of the document.

Sanders's (1979) middle-of-the-road reading of Puebla is particularly interesting coming from a nonecclesiastic or academic. He finds the press's emphasis on conflicts misplaced and insists on the religious nature of the meeting. The bishops are symbols of Church unity, and what is most significant is their "compromise and consensus" in defining the Church's role. Politics is interpreted according to religious norms and not vice versa. The bishops reject the assumption common to both "conservative authoritarians" and Marxists, that liberal democratic systems are outmoded and incapable of dealing with today's problems. "The position of Puebla unquestionably places the institutional Church once again on the side of participatory democratic, systems, mixed economies and reformist social policies" (p. 23). Sanders thus sees the Church as a positive force during the coming years when a number of countries are scheduled to return to "democratic" governments, since it can emphasize what binds people together. At the same time he already foresees the likelihood of these attempts failing and occasioning another round of authoritarian regimes and polarization.

All liberationist interpretations, to one degree or another, assume the existence of opposed visions in Puebla (e.g., Sobrino, 1979; Richard, 1979; Betto, 1979; Vidales, 1979). Gutierrez's (1979) reading of the whole document takes the "preferential option for the poor" as its interpretative key.

Pablo Richard insists that it is not a "consensus text but a contradictory text" with differing social analyses and theologies. It would be an error to try to find the hegemonic or central position. Only by putting each text or piece of text into its own theology can its real meaning be determined.

> There are clear and definite texts for or against a Christendom model of the Church, and for or against a prophetic or liberating pastoral practice. But there are also many confused and ambiguous texts with a mediocre and undefined theology [p. 192].

Thus a selective reading is legitimate, beginning with "positive" texts, going on to confront them with "dangerous" texts, and finally clarifying "ambiguous and confused" texts. Using this method he has interpreted the whole document taking criteria from the opening "Message." Rather than dispute the "communion and participation" line, he agilely says that it must be understood as "*liberating* communion and participation" (p. 191).

After making a series of positive comments, L. Boff (1979) points out a number of shortcomings in Puebla which should be overcome: "parallelism" (doctrinal elements run parallel to social analysis but do not shed light on them); "theologism" (self-sufficiency from a theology unwilling to learn from the social sciences); "moralism" (prescribing what should be done with insufficient attention to objective conditions); "ecclesiasticism" (clerical viewpoint, with the result that, e.g., the poor seem to be a group outside the Church for which it must "opt"). Finally he calls for more humility and less rhetoric.

All the major controverted issues at Puebla remain open. The meeting did not *decide* anything—except to assure that the debate (or ideological struggle) will continue in the Church even at the hierarchical level.

I would insist that Puebla, after all, was an epiphenomenon—the manifestation of an ongoing struggle involving Latin America as a whole (and, to a degree, the rest of the world). This observation may seem anticlimactic after spending so many pages on this account, much of which is about church politics. But it is emphatically not a question of angels dancing on pinheads.

For many Latin Americans, involvement in the struggle for liberation is an expression, and even an exigency, of their faith. At the same time there are those who defend torture, assassination, and even genocide—I am writing in the midst of the Nicaraguan civil war—as necessary to defend Western Christian civilization.

This larger context gives Puebla its meaning and will continue to do so.

NOTES

1. Fausto Fernandez (1979) writes in the Mexican daily *Excelsior* that President Carter has ordered U.S. intelligence agencies to intensify their activities of "study and examination" (considered euphemisms for "infiltration and vigilance") of the Catholic Church in Latin America to identify the influence of religious movements in popular struggles. According to the story, members of the Senate Foreign Relations committee expressed a fear that Latin American countries could include "another Iran." Lernoux and Winiarski (1979) tell of a Pentagon Latin American expert contacting the U.S. Catholic Conference to inquire about the Latin American Church.

2. CELAM (1979a) is the text which emerged in mimeograph at the close of the Puebla meeting and CELAM (1979b) is the definitive text approved by the Pope and published at Bogotá. The quote here is from *"Mirada de Conjunto,"* a preface eliminated in the revised version. In general, the revision weakened the text from a liberationist point of view, as will be noted in several places in the present article.

3. Examples of various tendencies: conservative (López Trujillo, and the Colombians and Argentinians in general); liberationist (Proaño of Riobamba Ecuador, and the Brazilians in general); center (McGrath of Panama, Silva Henriquez of Chile, Manresa of Guatemala). We will occasionally use other terms, such as "progressives" or "radicals," for the liberation tendency.

4. "Christendom" denotes the symbiosis of Church and society from Constantine-Theodosius until the modern movement of secularization. After fighting a rear-guard action for centuries, the Catholic Church renounced this ideal officially at Vatican II. The term "new Christendom" is sometimes applied to the ideas emanating from Thomist Jacques Maritain.

5. MacEoin (1979) reports that according to Cardinal Aponte of Puerto Rico, head of CELAM's finance committee, the Puebla meeting was paid for with contributions from the De Rance Foundation ($140,000), the German agency Adveniat ($100,000) and the U.S. Catholic Conference ($70,000).

6. Letter of López Trujillo to Archbishop Luciano Duarte of Aracaju, Brazil. López makes slighting remarks about some of the Brazilian bishops and says that some would like Puebla postponed or cancelled so as to leave things confused or ambiguous. He insists that it is necessary to lay down an ideological platform for the coming CELAM elections. He exhorts his friend: "Prepare your bombers, get some of your delicious 'venom' ready." He should train like a boxer. "May your blows be evangelical and on the mark" (López Trujillo, 1979a). Since the leak apparently came when a journalist found three such letters dictated on a tape which López had passed him, the incident was inevitably called a CELAM-gate.

7. The following is the outline of the Puebla documents. Title are slightly changed to indicate contexts better. Titles of "nuclei" at left and documents themselves at right:

Message to Latin America

1. Pastoral Vision of Latin America	History of the Church in Latin America; Sociocultural Context; Pastoral Work Today; Trends in Evangelization
2. God's Design (Evangelization), Content (Doctrine),	Jesus Christ; the Church; Man and Human Dignity
Evangelization	Criteria; Evangelization and Culture; Popular Religiosity; Liberation and Human Promotion; Ideologies and Politics
3. Evangelization in the Church	Family; Base-Communities, Parish and Local Church; Hierarchy and

	Clergy; Religious Orders; Laity; Promoting Vocations to Priesthood and Religious Life; Prayer and Liturgy; Witness; Catechesis; Education; Mass Media; Dialogue with Non-Catholics
4. Missionary Church	Option for the Poor; Option for Youth; Action with Leaders in a Pluralistic Society; Defense of the Human Person
5.	Pastoral Options

8. Puebla's language is incurably sexist by today's standards in English. We will not correct it nor sprinkle this essay with (sic).

9. A good illustration of the more than stylistic editing done by the CELAM secretariate is the change in the order of the "faces" passage. The original order was: indians and Afro-Americans, peasants, workers, shantytown dwellers, underemployed and unemployed, youth, children, old people. The revised and official version lists: children, youth, indians and Afro-Americans, peasants, workers, unemployed and underemployed, shantytown dwellers, old people. This change was obviously not motivated by "lifecycle" psychology, but by a concern to weaken the reference to the production process and hence the class nature of the passage.

10. The fact that the original italicizing of the phrase was edited out of the final version may be a hint that the CELAM secretariate also foresees this possibility.

11. "Therefore" not in original text: "los pobres, tambien alentados por la Iglesia, han comenzado a organizarse para una vivencia integral de su Fe y para un reclama de sus derechos" (CELAM, 1979b: para. 902). This passage sees CEBs and popular organizations coming from the same root, while the revised text conveys a picture of the poor being evangelized and then claiming their rights. I find the original more dialectical and more interesting, if I may be permitted some subtle exegesis.

12. *Individual rights:* to life (to be born, to responsible procreation), to physical and psychic integrity, to legal protection, to religious freedom, to freedom of opinion, to participation in goods and services, to work out one's own destiny, to access to property. *Social rights:* to education, to association, to work, to housing, to health, to recreation, to development, to good government, to freedom and social justice, to participation in the decisions which concern the people and nations. *Emerging rights:* to one's own image, to privacy, to objective information and expression, to conscientious objection, and to one's own view of the world (1271-1273).

13. Dialogo (1979), a Guatemalan magazine, reprints a summary of political violence compiled from newspaper sources. During July-December 1978, there were reports of 413 people from the popular classes killed, plus 37 students and professionals identified with the poor and one guerrilla vs. 11 politicians, 5 landowners or big businessmen, and 8 administrators or small businessmen. In addition 30 members of security forces were killed. These figures should be qualified by noting that some of the politicians seem to have been killed by the right and that not all the members of security forces were victims of the left.

14. Usually in CELAM elections there is a gentlemen's agreement to balance officers, e.g., a conservative first vice president after a liberal president, but this time there was

straight bloc voting. Some bishops cast blank votes in protest. Some of the heads of CELAM departments, however, are not straight *lopeztrujillistas,* e.g., Bishop Bambarén of the Department of Social Action.

15. Examples: The national security doctrine "is opposed to a Christian vision of man," is changed to "Would not be in harmony with"; "anti-witness of priests and religious" is changed to "the lack of witness on the part of some priests and religious." Many statements are weakened by the additions of "sometimes" and "frequently."

REFERENCES

AGUDELO, G. (1978) "Analisís del Esquema-Guia." CELAM 123 (enero): 5-24.

ASSMANN, H. [ed.] (1978) Carter y La Lógica del Imperialismo. San Jose, Costa Rica: Educa.

Anonymous (1978a) "Una Buena Noticia: La Iglesia Nace del Pueblo Latinoamericano." Panamá: Centro de Capacitación Social.

———— (1978b) "Reflexiones y Problemas de la Iglesia que Nace del Pueblo." UCA Editores (1978): 207-249.

———— (1978c) "Voice from Northeastern Brazil to CELAM III." LADOC 8 (May/June): 1-19.

BERRYMAN, P. (1973) "Latin American Liberation Theology." Theological Studies 34 (September): 357-395.

BETTO, F. (1979) "Tendencias Políticas en Puebla." Christus: 56-62.

BOFF, C. (1979) "Puebla: A Graca da Confirmacáo de Medellín." Puebla! E Entáo? CEI Suplemento 24 (maio): 10-20.

———— (1978) "The illusion of a new Christendom: a critique of the PD of CELAM III." LADOC 9 (September): 1-18.

BOFF, L. (1979) "Puebla: Avances e Interrogaciones." Diakonia 3 (mayo-julio): 24-38.

CARVALHO, F. (1979) "Brazilian bishops elect progressive leaders." Latinamerica Press 11, 22: 8.

Centro de Estudios Sociopoliticos y Eclesiales Antonio de Montesinos (n.d.) "Puebla: Aportes y Comentarios." Numero 2.

CELAM [Consejo Episcopal Latinoamericano] (1979a) "La Evangelización en el Presente y en el Futuro de America Latina." Puebla, Mexico. (mimeo)

———— (1979b) La Evangelización en el Presente y en el Futuro de America Latina. Bogotá.

———— (1979c) Bulletin. marzo.

———— (1979d) Bulletin, abril.

———— (1978a) "Documento de Consulta." (mimeo)

———— (1978b) "Documento de Trabajo." (mimeo)

———— (1969) La Iglesia en la Actual Transformación de America Latina a la Luz del Concilio. Vol. II Tercera Edición: Bogotá.

Cencos [Centros Nacional de Comunicación Social, A.C.] (1978) Daily documentation at Puebla.

Christus (1979) "Puebla: Crónica y Análisis." (marzo-abril): 520-521.

Crie [Centro Regional de Informaciones Ecumenicas] (1979a) III Conferencia del Episcopado Latinoamericano: Puebla '79.

———— (1979b) Daily reproduction of press reports on CELAM III in Mexican papers.

CRT [Centro de Reflexión Teológica] (1978) Cruz y Resurrección: Presencia y Anuncio de Una Iglesia Nueva. Mexico: CRT-Servir.

DELGADO, J. (1978) "Reflexiones Teológicas Sobre el Documento Preparatorio a la Reunión del CELAM en Puebla." (mimeo)

Dial [Diffusion de l'Information sur l'Amerique Latine] (1979) "Latin America: ten years of repression against the Church." (translated and printed by New York Circus)

Dialogo (1979) "Violencia Política en Guatemala: Julio-Diciembre 1978." 45: 24-49.

DUSSEL, E. and F. ESPINOSA (1979) "Puebla: Crónica e Historia." Christus: 21-37.

FERNANDEZ, F. (1979) "Pide Carter Espiar a Religiosos Liberales." Excelsior (3 febrero): 1, 14.

GOROSTIAGA, X. [ed.] (1979) Para Entender America Latina: Aporte Colectivo de los Científicos Sociales en Puebla. San Jose, Costa Rica: Educa.

GUTIERREZ, G. (1978a) "Sobre el Documento de Consulta para Puebla." CRT (1978): 3-45.

———— (1978b) "La Fuerza Histórica de los Pobres." Celadec 6: 39-69.

LERNOUX, P. and M. WINIARSKI (1979) "CIA ordered to survey Latin American Church." National Catholic Reporter 15 (February 16): 48.

LOPEZ TRUJILLO, A. (1979a) "Documento Confidencial: Carta de Mons. Lopez Trujillo al Arzobispo de Arcaju [sic] Brasil." Cencos, Servicios Especiales de Prensa 33: 1-2.

———— (1979b) "Editorial." CELAM (abril): 3-6.

MacEOIN, G. (1979) "Sobre Puebla: Quien Pagó?" Noticias Aliadas 6 (Febrero 15).

McGRATH, M. (1979) "Puebla: Vision General." (mimeo)

OLIVEROS, R. (1977) Liberación y Teología: Génesis y Crecimiento de una Reflexion (1966-1976). Lima: Centro de Estudios y Publicaciones.

RICHARD, P. (1979) "Para Entender el Documento Final de Puebla," pp. 186-192 in X. Grostiaga (ed.) Para Entender America Latina. San Jose, Costa Rica: Educa.

SANDERS, T. (1979) Untitled. (mimeo)

Sep [Servicios Especiales de Prensa] (1979) "Comentarios Sobre las Ultimas Personas Designadas Para Asistir a Puebla." 9 (16 Octubre).

SOBRINO, J. (1979) "Puebla: Serena Afirmación de Medellín." Diakonia 9 (abril): 27-56.

———— (1978) Resurrección de una Iglesia Popular." CRT.

————(1977) Cristologia desde América Latina: Esbozo a Partir del Seguimiento del Jesús Historicó. Mexico: Ediciones CRT.

TAMEZ, E. and S. TRINIDAD [eds.] (1978) Capitalismo: Violencia y Anti-Vida: La Opresión de las Mayorías y la Domesticación de los Dioses. San Jose, Costa Rica: Educa.

UCA Editores (1979) Iglesia de los Pobres y Organizaciones Populares San Salvador: Author.

VON RECHNITZ, A. (1979) "Cambios en el Documento de Puebla." Diakonia 10 (mayo-julio): 81-87.

VIDALES, R. (1979) "Puebla: Ni Mas Ni Menos." (mimeo)

WILDE, A. (1979) "Ten years of change in the Church: Puebla and the future." (mimeo)

WOJTYLA, K. [Pope John Paul II] (1979) "Homilies and speeches in México." Cencos, Servicios Especiales de Prensa Informativo 30.

4

LATIN AMERICAN EVANGELICALS
Oaxtepec and Beyond

T. S. MONTGOMERY

The Spirit of the Lord is upon me, because he has chosen me to bring good news to the poor. He has sent me to proclaim liberty to the captives and recovery of sight to the blind, to set free the oppressed.

Luke 4:18

Everyone must obey state authorities, because no authority exists without God's permission, and the existing authorities have been put there by God. Whoever opposes the existing authority opposes what God has ordered.

Romans 13:1-2

During the closing days of September, 1978, 200 official delegates from 110 Evangelical[1] Churches and 10 ecumenical organizations in 19 Latin American countries gathered in Oaxtepec, Mexico. Their stated purpose was to seek "greater unity of the Christian people in order to be more faithful to the gospel in today's Latin America" (Libro de Trabajo, 1978: 1). Unlike the Roman Catholic Conference of Latin American Bishops (CELAM III), which met in Puebla, Mexico, four months later and which began with a fundamental unity born of common allegiance to the Holy See in Rome,[2] the Protestants had as their only undisputed

AUTHOR'S NOTE: Research for this chapter was begun under City University of New York Research Foundation Grant 12213 during the summer and fall of 1978. I am grateful to the foundation for its support; to Juan Marcos Rivera who made it possible for me to attend Oaxtepec as a fraternal delegate; to CENCOS and J. Gary Campbell who provided most of the pre-Oaxtepec documentation; to Orlando Costas for his running analysis during Oaxtepec and his bibliographic assistance later.

source of unity their common agreement on the New Testament as final authority for the Christian faith.

At the same time, representatives from the Evangelical Churches were confronted with many of the theological and ideological conflicts that characterized the proceedings in Puebla. In the end, both conferences reached similar political and theological conclusions, and the evangelicals took another step closer to the unity that has eluded them throughout their history in Latin America.

This chapter examines the themes that dominated the Evangelical Assembly in Oaxtepec and the socio-politico-religious context in which the conference took place. The recurring themes during the six days of discussion included human rights, the national security doctrine, social change, cooperation between Roman Catholics and Evangelicals, and above all, the search for unity. The context was defined in the preparatory document and in greater detail by the participants themselves. Carmelo Alvarez, President of the Latin American Biblical Seminary in San José, Costa Rica, argued forcefully in his opening-day *ponecia* called "The Role of the Church in Latin America" that colonial and neocolonial crises have dominated Latin American history and that a "situation of domination, exploitation and dependency have characterized all levels of life on our continent." In this situation, Alvarez continued, our "history testifies to a church handed over to the dominant classes, but also shows the face of a church that opts for living from the 'underside of history'" (1978: 1). In Oaxtepec, as in the history of the Christian Churches throughout Latin America, both aspects of the Church were represented. But Oaxtepec, like Medellín ten years earlier, was a turning point for the Evangelical Churches.

Historical Background

The historic path leading to Oaxtepec is anything but straight and narrow. Indeed, there is no single path, in the way that one may metaphorically speak of the Catholic Church. Protestants did not appear in Latin America in any significant numbers until the first third of the nineteenth century. During that period European settlers in the southern cone received permission to construct houses of worship and to have chaplains (Dehainaut, 1972: 5, 8-9). These Protestants were ethnically, culturally, and linguistically separate from their Latin

American neighbors. The immigrants tended to settle close to each other and generally did not engage in proselytizing (Liggett, 1979: 59). As a result the immigrant churches remain among the smallest of the more than 300 Evangelical groups in Latin America.

Protestantism penetrated the southern hemisphere via another means during this period. Until the late 1700s the Bible was banned in Latin America by the Pope and King who did not want their subjects exposed to the heresy of the Reformation. By the early nineteenth century, however, Bibles began to appear, thanks to the American and British Bible societies. Within a short time Bible colporteurs began distributing the word, often in the face of great persecution and occasional martyrdom. Their efforts paid dividends, for churches were founded in unexpected places. Many pointed to a pattern: "first a Bible, then a convert, then a church" (Read et al., 1969: 40; see also Liggett, 1979: 59). Thus the indigenous churches took root in various parts of the continent.

Until much later in the century there was little missionary activity, the Protestant churches of North America and Europe preferring to direct their attention to the un-Christianized areas of Asia, Africa, and the Pacific (Dehainaut, 1972: 5, 8-9). So insignificant was Latin America as a mission field that the World Missionary Conference of 1910 declined to invite mission societies working there. This slight led to a decision on the part of those societies to organize their own conference, the Congress on Christian Work in Latin America, which met in Panama in 1916. By then missionary efforts, though limited, were 60 years old. Presbyterians, Methodists, Baptists, Lutherans, United Brethren, and the YMCA were the principal participants among the 44 mission boards; yet of the 304 delegates, only 26 were Latin American (Read et al., 1969: 44).

The issues in Panama reflected the mentality of the missionaries who ran the conference; primary among their concerns were division of territory and plans for cooperation in various areas such as literature production (Read et al., 1969: 44) Yet already there were signs of the tensions that would plague ecumenical efforts through the years. One the fundamentalists' opposition to any accommodation with the Catholic Church (Beach, 1916: 8); another, which would reappear in different form at Oaxtepec, was an emphasis on the Social Gospel instead of individual conversion. The latter was not dismissed, but those who advanced the Social Gospel argued that the two must be combined (Dehainaut, 1972: 5-10). "It [the social approach], the conference report read, kindles gratitude, gains their confidence, wins their affections, and in some measure reveals the Christian spirit" (Committee on Cooperation in Latin America, 1916: 292). We will see how this social concern transforms itself by the late 1970s into a radical critique of the Latin American socio-economic reality and a radical theology that seeks to transform the society of which it is a part. Meanwhile, in the early years of mission work this theological orientation led to the founding of many Protestant educational institutions, social service agencies, orphanages, and hospitals through the continent (Dehainaut, 1972: 5-10; Costas, 1976: 50-51).

Thus the third means by which Protestantism gained a foothold in Latin America was through the establishment of *mission churches* and institutions. Often these efforts had at least the tacit support of Latin American liberal leaders who, in the wake of struggles for independence, were ideologically a part of the international liberal-modernist movement and its concomitant economic system, capitalism (Míguez Bonino, 1975: 11 f.). José Míguez Bonino (1972: 4) a leading Latin American Protestant theologian, has written:

> At the moment when our countries were slowly emerging from their colonial past and were seeking to integrate into the modern world, Protestantism constituted for them a call to change and transformation, centered in the religious sphere but with an effect on the totality of life and society. . . . Protestantism was incorporated into the "liberal-modernist" movement represented by such names as Sarmiento, Rivadavia, Lastarria, Bilbao, etc., with their anti-clerical battle against the traditional pre-modern ethos. It is significant that without becoming Protestant Christians, the leaders of this movement were favorable to the coming of Protestantism, both as immigration and mission. This inevitably linked Protestantism to the neo-colonial-imperialist expansion of the largely Protestant countries into Latin America. The external link is historically evident. The internal ties are less clear but relate to ideas of liberty, progress, and individuality, and has both an ethical, personalising liberating aspect as well as a political, economic aspect that binds them to imperialist capitalism.

This history, Míguez writes, has placed Protestantism in an ambiguous situation. For one part, the movement has played a critical, if minor, role in the overthrow of traditional society "by introducing new norms, values and institutions contrary to the existing ones." For the other part, there is a perception that liberalism today contains "negative consequences (imperialism and domination), and [has] no real future." Even though Protestant participation in these developments has been for the most part unintentional, Míguez concludes, this "does not solve the problem of [the] ambiguity [of Protestantism]. . . . We find ourselves participating in the creation of an order whose inhumanity and perversion are more evident every day" (1972: 4).

There are many Protestants in Latin America who would not agree with Míguez's harsh conclusion—a fact that he is the first to recognize. Where this analysis leads him is to a three-fold typology of Protestant ideology. Using Míguez's categories as a starting point, we will examine some critical ideological and theological differences among Latin American Protestants. This will enable us to better understand political positions that the various Evangelical Churches have taken in recent years and the positions that were taken at Oaxtepec.

Ideological Divisions

The first group Míguez (1968) identifies are those who, in the words of Laliv D'Epinay, have gone on "a social strike."[3] They "refuse to take any responsibility for social processes. To them, religion belongs to the individual, private sphere." On becoming a Christian, one should of course reflect a particular quality of life that will redound to the benefit of society. "But every intent to relate faith and Christian doctrine to the public sphere is considered an 'intrusion' which violates both the 'lay' character of the public sphere (remember the anticlerical heritage) and the 'spiritual' purity of the faith" (Míguez, 1972: 4).

Orlando Costas correctly points out that going on a "social strike" may have opposite results. On the one hand it may lead groups "to withdraw from socio-political responsibilities," but on the other hand "it has also led them to affirm respect for established authority, thereby making them militant advocates of law and order" (Costas, 1976: 39). In other words, "social strikers" of the first variety tend to be a-political; those of the second tend to be supporters of the existing regime, however right-wing. In Latin America it is possible to identify both kinds of response. Pentecostals in Mexico often reflect the first type, while Lutherans of Brazil have reflected the latter.

Míguez's second group consists of those who "insist on supporting the liberal project" (1972: 6).[4] Costas describes these Evangelicals as "defenders of institutional democracy, classical forms of freedom; socio-economic developmentalism and the Western capitalistic enterprise" (1976: 38). But, Míguez adds, they fail to understand that within the "existing conditions of Latin American society, the formal concept of 'freedom' is merely a game with rules that favor those who possess [political, economic, and military] power" and that the developmental model "has failed in its announced purpose of achieving a 'take-off' for accelerated progress in our countries" (1972: 6).

The last group Míguez calls "revolutionary" (1972: 7). As Costas (1976: 38) puts it,

> These Christians advocate active participation in the process of liberation from the situation of economic dependence on foreign capital and technical know-how and the internal domination of national oligarchies and corrupt politicians. They call for the radical transformation of the social, economic, and political structures of the Continent. In this sense, they try to recapture the "subversive" role that Protestant Christianity once played, but then from "within the radically different situation" in which Latin America finds itself today.

In other words, these Evangelicals have opted for the poor in place of the rich, for human rights against political repression, and in favor of liberation theology in place of the "Let's wait for the second coming" mentality that characterizes the "social strikers."

In recent years it has become increasingly clear that these ideological types cannot be used simply to distinguish among denominations, but must also be used to distinguish different groups *within* denominations. For example, it would be erroneous to place all Pentecostals in the first category, as the inclination would have been even a decade ago. The Pentecostal Church of Chile, which has given unequivocal and even enthusiastic support reminiscent of the church in Nazi Germany to the military junta,[5] is 180° away in its theological hermeneutic and its social consciousness from the Pentecostal Church in Cuba, whose ministers did not leave after the revolution in 1959 and whose members today are among their government's most dedicated supporters (Interview with Cuban Protestants in Mexico City, 1978). Methodists in Brazil supported their military regime until the early seventies when an excess of human rights violations pushed them to begin working through the Ecumenical Service Commission (which includes the Catholic Bishops' Conference) in support of human rights (Wright, 1979). By contrast, Argentinian Methodists joined with other church groups following the military coup in 1976 to create the Ecumenical Movement for Human Rights (see Smith, this volume). In yet another example of denominational differences, the Lutheran Church in Chile split over whether to support the junta; Lutherans in the South consistently have given strong support to the regime, while Lutherans in and around Santiago joined the ecumenical Committee for Peace and broke early with the junta, leading to the expulsion of Bishop Helmut Frentz (see La Iglesia y La Junta Militar, 1975: 127-136).[6]

It is pertinent to look for a moment at why the conservative ecclesiology has been so pervasive. Rubem Alves (1971), following Mannheim's disinction between ideology and utopia, has argued that, in the contemporary Latin American context where a consciousness of the need to create a new society exists, "Protestantism could act . . . as a catalyzer, if its utopian possibilities . . . with all of its promises of trans-formation . . . would find a way to insert themselves in our historic moment." But he continues,

Its forms of thought have been dominated in such a way by indi-vidualism that Protestantism cannot produce categories to under-stand problems of a structural nature.

This seems very strange. . . because the contradiction between the personal and the structural, so characteristic of Protestantism, could and should have created an ethic through which the personal would have accepted as its own vocation the transformation of the very structures which it opposes, in order to reconcile itself with them. But it did not work this way and the reason is very simple. . . . *Protestantism, instead of considering the contradiction between the personal and the structural in dialectical terms, interpreted it in dualistic terms.* . . . Thus the typical formulation of the dom-inant ecclesiology: the church, as community, does not participate in social transformations. Its task is to convert unbelievers and protect the converted [Alves, 1971: 16-17].

How then does he account for the emergence of a radical theology and accompanying social action among the Evangelicals? Alves suggests that it is through small groups who have begun to "reinterpret the symbols of their faith, but in the direction of the utopia or prophetic messianism of the Old Testament." Furthermore, he sees this process taking place among "certain groups which have been marginalized by the official structures." It is this conflict, he suggests, that explains "the fractures that presently divide . . . Protestant denominations" (1971: 20). Costas (1976: 36) notes that for Alves there are only two kinds of Protestants: conservatives and revolutionaries.

While the whole Evangelical experience suggests that Alves is right on the mark in pointing to the option for a dualistic rather than a dialectical interpretation of the relationship between faith and society, his account of the prophetic few overlooks those whom Costas calls "Mainline Protestantism" (Methodists, Presbyterians, and so on) who have been in the forefront of social action and ecclesiastical reinterpretation (1976: 50-55). More recently these groups have been besieged by what Costas (1976: 54) calls a "crisis of mission."

> As Protestants become aware of their cultural alienation from the mainstream of society, their imported institutions, transplanted methods, imitative and repetitious theology and their conscious or unconscious alignment with neocolonial powers, they begin to question their traditional understanding of their nature and mission in Latin America and to reevaluate their performance. The crisis . . . is highlighted by the participation of many church young people in the continental struggle of the 60's against oppressive foreign powers and local oligarchies. It is further strengthened by the awareness of the ideological manipulation of the faith for the maintenance of the status quo, and by the signs of renewal in the Catholic Church.

Thus Costas summarizes nicely the pressures that have pushed Evangelicals throughout Latin America to reexamine the role of the Church. This reexamination began in the early sixties and may be traced through a series of conferences of which Oaxtepec is the most recent. Let us look briefly at the evolution of theological and political positions reflected in the Second Latin American Evangelical Conference (II CELA)[7] held in Lima in 1961, and the Third Conference (III CELA) which met in Buenos Aires in 1969. After that we will be able to discuss the significance of Oaxtepec and suggest directions in which the Evangelical Churches of Latin America are headed in the 1980s.

Political and Theological Evolution

A number of writers have pointed out that a major problem of Protestantism in Latin America has been "its concentration on the individual aspect of salvation to the exclusion largely, although not entirely, of a sense of the Church as divine community" (Rycroft and Clemmer, 1963: 221). In a paper prepared for II CELA, Míguez Bonino (1961) prefigured liberation theology including his own later writings by challenging the conference to deal with this issue:

> Has not the insistence on the personal character of salvation resulted in an individualism obsessed with one's own well-being, and arrogantly disinterested in the fate of the world? . . . Has this not been the cause of our Christian joy deteriorating into an insolent self-sufficiency, and a proud self-assertion?

Rising to the challenge, the delegates made a concerted effort to become more contextual and concrete in their analysis of the Latin American social reality. They revealed a general awareness of the condition of underdevelopment, the need for change in societal structures, and the accompanying need for a commitment to freedom and justice. They argued that "the problem of Latin America is much more profound than what kind of a social or political system the area must have. . . . The deeper problem is, 'What kind of man must we have?'" They also recognized that they could not "offer easy solutions for the problems of our America, and that we must resist the temptation to superficial optimism, and dedicate ourselves seriously to a persistent and creative effort to discover what are the consequences of the Gospel message for the totality of the life of our peoples" ("Cristo la Esperanza para America Latina," 1961: 121, 127).

In spite of this analysis, Míguez notes that "the concrete perspective of these changes [were] basically developmentalistic" (1973: 185; see also Costas, 1976: 86-87). Perhaps most significant, the delegates for the first time at an international gathering were faced with a fundamentalist-modernist theological controversy (Costas, 1976: 102), one that would cause explosions at III CELA eight years later.[8]

There was a period during 1967-1969 when there was some question as to whether or not III CELA would be held. Originally scheduled for Rio de Janeiro in December 1967, it was postponed a month and then another year, only to be cancelled altogether in December 1968. Why? The evidence suggests that the Brazilian Protestant Confederation of

Churches, which was organizing and hosting the conference, feared the political consequences within Brazil of a conference that was very likely to level criticism at the Brazilian status quo (Costas, 1976: 104).

The Argentinian Confederation of Churches, however, stepped in and assumed responsibility for the conference's organization. Thus III CELA met in the summer of 1969 in Buenos Aires. Costas (1976: 85) writes that this meeting was a landmark in the ecumenical history of Latin American Protestantism because it provided an inventory of what was taking place within Evangelical Christianity. In contrast to II CELA, there was a clearer focus and a deeper perception of continental social reality. The clearest example of this was the report from Commission Five, one of six study commissions that met during the conference. This commission reflected the theological and ideological divisions more profoundly than any other group, and it was the only commission to submit both a majority and a minority report.

The (bare) majority distinguished between conscious, revolutionary and unconscious, nonrevolutionary youths. It identified with the former who "have inherited unjust situations and inhuman systems, which [have in turn] led the more conscientized ones to take 'a revolutionary attitude'" and make a commitment to the "process . . . of liberation." This sector within the church expects the church "to commit itself" to the liberation process, thereby taking "the gospel to its ultimate consequences" rather than continuing to be an institution that "maintains the status quo" (Duedores del Mundo, 1969: 50).

Bewildered and outraged by this onslaught, the minority took the opposite tack and began by making a traditionalist argument that "just solutions" to Latin America's problems could be found only "in Christ." Yet the report went on to condemn dictatorships and oppressive governments of the right and the left that attack the dignity of the person; to oppose revolutionary violence *and* institutionalized violence; and they declared themselves in favor of the developmentalist model, yet condemned in the same sentence "the economic measures of the USA and some European countries that obtain our raw material at despicable prices and sell their manufactured produces at confiscatory prices" (Deudores del Mundo, 1969: 38; for a full discussion, see Costas, 1976: 102-108).

Here we see the dilemma of many Latin American Protestants (and Catholics). On one hand there is a genuine, sincere faith that is unable to escape its social consequences. On the other hand, there is deep confusion about what this means in terms of social commitment and action. The dilemma was not resolved in Buenos Aires. By the time delegates gathered in Oaxtepec, however, those caught on its horns no longer con-stituted a sizable minority.

There were several other developments at III CELA that foreshadowed events of the 1970s and the next major gathering in Mexico. First, there was an acknowledgment of the cultural alienation between church and society, as well as the alienation among denominations. Second, they not only acknowledged the winds of renewal and change within the Catholic Church, but also confessed for the first time collectively that, as Protestants, they had not always acted in a spirit of love toward Catho-lics.[9] Third, there was a new concern with the marginalization and dependence of Latin American women. In this connection they asserted that the church was compelled to actively promote the liberation of women from oppression (Costas, 1976: 89, 91, 97-98).

Finally, the elusive search for unity continued in Buenos Aires. During II CELA in Lima eight years earlier the suggestion that a "con-tinuation organism" be established led to the creation in 1976 of UNELAM (Pro-Protestant Unity Movement), which was seen as a "permanent organism for consultations and encounters among the Protestant churches of Latin America" (Perez-Rivas, 1971: 278). In effect, III CELA caused the transformation of UNELAM from a "provisional commission" to an organized movement by passing a resolution that charged UNELAM with the promotion of "the common insights and concerns" reflected in the III CELA documents, and by asking it to organize and coordinate the IV CELA (Costas, 1976: 114). So, in 1970, UNELAM was set up as a regional ecumenical coordinating organiza-tion.

There was, however, one oversight in the resolution. It failed to take account of the ecumenical bodies such as ISAL and CELADEC[10] which have often been on the cutting edge of ecumenical efforts and social action, forging ahead while denominations muddled along. This over-sight, along with the refusal of many churches to join UNELAM, a series of leadership crises, and conflicting interests, condemned the organiza-tion to a rather ineffectual existence (CENCOS, 1978). Indeed, it was not able to organize IV CELA, as it had been charged to do.

During the 1970s ecumenical efforts among Protestants as well as between Protestants and Catholics waxed even as UNELAM waned. Yet even in this context, discussion of a Latin American Council of Churches developed. Finally, during 1976 UNELAM held a consulta-tion among 114 national churches which led to the selection of 20 repre-sentatives, one from every country, who gathered with 4 members of

UNELAM's Executive Committee in Panama in March 1977. The purpose of the meeting was to "discuss and decide about the affair of the proposed organism of churches. The presence of UNELAM was only to serve, in whatever manner, the process of transition" (Santana, 1978).

The Panama meeting led to a larger gathering in Bogotá six months later. There the decision was made to convene an Assembly of Latin American Evangelical Churches and ecumenical organizations in Oaxtepec during September 1978. In a letter addressed to all these groups, Benjamin Santana (1978), president of the organizing committee for the assembly said that after 14 years, UNELAM

> is set aside to give way to the formation of a body which will, this time, represent the churches, thus becoming more vigorous and more effective in the proclamation of the Gospel and in the efforts of Christian cooperation, without sidestepping the integral liberation of the human person in the totality of his/her being or the collective society to which he/she belongs.

The empirical support for this burst of optimism is absent but the optimism persisted on the part of many at Oaxtepec.

In November 1977, two months after Bogotá, member churches of the World Council of Churches met in Huampaní, Peru. They accepted an invitation to participate in the assembly, but only on the condition that it have a strictly *consultative,* not a *constitutive,* character. Nevertheless, all announcements and preparatory documents referred to an assembly called to constitute the "Latin American Council of Evangelical Churches" (CLAI) (CENCOS, 1978). This division of opinion about the nature of the conference followed the delegates to Mexico.

Oaxtepec[11]

The one word that will serve to characterize the six days in Oaxtepec is "tense." Tension was brought into the conference by the fact that, in certain countries, some denominations are not on speaking terms, though their leaders may sit together in ecumenical organizations. Tension was produced by theologically conservative churches that elected not to participate in the Assembly and by communications gaps. For example, the Rector of a Presbyterian Seminary was asked a week before the convocation for his prognosis, to which he replied that he did not know anything about it because he had not received an invitation. However, a member of the organizing committee said in a separate interview that not only had the rector been apprised of developments, there was also agreement that Oaxtepec would be considered at the church's General Assembly.

More tension appeared when the traditionalist-modernist theological differences that had first erupted in Lima 20 years earlier reemerged. Manual Gaxiola, the Pentecostal Bishop of Mexico and one of the commentators on Carmelo Alvarez's paper, quoted earlier, expressed the conservative position of many present in arguing that Alvarez had placed "more emphasis on man than God" (Gaxiola, 1978). Immediately thereafter Luis Reinoso, a Peruvian Methodist and General Secretary of CELADEC, praised Alvarez's paper, pointing to its rich reading of history, the crisis of Evangelical identity in Latin America, and the importance of the common people becoming subjects for doing theology (Campbell, 1978). By the end of the week there was still unhappiness. Ramon Reinfelds, a Lutheran pastor from Caracas, said in an interview on the last day, "I expected more theology . . . more talk about church work and the real purpose of the church, that is to reach the souls of our fellow men, and not so much political element."

In a related area, some delegates argued that there is no Bibical basis for church action in the areas of human rights, illiteracy, and ecology. And the position that the church must, in its prophetic role, denounce repressive military regimes was challenged by citing Romans 13.

Another source of tension was political. There were delegates who supported the military regimes under which they lived—and there were those who did not. One member of the Brazilian delegation rose on the last day to object to the inclusion of Brazil in a statement condemning the systematic violation of human rights. The new Brazilian president was a Lutheran, he said, and should not be condemned before he had an opportunity to implement new policies. Some Chilean delegates were unabashed supporters of the junta. Others, very quietly, made it known that they opposed the regime but were afraid to speak out in support of the progressive positions being put forth largely because they had reason to believe that two members of the Chilean delegation were agents of DINA, the Chilean secret police.

TO BE OR NOT TO BE:
A LATIN AMERICAN COUNCIL OF CHURCHES?

Of greatest significance, however, was the tension over whether to create a Council of Churches. This issue monopolized plenary sessions during the first four days of the assembly. Opposition to the Council came from a number of groups. Some conservatives feared the Council would affiliate with the World Council of Churches—with whose politics and theology they did not agree. But other conservatives wanted to establish a council immediately so that they, as founding members, could be in a position to exercise control over programs and money. In this connection, some progressives expressed fear that control by the conservatives, Miguez's "liberal project" folk, would block the work of the most progressive Christians in their sociopolitical commitments on behalf of the liberation of oppressed people (CENCOS, 1978).

The progressives had still other concerns. They placed little hope in what appeared to be just one more superbureaucratic ecclesiastical body. And there was fear expressed in some quarters that a Latin American Council could be an expression of what many Latin Americans perceive to be the strategy of North American imperialism and the Third World policies of the Carter Administration. Through those policies, it is charged, the United States "seeks to utilize ecclesiastical structures in order to penetrate, acculturate, and impede the organization and action of the popular social classes" (CENCOS, 1978; for a radical perspective on this process, see Fazio, 1978). Finally, progressives were concerned that a unity based on neutrality would ignore the real divisions in church and society and in the long run benefit only the interests of the rich and oppressors (CENCOS, 1978).

Interestingly, the most vehement opposition to the Council came from the Cuban delegation. They arrived in Oaxtepec tempered by the experience of having had to rebuild their churches in membership and leadership following the exodus of missionaries, Cuban pastors, and thousands of members after the revolution. They had also lived for 20 years under a government that, to say the very least, had not encouraged religious activity. One result of this experience was a rich ecumenical experience among the Protestant churches of Cuba and cooperation in various areas, such as youth activities, between the Cuban Council of Churches and the Catholic Church (Interview with Cuban Protestants, Mexico City, 1978). So the Cubans came to Oaxtepec with the deep conviction that ecumenism cannot be imposed from above, through the creation of a supranational body, but must grow up from the grass roots.

Dora Arce, a Presbyterian, flatly termed ecumenism on the continent "a lie." In his commentary on the *ponencia* "The Unity Which We Seek"[12] Hector Mendez, a Presbyterian pastor from Sancti Spiritus, pointed to the large number of churches that had declined to attend which "leads us to affirm that it would be impossible to believe that from Oaxtepec any type of organic structure could be considered an expression of continental unity." He emphasized the inadequate representation of youth, women, and ecumenical bodies,[13] and asked the delegates to consider Oaxtepec a call to repentance "for the great sin of Latin American Christianity in having ignored the true evangelical function of service to humanity."

In the end, after four days of fierce debate, the assembly rejected the idea of creating immediately a Latin American Council of Churches— in favor of a *"consejo en formacion,"* a council in formation. In a classic example of compromise, neither side came out exactly the winner. In a ceremony on the last day, all powers and properties of UNELAM were passed to the newly elected steering committee[14] leaving one with the impression that a Council of Churches had, in fact, been constituted. Yet both sides seemed curiously satisfied. Progressive supporters saw the council as a "committee of continuation" that would promote ecumenism at the local level. On the other side, conservatives who had opposed the idea of an international council were relieved that there would be no formal organization that could be susceptible to "Marxist" influence (Campbell, 1978).

. . . AND OTHER RECURRING THEMES

While the debate over the meaning of unity and the formation of a council was consuming the plenary sessions, study groups, each organized around a particular topic, were meeting to formulate position papers that would be presented to the assembly for amendment, acceptance, or rejection. Among the issues covered by these groups were power structures, human rights, indigenous communities, Christian presence in the community, and forgotten sectors (women, youth, the elderly, et al.). All the papers presented to the assembly would fall under Míguez's "revolutionary" category. Perhaps the paper presented by the group examining power structures was, in its analysis, the clearest and most radical of all. It began:

The economic system that exists in Latin America determines the development of the first world countries and the underdevelopment of the third world countries. Transnational capitalism subordinates those countries called the Third World to its interests of profit and accumulation, generating a growing external debt, technological dependence . . . [and] military control of politics. . . . The doctrine of National Security provides the justification for the power exercised for the first world capitalists and the dominant social classes within each country. These power structures are ultimately the causes of . . . malnutrition; infant mortality; unemployment; short life spans; inadequate health care, education and social security.

The churches, this document continued, must reject Paul's charge in his letter to the Romans (13:1-6) regarding obedience to one's governors. The churches that cooperate with despotic regimes, said the document, "represent an alliance with and support of Pharaoh against Moses and the people of God who look for their liberation."

The other papers were equally pointed. Those examining the "Christian presence in the community" noted that "for the majority of our continent, the marginal, the impoverished, and the oppressed, the gospel is a voice of hope." But, it continued, "for others, who have enjoyed abundance and have failed to use that abundance such that they have caused the suffering of many, the gospel is a denunciation and exhortation to repentance for a change of life in Christ."

Yet another group studying "priority areas for action" insisted that "this critical hour demands a ministry directed to the victims of all types of violations of human rights: families of the missing, political prisoners, prisoners without lawyers, refugees, those enduring torture, those who suffer military repression." This same group summarized the situation of campesinos in one word: "exploitation." They pointed out that the health of the great majority does not meet minimal standards, and they condemned the wanton destruction of irreplacable natural resources.

Finally, in the most immediate and specific denunciation and recommendation to the assembly, the study group on "human rights" condemned rights violations in Nicaragua and called on the assembly to (1) send a letter of solidarity to the Nicaraguan people; (2) send letters to the National Council of Churches in the United States and to the United Nations calling on those bodies to exert pressure on the U.S. administration; (3) take up a collection for humanitarian aid in Nicaragua; and (4) send a delegation from the assembly to meet with local churches and assess more directly the situation and needs. The assembly not only adopted all these recommendations with only one or two dissenting voices. it also decided unanimously to send a cable to President Somoza calling on him to resign as his "contribution to national reconciliation."

These acts must be considered among the most prophetic positions taken at Oaxtepec. This is particularly true in light of the assembly's failure to approve the fifteen-page "Pre-Informe" produced by the study groups (and quoted from above) as an official statement. It was accepted as a study document, to be circulated among those attending and other interested churches and groups.

The only official document to come out of Oaxtepec (in marked contrast to CELAM III) was a three-page "letter to the Christian churches and ecumenical bodies in Latin America." This letter summarized in general and noncontroversial terms the conclusions of the study groups, the decision to create a council-in-formation, and the specific human rights actions.

The other significant events can only be described as reconciling. Continuing the tradition begun at Medellín and III CELA, there were Roman Catholic observers at Oaxtepec (as there would be official Protestant observers in Puebla). Then, in a moving demonstration of ecumenism, Bishop Sergio Mendez-Arceo of Cuernavaca, in whose diocese Oaxtepc is located, appeared the first day to bring *bienvenidos* and to join in for a time as observer and commentator. He arrived while Carmelo Alvarez was delivering his paper, after which Mendez-Arceo commended the presentation for its self-critical spirit and its emphasis on "the announcement of the Kingdom to the poor from the position of the poor." On Sunday of that week the Bishop honored the Protestants during a special mass in Cuernavaca's cathedral.

Conclusions

Clearly, Oaxtepec did not resolve all the tensions, nor solve the massive problems Protestant churches face in Latin America. Evangelicals constitute only ten percent of the population in an overwhelmingly Catholic continent. The churches must frequently try to be faithful to the gospel in the face of repressive regimes. There are historic, theological, political, and ideological divisions that must be overcome. And, at some point, the churches must grapple with the fact that if they have really opted for the poor they will be in opposition to the rich. This issue, the extent to which we are talking about the reconciliation of irreconcilable forces, has never been addressed in any systematic way by the Evangelical Churches of Latin America.

In one sense, with regard to this issue, it can be argued that the Evangelical Churches are in an easier position than the Roman Catholic Church. Catholics will do whatever they must to avoid even the appearance of schism. Since institutional schism already exists among Protestants, if (when) the point comes that Míguez's "revolutionaries" are compelled to say, "here we stand," it will be the "social strikers" who fall away and withdraw into their own ecclesiastical womb. For all Latin American Evangelicals, that will be a regrettable but manageable event. The Catholic Church would not be so lucky.

I said at the beginning of this essay that at Oaxtepec the Evangelicals took another step closer to the unity that has eluded them throughout their history in Latin America. In light of the differences, conflicts, and divisions discussed above, one may legitimately question this assertion. It is however, a guarded conclusion.

The divisions that marred the earlier meetings were less evident at Oaxtepec because of developments that could have papered over significant differences. First, growing Latin Americanization of the Evangelical Churches has created a common frame of reference. Then, a common language (provided by liberation theology) has emerged that virtually all churches are buying into, even the most conservative. This means that one often must read carefully between the lines to detect the absence of a genuine commitment to the demands of Luke 4.

In a strictly institutional sense, the possibility does exist that CLAI (in formation) will be better equipped to coordinate certain ecumenical activities in Latin America than was UNELAM. But because of the above-mentioned factors, it is not clear that Oaxtepec represents a threshold of genuine understanding among Latin American Evangelicals.

NOTES

1. In the English-speaking world Western Christian churches that are not Roman Catholic are generally called Protestant. The term Evangelical often refers to a conservative theological position. In Latin America however, "Evangelical" is used to describe all Christian churches that are not Catholic or Orthodox. It derives from the Spanish "evangelio," which means gospel or New Testament.

2. This meant that, regardless of the theological or political divisions at Puebla, there was never any doubt that there was *one* Church and that *one* final document would be produced.

3. Not everyone agrees with this characterization. See, for example, Willems (1967) and Wagner (1973).

4. The idea of "project" is defined by Miguez "as a midway term between an utopia, a vision which makes no attempt to connect itself historically to the present, and a program, a technically developed model for the organization of society" (1975: 38).

5. Brian Smith (1978) has written that

most fundamentalist Evangelical churches (which account for the vast majority of the 1,000,000 Protestants in Chile) . . . were openly supportive of the junta from their first days in office and most did not participate in ecumenical human rights activities. Soon after the coup, the new government gave significant subsidies to the Evangelicals for the completion of a large temple in downtown Santiago. In December 1974 Pinochet attended the dedication ceremonies of the edifice (where he was warmly received by a capacity crowd of several thousand Pentecostals), and he affirmed his support for freedom of conscience and religious practice for all Churches in Chile.

6. From this discussion it can be seen that the long-held North American social science finding of a positive correlation between religious and political conservatism simply does not hold up when one examines Latin American Evangelicals. The exceptions to the rule are so numerous and widespread that one must argue, at least in the Latin American context, for a new rule. I believe it is necessary to look beyond denominational labels to the theological hermeneutic of the particular church or subdivision thereof. To oversimplify, is Luke 4 : 18, the Exodus story, Jeremiah, or the Magnificat emphasized, or is the guiding word Romans 13 : 1-5? In any event further discussion of this point is beyond the scope of this chapter, but it is an issue deserving of careful study.

7. The First Latin American Evangelical Conference was held in Buenos Aires in 1949. Now numerically dominated by Latin rather than North Americans, the conference still reflects the Social Gospel orientation manifested 33 years earlier in Panama. They attacked the "caudillismo" which had "sown hatred, intolerance, and irreconcilable division in many aspects of civil, political and religious life. There has grown up a kind of intellectual aristocracy which has expressed itself in ambition and materialistic selfishness." But the appropriate response to this situation was to "preach tolerance, respect for life and other peoples' ideas, the obligation to use material possessions for the Glory of God and the good of one's neighbor." The quote is taken from the 1949 Report on the First Latin American Evangelical Conference.

8. Recall that the earlier version of this conflict had appeared during the Panama conference as a debate between advocates of the Social Gospel and those whose attention was confined to individual conversion.

9. There was a reciprocal exchange of observers at Medellín and Buenos Aires.

10. ISAL, the Church and Society Movement in Latin America, has been described by Orlando Costas as "the most consistently radical Protestant ecumenical organization" on the continent. CELADEC, the Latin American Protestant Commission of Christian Education, was founded in 1962 and charged with coordinating all the efforts to promote Christian education.

11. Much of the information in this section derived from my own status as a partici-pant-observer at Oaxtepec. Unattributed material was gathered in informal interviews and conversations during that week.

12. The ponencia was delivered by Emilio Castro, a Uruguayan Methodist and cur-rently director of the Department of Evangelism of the World Council of Churches.

13. Of 193 official representatives from 19 countries, 25% came from Pentecostal churches and almost one-quarter were Lutherans. Both groups had barely been repre-sented in previous gatherings. There were two youth delegates from each country, with voice and vote. The coordinating committee had called for half of each national delegation to be women, but only 12% of the total number of delegates were women.

14. After deciding to create a council-in-formation, discussion shifted to how the con-tinent ought to be divided for purposes of representation. Six regions were created with two representatives elected from each region. Heated debate preceded the decision to make the ecumenical organizations a "seventh region," also with two representatives. Míguez Bonino was the most influential speaker here when he pointed out that denomina-tions do not exhaust Christian organizations and noted that when the churches fail to practice the Social Gospel it is often these groups that fill the void. Míguez also reminded the delegates that the churches of Latin America are imported, bu the ecumenical move-ment is indigenous.

Bishop Federico Pagura of Argentina, who had been elected president of the assembly on the first day, was elected president of the steering committee of the council on the last. Five Methodists, three Pentecostals, three Lutherans, one Episcopalian, one United Church of Christ, and one member of the Salvation Army were elected by the delegates from a slate of candidates nominated by the several regional groups and ecumenical organizations. Notably absent are representatives from the Presbyterian or Reformed Churches. Members come from eight countries, including Puerto Rico, but excluding Cuba, whose candidate, Sergio Arce Martinez, Rector of the Protestant Seminary in Matanzas, lost by one vote. There are two women on the committee.

The political constitution of this group ranges from Miguez's "liberal project" types to "revolutionaries"; however, the overall makeup is slightly left of center.

REFERENCES

ALVAREZ, C. (1978) "The role of the Church in Latin America." Presented at the Evangelical Assembly, Oaxtepec, Mexico.

ALVES, R. (1971) "Function ideologica y posibilidades utopicas del protestantismo latinoamericano," in De la iglesia y la sociedad. Montevideo: Tierra Nueva.

BEACH, H. P. (1916) Renaissant Latin America: An Outline and Interpretation of the Congress on Christian Work in Latin America. New York: Missionary Education Movement of the United States and Canada.

CAMPBELL, G. (1978) "Latin American Protestants move toward unity and demand human rights." (mimeo)

CASTRO, E. (1975) Amidst Revolution. Belfast: Christian Journals, Ltd.

CENCOS (1978) "Oaxtepec '78—Protestant version of 'Puebla '78'?" Press release, Mexico City, June 21.

Committee on Cooperation in Latin America (1916) "Christian work in Latin America."
    Reports of Commissions I, II, and III presented to the Congress on Christian Work in
    Latin America, February 1916. New York: Missionary Education Movement.
COSTAS, O. E. (1976) Theology of the Crossroads in Contemporary Latin America.
    Amsterdam: Rodopi.
"Cristo la Esperanza para America Latina." (1961) Report of the Second Latin American
    Evangelical Conference, Lima, Peru.
DEHAINAUT, R. K. (1972) Faith and Ideology in Latin American Perspective. Cuerna-
    vaca, Mexico: CIDOC.
Deudores del Mundo (1969) Montevideo: UNELAM.
FAZIO, C. (1978) "Misioneros al servicio de la politica de Estados Unidos." PROCESO
    (Mexico City), September 18.
GAXIOLA, A. (1978) "Reaccion a la Ponencia: Rol de la Iglesia en America Latina."
    Oaxtepec. (mimeo)
La Iglesia y la Junta Militar (1975) Buenos Aires: Tierra Nueva.
LALIVE D'EPINAY, C. (1968) El refugio de las masas. Santiago: Editorial El Pacifico.
Libro de Trabajo (1978) Asamblea de Iglesias de America Latina. (mimeo)
LIGGETT, T. J. (1970) Where Tomorrow Struggles To Be Born. New York: Friendship.
MENDEZ, H. (1978) "Reaccion al tema sobre unidad." Oaxtepec. (mimeo)
MIGUEZ BONINO, J. (1975) Doing Theology in a Revolutionary Situation. Phila-
    delphia: Fortress.
——— (1973) "Vision del cambio social y sus tareas desde las iglesias no-catolicas," in Fe
    cristiana y cambio social en America Latina. Salamanca: La Aurora.
——— (1972) "The Political attitude of Protestants in Latin America" (J. and M. Goff,
    trans.). Noticiero de la Fe 37 (July). (mimeo)
——— (1961) "Los Factores Religiosos en la Situacion Actual." Study Paper for the
    Second Latin American Evangelical Conference. Lima.
OLIVA, P. P. (1975) Posicion Evangelica. Santiago: Editora Nacional Gabriela Mistral.
PEREZ-RIVAS, M. (1971) "El ecumenismo en America Latina," in N. Goodall, El movi-
    miento ecumenico. Buenos Aires: La Aurora.
READ, W. R., V. M. MONTERROSO, and H. A. JOHNSON (1969) Latin American
    Church Growth. Grand Rapids. MI: Eerdmans.
RYCROFT, W. S. and M. M. CLEMMER (1963) A Factual Study of Latin America.
    New York: Commission on Ecumenical Mission and Relations, the United Presby-
    terian Church in the USA.
SANTANA, B. (1978) "Prologo," to De Panama a Mexico via Bogota. San Juan, Puerto
    Rico: Comision organizadora pro Consejo Latinoamericano de Iglesias. (mimeo)
SMITH, B. (1978) "The Catholic Church and political change in Chile, 1925-1978." Ph.D.
    dissertation, Yale University.
WAGNER, C. P. (1973) Look Out! The Pentacostals Are Coming. Carol Stream, IL:
    Creation House.
WILLEMS, E. (1967) Followers of the New Faith: Culture Change and the Rise of
    Protestantism. Nashville.
WRIGHT, J. (1979) Interview in New York City, April 11.

Part II

RELIGION AND POLITICS:

POINTS ON THE SPECTRUM

Introduction

In recent years, church leaders have consistently tried to withdraw from politics and develop an autonomous, nonpolitical stance. But this has proven difficult, for politics is everywhere. Divisions along political lines split the churches internally, while setting their organizations and activists into increasing conflict with political (and especially military) authorities. Politics is both of interest to many in the churches and also a crucial element of context. Thus, church people reach out to understand and deal with political issues, while politics itself intrudes more and more on the churches as public authorities seek to expand and tighten their control.

Ideological conflict is thus very salient in the Latin American churches today. Indeed, much of the tension and debate in Catholicism can be understood as a struggle to control and orient the social and political content of Christian symbols. For radicals, this process involves a *demythologizing* of Christian symbols, cutting the ties that bind them, unnecessarily, to the existing order. The intellectual and organizational origins of the Christian Left in Latin America are explored here by Michael Dodson. He examines radical Catholicism both as an innovative religious theology and as a new political theory, and shows how these new insights led to the formation of religiopolitical movements to promote change in several countries.

As we have seen, the struggle is not only within the churches. Indeed, the contemporary Latin American scene is marked by extremely high levels of church-state conflict. Of course, disputes between church and state are nothing new in Latin America. Conflicts over school subsidies, marriage and divorce laws, birth control, and similar issues have been a prominent feature of Latin American life for many generations. But in recent years church-state conflict has taken a new turn. As Catholic individuals and institutions have increasingly moved to positions of radical social and political criticism, they have come up against the new totalizing ideologies of national security elaborated by military regimes throughout the region. Roberto Calvo examines the sources and key elements of the doctrine of national security, while laying out the main lines of the Church's analysis and doctrinal response.

What are the implications of this clash between churches moving toward greater political interest and activism and governments concerned for ever more extensive "security" and control? At the very least, it is clear that a middle ground—some neutral, nonpolitical space—is harder and harder to find. Often, the churches have, in effect, become shields for dissent in societies where independent political expression and action is impossible. The issue of human rights in Latin America has become an important expression of these conflicts, and in his contribution, Brian Smith explores the developing organizational basis of church response to authoritarian rule and its implications for the future. He further analyzes the way in which the very concept of human rights has expanded beyond the limits of traditional civil liberties to include the demands for more just and equitable social, economic, and political structures which have been so central to the debates in the Latin American churches since Medellín.

5

THE CHRISTIAN LEFT
IN LATIN AMERICAN POLITICS

MICHAEL DODSON

After decades of neglect, interest in the political significance of Latin American Catholicism increased sharply in the late 1960s when it began to appear that the Church might have unimagined potential for promoting social change, particularly in a continent plagued by social upheaval and political instability (Drekonja, 1971: 59-65). In both word and deed, the postconciliar Church manifested a changing social orientation which entailed open involvement in political issues on behalf of the poor. In fact, by August 1968 and the convening of the Council of Latin American Bishops (CELAM) in Medellín, Colombia, the Church seemed to be changing its social and political attitudes so profoundly that reports of a revolutionary Church began to accompany discussions of the political situation in Latin America. Since Medellín, an important literature has evolved from efforts to understand this change in Latin American Catholicism. The experience sent students of the Church back to the question first posed by Marx and Weber: can traditional religious institutions be a source of energy for changing society (Silvert, 1967; Smith, 1975)?

The search for an answer to this question has resulted in a variety of perspectives and arguments about the relationship of religion to social change in Latin America. Depending on which country one studied and at what point in time, writers have seen the Church as a dynamic force for social change (D. Smith, 1970; Sanders, 1970; Drekonja, 1971; Williams, 1969, 1973; Turner, 1971; Vallier, 1967, 1970), a moderate force for social change (B. Smith, 1975, 1976; Levine and Wilde, 1977), a mild obstacle to social change (deKadt, 1967, 1970, 1971), and a serious obstacle to social change (Mutchler, 1969; Vekemans, 1964).[1] Such diverse points of view are not necessarily contradictory because the postconciliar Church has spawned a wide range of groups possessing an array of strategies for political action. There is, however, a strong tendency in the literature to explain and judge the entire range of groups and points of view from a single interpretive framework. Until recently the predominant conceptual approach to the study of the Latin American Church and its role in social change was drawn directly from the developmental paradigm which informed the broader study of comparative politics in the 1960s.[2] Thus, there is more overlap in the interpretations mentioned above than first meets the eye.

In sifting through the literature, one is struck by the tendency of many North American writers to generalize about the "progressives" who changed the Church in the aftermath of Vatican II. Although the word "revolutionary" is sometimes used, it usually serves as a synonym for progressive. The impression thus developed is that progressives have been the dynamic force in changing Latin American Catholicism and have effectively defined the Church's viable range of sociopolitical options. The right and left have received far less attention. Both conservatives and radicals are either ignored in the theoretical writings, or assigned a negative, counterdevelopmental role. This article questions the assumption on which that orientation rests and examines the case of the radicals, whose explicit goal is to make the Church an agent of social change.

The article examines three writers who have been prominent among the students of the Latin American Church. I explicate briefly the framework of interpretation they have used to criticize and evaluate the political behavior of progressives and radicals in the Church. It is important, I believe, to clarify how the developmentalist perspective shapes the way in which these writers distinguish the progressives from the radicals. (Later I will show how the distinction looks from the point of view of the radicals.) Analysis will be based on a comparison of religious change in two countries—Argentina and Chile—where struggle and innovation in the Church has been notably intense. In each country both progressive and radical groups have emerged among the clergy, becoming sufficiently organized to have an impact in the political arena. Through comparison of the Argentine Movement of Priests for the Third World and the Chilean Christians for Socialism, I will evaluate the strengths and weaknesses of the developmentalist approach to the study of the Church and social change in Latin America.

A second issue guiding this analysis follows logically from the first. What intellectual framework is employed by the left to explain and criticize the Latin American Church's role in social change? The answer

to this question entails an implicit critique of the development paradigm. Hence, I propose to examine the way recent church involvement
in social change looks from the point of view of the left. Of course,
the radicals themselves must be criticized, but in relation to *their own*
intellectual frame of reference and normative goals as well as those
of development theory.

Developmentalism and the Study of the Christian Left

Religious innovation raised high expectations that the Church might
assume a constructive role in promoting social change and political
development. Imbued with the hope and optimism which pervaded
the "decade of development," North American writers were attracted to
the prospect that so traditional and conservative an institution as the
Roman Catholic church would embrace and promote the values of
modernization. With the Church at least nominally commanding the
loyalty of over 90% of the Latin American people, a visible shift on its
part in a modernizing direction was envisioned as a great stimulus to
the "nation builders." The case of the Chilean Church stood out among
the national churches of the region; indeed, it became a model in the
minds of North American observers. Just as United States policy
makers looked to Chile as a test case of political development, so
prominent students of the Church looked to Chile as a test case of
"religious system development" (Vallier, 1967: 466). It is no coincidence,
then, that the bulk of this literature on religion and social change
shares so fully in the language, concepts, and perspectives of the broader
development literature (Almond and Powell, 1966; Pye, 1966; Huntington, 1968, 1971).

Several authors have conceived modernization in the Church as a
process of reformulating religious values to promote a natural social
consensus and heightened integration. The Church has always promoted
value consensus, of course, but the new consensus would allow for
innovation while at the same time helping "to minimize the competition
between the old and new elites and [also] to avoid unnecessary and
counterproductive conflict" (Williams, 1969: 334-335). This language
and conceptual framework are based on a view of Chile in the mid-
1960s, which set a reform-minded Church in a pluralistic society.
Williams labels this church "prophetic," but ignores entirely the possi-

bility that religious change (and prophetic values) might clash with developmentalism, as he sees it, or be accompanied by social conflict. One finds a similar, though more discriminating analysis, in the work of Einaudi et al., (1969), who also focus on the Christian Democratic experience in Chile and the early liberalization of the Church there. Einaudi's conception of a "prophetic church" also envisions a reformist or modernizing Church dedicated to the building of western, pluralist democracy. He recognizes that change-oriented members of the Church have diverse orientations, and that no single, homogeneous, progressive Church emerges from Vatican II and Medellin. So he distinguishes between prophetic *liberals* who seek to transcend "partisan politics," promoting nation-building through social harmony and consensus, and prophetic *radicals* who engage in "movements" or in partisan politics which generate conflict and disunity (Einaudi et al., 1969: 48-50). The latter are dismissed as utopian and counterproductive.[3]

This general perspective is most fully elaborated in the work of Vallier (1967, 1970, 1972). Vallier built a model of Church development in which the Church initiates and sponsors "a framework of order" relevant to "injustice" and "a generalized need for rapid and deep changes in the institutional system." Vallier's developed Church, in fact, represents "a new conception of order." His theory requires that Church development produce "symbols and normative principles that legitimate fundamental change but in such ways that continuity with certain elements can be observed" (1967: 466). Achieving this objective requires the *avoidance* of "partisan politics." Success promotes social integration and political stability, which in turn enable the Church to remain above partisan politics. Remarkably, Vallier's developed religious system is to promote "fundamental" social change without ever soiling itself with what one writer has called the "messiness" of politics. The Church exercises its religious power in socially relevant ways without exercising political power.

Vallier is aware that Medellin stimulated many approaches to religious innovation, and he captures this diversity by distinguishing "pastoral" from "clerical" radicals (1972). His virulent criticism of the clerical radicals typifies the normative framework of the developmental approach. Here he shows clearly what was only implicit in his earlier work as well as that of Williams and Einaudi—that a prophetic "modernizing" church is not radical but liberal and, indeed, apolitical. Taking Chile and Colombia as polar types of Church political involvement, Vallier expounded the differences between "pastoral radicalism" and "clerical radicalism" as seen from a developmental perspective. In pastoral radicalism the priest avoids using his religious office as a basis for building up social and political authority. He carefully sidesteps all partisan political involvement or identification. In his pastoral activity "the religious floor is a generalized source of certainty and identity for other roles in society, but it is not the base on which all choices are made" (1972: 22). The religious norms fostered by the priest are suprapartisan in this model, transcending specific political options and therefore rising above political conflict. Thus, pastoral radicals can promote the "Christian revolution," while at the same time helping to "depoliticize" society and foster "civic development" and "nation-building."

The clerical radicals present a sharp contrast. By stressing the Colombian example, Vallier generalizes the case of Camilo Torres, the well-known guerrilla priest who died in a skirmish with government troops in February 1966, into a prototype of clerical radicalism. By doing so he identifies the Christian left with Camilismo, guerrilla warfare, and in his words, violent "assaults on the establishment." In Vallier's view, the clerical radicals are politically "retrogressive" (counterdevelopmental) for several reasons. First, they engage in direct political action through religiopolitical movements of the left: they try to "lead the social revolution." Since such activity is partisan, it must be conflictual in its impact and therefore retrogressive with respect to nation-building which is conceived in terms of harmonious integration. Second, they organize their religious roles from the perspective of a "comprehensive closed religious framework." Like the protagonists of the Protestant Reformation, the clerical radicals are fanatical men who define all issues in terms of a single, unchangeable religious perspective. Third, Vallier charges the clerical radicals with having a unidimensional and dogmatic religious perspective *because* they utilize Marxist social analysis, which is intrinsically dogmatic. Finally, the clerical radicals make a "traditionalizing demand" for the laity to "defend" the Church's institutional structures and dominance in society, or to augment the corporate interests of the religious institution (1972: 22-23). The analysis which follows examines this dichotomy between pastoral and clerical radicals, measuring it against the actual experience of the religiopolitical movements of the left in Argentina and Chile. I will try to determine the extent to which these characteristics do in fact appropriately describe the Christian left. Are the clerical radicals uniformly committed to

Camilismo? Vallier's approach prejudges these issues, for within the theoretical framework of developmentalism there is no place for the left. For this reason we must judge the left in terms of its own goals, and then relate our findings back to the charges made by Vallier.

The terminology, then, which has been used to describe Church change in Latin America has been too broad. Some writers have lumped everything from Chilean Christian Democracy to Camilo Torres under the label "progressivism," suggesting that a single, homogeneous, change-oriented Church has evolved in Latin America. The developmentalists have been guilty of this, but have in fact systematically excluded the radical left from their analysis. Indeed, I contend that their intellectual framework leads students of the Church away from the study of priest groups consciously organized for direct political action. Such groups have appeared in most countries in Latin America, yet they have scarcely been noticed by North American writers preoccupied with the search for agents of development.[4]

In this regard, it is important to be clear on the composition of the "Christian Left." In my view, an effective definition of the Christian left lies between the two extremes of Christian Democracy, which represents a liberal progressivism, and Camilismo, which represents a fully developed revolutionary position. A significant field of Christian radicalism lies between these positions and is notable for its rejection of both reformism and violent revolution, along with the unstated assumption that these are the only options Latin Americans possess. The fact is that the religiopolitical movements discussed here look extremist only when compared to the Christian Democrats and when evaluated in terms of developmental criteria; when compared to Camilismo the Third World Priests look moderate, while the Christians for Socialism, though more radical than the Third World Priests, hardly appear to be a band of guerrilla revolutionaries. The Christian left is united by a common political theory, the theology of liberation, which encompasses a radical theology, a radical social analysis borrowed largely from the neo-Marxist literature on dependency, and a radical, but not revolutionary, political program of democratic socialism. Therefore, the Christian left does include those who have engaged in direct political action and who utilize Marxist analysis, as Vallier contended. But it remains to be seen whether this has made their activities inherently retrogressive.

Liberation Theology:
The Normative Criteria for Religiopolitical Action

It is essential to examine the relationship between thought and practice in the study of the Latin American Christian left. Below, I discuss briefly the crisis in the Church with respect to development which occurred after 1965 and the subsequent turning away from the capitalist model toward socialism. This crisis in perspective made necessary the creation of new "prophetic" clerical roles, "prophetic" roles which seemed to require the organization of individual ministries into religiopolitical movements of the left. Let us examine this process and the liberation values which inform the political programs of two such movements.

Officially, the Catholic Church acknowledged that capitalism as well as socialism produced detrimental social consequences as early as 1891 with the publication of Pope Leo XIII's encyclical *Rerum Novarum*. But as recently as 1960, the Latin American church had shown no inclination to condemn capitalist expansion in Latin America because it failed to improve the lives of the vast majority of people. Only in Chile (Sigmund, 1973) and Brazil (deKadt, 1970) had criticisms of capitalism been clearly voiced within the Church. In the case of Chile, the Christian Democratic movement attempted to carve out a "third way" between capitalism and socialism. With the election of Eduardo Frei to the presidency in 1964, Chilean Christian Democrats got a chance to demonstrate that a "third position" could transform social structures and bring real change for the better in the lives of the poor. In power, Christian Democracy became closely identified with the reformist position of the Alliance for Progress, a position supported by the United States and based on capitalist development. Frei's "revolution in liberty" meant reform within capitalist economic structures and formally democratic electoral processes; it excluded the more profound change implied in socialism.

The general failure of the Alliance for Progress, and the specific failure of the Frei regime to bring about land reform, to "denationalize" the Chilean economy, or to raise the living standard of the great mass of poor, undercut the appeal of a reformist path to development. Indeed, these failures led to a rethinking of the very concept of development and a gradual rejection of its premises. Activist clergy began to sense that capitalist development implied not progress, but deepening poverty in their countries and *less* likelihood that democratic institutions of a participatory nature would flourish. Gradually there emerged in the Church (as in society at large) a perspective which saw "development" as exploitation, benefiting the rich nations and select elites in Latin America at the expense of the great majority of ordinary people. From this changing awareness came the development of a theology of liberation, which adopted a conflict model of social analysis to replace the consensus model of the developmentalists and attempted to articulate a vision of the good society quite different from that presented by western capitalism. Let us turn first to the prophetic ministry which is developed to meet the exigencies of a conflictual social order; then we will examine the political alternative envisioned in liberation theology.

When seen from the vantage point of the poor, Latin America's social order appeared laden with "structural" obstacles to change. Thus, poverty was less a function of individual failure than "systemic" failure. The political interests and policies of both local and foreign elites seemed to become not only inconsistent with, but diametrically opposed to, those of the Latin American masses. This appraisal of the social order recalled the prophetic ministry of Old Testament gospels: that ministry had been fashioned precisely to meet a condition of captivity, exploitation, and oppression. Priests adopting this new perspective found it necessary to revise both their theology and their ministry in terms of the ancient prophetic tradition in order to struggle against "structural sin" (Schillebeeckx, 1970: 27).

Moving out of a purely confessional role and into the public domain brought with it the need to clarify the priests' social role. Two broad themes evolved. First, for radical priests a prophetic ministry involves the interpretation of the gospel in light of social conflict and exploitation, not with an eye to transcending or avoiding such conflict for the sake of some "higher" consensus. A prophetic ministry interprets the "signs of the times," an activity with two dimensions—one negative, the other positive. Negatively, a prophetic ministry calls for the denunciation of structural sin. This means attempting, through social analysis, to determine where the chain of exploitation begins, and requires exposure and criticism of its social roots. Radical clergy see this as "desacrilizing" or delegitimizing the current social order. Obviously, Christian radicalism differs sharply from Christian reformism. The latter has no provision at all for a denunciatory role, for it is not imagined that the social and political orders could require "desacrilization" (Williams, 1969, 1973; Vallier, 1967, 1970).

Second, the tearing down of unjust structures must be accompanied by the building up of a new order. Hence, radical clergy also have assumed a role of community leadership by attempting to organize their followers for political action, guided by a vision of the Christian eschatology and a "hope" for the future that is both spiritual and temporal, and therefore political. Liberation theology (theory) and priests organizing for social change (praxis) are bound together in a single prophetic action.

Finally, as to the social goals which inform this prophetic Christian vision, two themes lie at the core of liberation theology. First, liberationists argue that meaningful social change in Latin America implies the full participation of ordinary people in the shaping of their own lives. Profound dependence and passivity must give way to an equally profound participation. Second, social structures must be reordered to promote human cooperation and to redistribute social values in a more egalitarian fashion. Participatory democracy and humanist socialism thus go together.[5]

In this vein, it is clear that radical Latin American clergy follows the democratic tradition associated with the name of Rousseau rather than the more cautious and skeptical tradition deriving from Locke (Sabine, 1952). The "freedom" each tradition espouses is quite different. Lockean concepts of freedom are based on a model of "bourgeois" social relations (MacPherson, 1964) appropriate to a market society which rewards egocentrism, individualism, and competition. Such a society is inherently conflictual, and its core value of freedom is "freedom from" norms imposed by the collectivity (Berlin, 1967). In the eyes of radical clergy this view of freedom corresponds to the social conditions of liberal democracies and implies materialism, social conflict, and exploitation. They opt instead for an egalitarian approach to freedom, which seeks not to protect individuals from the collectivity, but rather to enable them to be free within it. Liberation theology thus emphasizes a "positive" kind of liberty, a "freedom to," which stresses participation, self-determination, and the creation of social conditions to make both available to all citizens. Following Rousseau, liberationists stress the value of equality, making it inseparable from freedom.

The attempt to join the values of freedom and equality has led radical priests to promote socialism as well. For in practice, the stress on structural sin noted earlier means that capitalist social and political institutions are the chief obstacles to the fulfillment of democratic values. The only way to expand the range of choice within which poor and exploited peoples can identify and meet their own goals is to replace capitalism with socialism. Míguez Bonino's views are representative of liberation theology here:

> Humanization is for capitalism an unintended by-product, while it is for socialism an explicit goal. Solidarity is for capitalism accidental, for socialism it is essential. In terms of their basic ethos, Christianity must critique capitalism radically, in its fundamental intention, while it must critique socialism functionally, in its failure to fulfill its purpose [1976: 115].

Case Studies

THE FORMATION OF RADICAL MOVEMENTS

Radical priest movements seemed to burst on the Latin American scene quite suddenly in the late 1960s. In fact, however, a major factor which led to their creation had been developing for nearly a decade. The worker-priest experiment thrust priests into factory jobs to share the daily life of the working class as early as 1960 in Argentina. In Chile priests entered the *poblaciones* in the first years of the Frei government. In each case direct contact with the poor was a catalyst in politicizing clergy during the '60s. Although initially supported by the hierarchy as a move to revive the working class' declining interest in the Church, such experiments evolved rapidly as immersion in the life of working people brought priests face to face with massive poverty, social dislocation, and individual alienation. Worker-priests in Argentina discovered a large rift in the working class between a labor aristocracy and a mass a unemployed or underemployed workers for whom "development" brought no improvement in standard of living. Between the conclusion of Vatican II in 1965 and CELAM in 1968, worker-priests in virtually all countries of Latin America began to interpret this pattern as the inevitable consequence of "dependent" capitalist development.[6]

Thus, in Argentina and Chile the rejection of developmentalism and the turn to a liberation perspective evolved over nearly a decade, rooted in informal exchanges among priests with similar experiences. An early issue was how to acquire within the existing organizational structure of the Church the latitude necessary for effective social commitment. How far would the hierarchy permit activists to go? In Argentina radicalized priests found it necessary to expand their social role with little or no support from the hierarchy. In many areas of the country the hierarchy not only resisted the leftward drift of the clergy, but sought to crush such a move by suspending priests, moving them to remote parishes, and even collaborating with the government to deport foreign clergy. In Chile a more dynamic climate of Christian activism and a more liberal hierarchy made early efforts to work among the poor seem more fruitful in that country. As we shall see below, however, this did not mean that the Christian left would be in the long run more successful there. Before turning to that issue, let us take a closer look at the factors which fostered the transition from loose networks of social-activist priests to organized, nationwide movements of politically committed clergy.

In Argentina two factors stand out. The first is the maturity of the worker-priest experiment as discussed above. By May 1968, when the Movement of Priests for the Third World was formally created at Córdoba, the worker-priest experiment was a decade old. In urban, industrialized Argentina this meant that a "pooling" of highly motivated priests with common, radicalizing experiences had taken place. These priests were politicized to a working-class political culture heavily influenced by the legacy of Peronism. The result was a strongly unified perspective which gave a large measure of coherence to their movement even in its early stages. The second factor is the important, but changing, Argentine hierarchy. On the one hand, the obdurate resistance of certain bishops to the activities of radical priests in their dioceses and the heavy-handed penalties meted out by such bishops pushed the radicals to one another's defense. Priests expelled from one diocese were welcomed in another. Moreover, the complicity of government authorities in several such incidents made it seem all the more essential for priests to band together. Mutual assistance led to collective action and finally to the construction of an organizational apparatus. On the other hand, there were bishops in Argentina who openly supported radical priests when they needed that support most. As early as 1965, Bishops Antonio Quarracino, Alberto Devoto, and Jeronimo Podestá attended meetings of radical priests and gave them public support. In 1967 Bishop Podestá lost his diocese as a result of promoting social activism and worker organization (Dodson, 1972: 62), and thereby became a potent symbol to the fledgling Third World Priest movement. After the movement's formation in 1968, a small number of bishops gradually moved to open support for the Third World priests, including the influential Archbishop of Santa Fe, Vicente Zaspe. In short, both with resistance and with support, the Argentine hierarchy played an important role in the formation of the Third World Priest movement.

In turning to the Chilean experience we must recall that the developmentalist approach outlined above did not anticipate the appearance of *any* radical priest movement in Chile. In fact, however, a numerous and diverse Christian left emerged in Chile during the half-decade between 1968 and the military coup in September 1973 which halted all political activity. The Christian left in Chile included the Young Church, the Movement of Unified Popular Action (MAPU), Christian Left, The Eighty, The 200, and the Christians for Socialism. In part this broad range of groups represents the fragmentation of the left which occurred during the period, and in part it merely represents the evolution of groups with significantly overlapping memberships. Let us briefly examine the origins of these groups with the purpose of seeing how the largest and most radical of the groups, the Christians for Socialism, came to be formed.

It is important, first of all, to mention the prominent role played by Christian Democracy in Chilean political life prior to 1968. The existence of a lay political party of Catholic inspiration simply made clergy more aware of political issues than was the case in Argentina and other countries of Latin Amerca. In addition, the well-funded Jesuit research center, Centro Bellarmino, constantly publicized issues of social reform. Other Catholic orders in Chile also sponsored research and teaching centers, designed primarily to promote efforts at "development." In the crisis of Christian Democratic government discussed earlier, these centers also helped focus attention on underdevelopment. The Jesuit Latin American Institute for Doctrine and Social Studies (ILADES), for example, made the interpretation of the Church's social doctrine in relation to underdevelopment the central theme of its investigation. Its director in the late 1960s, Gonzalo Arroyo, became a leading figure in the Christians for Socialism.

In Chile the crucial year in the emergence of the Christian left was 1968. Until that year Christian activism had found its expression through Christian Democracy and a "pastoral movement" centered in the *poblaciones*. But the growing sense of the failure of Christian Democratic reform programs, together with the gradual mobilization and politicization of the working-class prior to the 1970 elections, began to draw these social activists leftward. A "rebel" wing developed in the Christian Democratic party. Then, on August 11, 1968, a group of radicalized Christians, including nine priests and about 200 lay people, occupied the Cathedral in Santiago, using the occasion to denounce both social injustice and the inadequacy of efforts by the institutional Church to alleviate it. This brief occupation of the Cathedral, timed to coincide with the Eucharistic Congress in Bogotá which inaugurated the CELAM meetings, received wide publicity in Chile and became a focal point for gathering discontent within the Church. The "Young Church" movement grew out of the occupation. The Young Church movement itself was only a stage, albeit a crucial one, in the transition to left political militancy within the Church. Although it managed to hold a national meeting in October 1970, to affirm its "complete support of the Government of Popular Unity," it did not remain the focal point of Christian left activism (Epica, 1973: 4-8). On the one hand, some early members of the movement helped to form MAPU in 1969, which became part of the united front of the Popular Unity coalition. For these members, direct involvement in secular party politics became the outlet for their social commitment. Others in the Young Church movement, particularly clergy who chose to focus their efforts at internal Church reform and pushing the institutional Church toward direct political action, subsequently formed a series of new movements culminating in the formation of Christians for Socialism. In retrospect, the major significance of the Young Church is that it represented, first, a crystallization of the shift to the left in the church, and second, "a moment of cleavage," a dividing point at which some Christians moved into secular party politics, some stayed within the parameters of official church doctrine, and some began the effort to build up a "'parallel' Church" which would ally the institutional church with the struggle for socialism (Rojas and Vanderschueren, 1977: 25).

The Christians for Socialism movement grew out of the April 1971 meeting of 80 priests whose common background was very like that of the members of the Third World Priests in Argentina. The Eighty, as they were initially called, issued a strong declaration urging cooperation among Christians and Marxists, calling for the mobilization of the working class, and asserting that criticism of the Popular Unity government must come from "within the revolutionary process" (Rojas and Vanderschueren, 1977: 42). By November 1971, the Eighty, which was composed primarily of priests from Santiago, had created the larger Christians for Socialism movement.

POLITICAL ACTION STRATEGIES

Let us turn now to the question of strategies for political action adopted by these movements. They can be compared in terms of the two roles outlined above, denunciation and organization, and further as to the degree of militancy taken with respect to radical social change. Of course, neither movement was ever fully united over a single strategy or level of militancy, so I will be speaking of general tendencies which predominated.

The Movement of Priests for the Third World brought itself national attention through effective exercise of the denunciatory role. Indeed, their skill in publicizing social problems and the ineptitude of the Onganía regime in dealing with them was remarkable. From the "Rebel Christmas" of 1968, in which Third World Priests organized a nationwide protest tied to the symbols of one the year's major religious seasons, through the coup of June 1970, the movement was a constant thorn in the side of the regime, as well as a perpetual goad to the Church hierarchy. The movement showed a great ability to become associated with workers' strikes, student demonstrations, barrio protests, and peasant mobilizations without alienating the hierarchy sufficiently to move it to active collaboration with the regime. Criticisms of the regime often hit home in telling ways. The Third World Priests publicized the government's neglect of the working class at a time when inflation was wreaking havoc with workers everywhere in the country. The jailing of priests along with union leaders heightened public awareness of the costs of proscribing political parties. In addition, the priests carefully cloaked all their actions in the rhetoric of Vatican II, Medellín, and statements of Latin American bishops from Helder Camara to their own Eduardo Pironio. Thus, when the government counterattacked, it seemed to attack the church as a whole. This tended to drive a wedge between regime and Church. Gradually, individual bishops, their own consciousness raised by the wide range of publications and activities of the Third World Priests in their dioceses, began to speak out in support of the movement; perhaps more significantly in the short run, a growing number joined their voices to the chorus of antiregime protest which originated with the Third World Priest movement.

Although this denunciatory role was notably effective at the national level, direct political organization was confined largely to the parish level. In this area, the movement's greatest effectiveness was clearly among shanty-town dwellers and rural workers. The industrial working class had its own organizations in the Peronist movement. After 1970 the movement's major organizational thrust was in linking the unorganized working-class poor to the Peronist movement.

Clearly, the Third World Priests followed a relatively moderate political strategy during the crucial early years, in spite of the radical character of their theology and social analysis. They became identified with the extreme left only in the eyes of a small minority of the public. Between 1969 and 1972 the movement served as the focal point of protest against the repressiveness and austerity of military rule. It bore a striking resemblance, through its peaceful protest, to the civil rights movement in the United States under Martin Luther King. By 1972 the Third World Priests were also a center of the movement for a return to electoral politics and full participation by Peronists in national political life (Dodson, 1974b: 63-67).

When the Christian left in Chile is compared with that of Argentina, the later and more rapid evolution of a radicalized movement in Chile is evident. This difference seems to be accounted for at least in part by the more open, fluid, and rapidly changing political context of Chilean society as a whole. Two factors will be stressed in the following discussion. The first is the bitterly contested nature of Chilean elections in 1970 and 1973, which involved all sectors of society, as compared with the very controlled and limited nature of political activity under military rule in Argentina. The second is the role of the hierarchy in relation to the radical movement in the Church and in relation to the existing regime. Let me briefly compare these in more detail, with an eye to assessing the appropriateness of the political action strategy adopted by each movement within its particular political and religious context.

We saw above how the Argentine Third World Priest movement comprehended both the limitations and the opportunities which their immediate political and religious environment provided them. They correctly perceived the existence of very widespread, but latent support for Peronism throughout the country. They skillfully linked their own denunciations of the Onganía and Lanusse governments to this grassroots Peronism in such a way as to become a highly visible source of political opposition to an increasingly unpopular regime from 1968 to 1973. Such a strategy not only gave them significant political credibility in the eyes of the working classes, but also helped to give them unprecedented influence with the hierarchy. At no point did the Third World Priests seek to establish a priestly authority independent of the hierarchy. They did not call on their hierarchy publicly to commit itself to Peronism. They did, however, mount attacks against certain individual bishops who clearly were guilty of imposing excessive limitations or harsh punishments on activist priests. By isolating such bishops within the hierarchy, while gradually gaining the outspoken support of other bishops, they were able to influence the highest levels of the hierarchy to take public positions against military rule and for political programs which met the needs of the poor.

The Chilean case offers an interesting contrast. In 1968 there was no ban on the political participation of any group; in fact, there was active, effective participation on the left, center, and right of the political spectrum. Moreover, in the wake of Christian Democratic government, the active political participation of Christians and the identification of the Church with political programs was uniquely strong. As was suggested above, a Christian left was forming in Chile at this time because of growing disenchantment with the failure of Christian Democratic reformism. A large number of these left Christians, persons of primarily middle-class background, joined MAPU and became part of the Unidad Popular. Within that larger political coalition, their own development as a distinctly Christian voice for radical social change was inhibited. As part of a secular political movement which openly competed for and then held power, MAPU could not play the highly visible, prophetic role of social criticism (denunciation) which the Third World Priests played in Argentina. As we shall see, MAPU was also outflanked on its own left by the more militant members of the Young Church movement who formed The Eighty and Christians for Socialism.

The latter two groups, which formed after the election of the Unidad Popular government, more closely resembled the Third World Priests. Composed primarily of clergy, they exercised the prophetic role in the fashion of an interest group rather than as part of a coalition, and focused much of their concern on persuading the church to become an agent of social change. These similarities, however, mask important differences in the political strategies pursued by the religiopolitical movements in the two countries. Like MAPU, the Christians for Socialism supported the UP in the early stages of its administration. What distinguished them was the latter's conscious effort to link the entire institutional Church to the socialist program of the UP. Indeed, although much of the movement's public efforts focused on the same denunciatory role which so distinguished the Third World Priests, it became increasingly preoccupied after 1971 with transforming the entire Church from within. Thus, as Christians for Socialism grew in membership and developed the organizational apparatus which made it resemble the Third World Priests, it in fact pursued a strategy which diverged sharply from that of the Argentine movement. It moved increasingly toward what Smith (1978: chap. 8) has called a "parallel magisterium" within the Church.

An extremely significant difference emerges here between the political and religious contexts of Argentina and Chile. In Argentina the radical priests could criticize the government, publicize unjust policies, voice the demands of the poor, and even criticize the church for inaction, without seriously implicating the hierarchy as a whole or appearing to challenge its authority. It was much easier for the Argentine hierarchy to follow the lead of the Third World Priests in a country with widespread popular unrest and virtually no political freedom, then for the Chilean hierarchy to accede to the demand of Christians for Socialism that they explicitly ally the Church to the UP government *in power* and against the very large number of Chileans who opposed that government. The strain this put on the relationship between Christians for Socialism and the hierarchy was further heightened by the former's continuous move leftward between 1971 and September 1973. In this period the Movement went considerably to the left of the UP. As that government came increasingly under attack from both left and right, as it sought compromise solutions to which the Church hierarchy lent its own prestige, the Christians for Socialism urged more intense revolutionary commitment by Christians and by the Church as a whole. An impasse was reached by early 1973, when the hierarchy began to distance itself from the beleaguered regime and moved to sanction the Christians for Socialism by banning participation in their movement. The military coup of September 11, 1973 preempted a final confrontation between the two.

The Movement of Priests for the Third World set out in 1968 to make their Church a voice and an instrument for social change, and they achieved notable short-run success. Their greatest success was in gaining a hearing within the institutional Church for a liberation point of view. The hierarchy's declaration at San Miguel in May 1969 bore the influence of the Third World Priests and provided a strong veil of legitimacy which the priests were able to utilize successfully over the next five years. Further, the movement helped force an open break between the Church and the regime of Onganía, and the loss of this ally certainly hastened Onganía's demise. The movement also turned the Church around from open hostility toward Peronism to a cautious acceptance, helping to pave the way for the return of elections and of Peronists to active political participation. Thus, the Third World Priests helped to change their Church, were a strong voice of protest during a period of national political crisis, assisted materially in discrediting military rule, and helped to promote a return to democratic politics.

But in their very strength lay a serious weakness for which there is a striking parallel in the experience of the Chilean Christians for Socialism. As the movement evolved, most of its members became convinced that the road to socialism and participatory democracy lay in Peronism. After 1972 they actively promoted Peronism and forged an alliance with the Peronist movement at a variety of levels. But, like many Argentines, they placed too much hope in the healing powers of the Peronist movement. They failed to recognize the serious splits latent in Peronism and overestimated the degree to which Perón would be willing or able to change Argentine society according to the norms of liberation theology. Once on the scene, Perón soon turned away from the masses to whom the priests were linked and, in his famous May 1, 1974 speech, read the left, including the Third World Priests, out of his movement. The disillusionment which followed revealed that the priests had failed to lay the foundation for grassroots organization which would enable the movement to retain its coherence through this crisis. With Perón's death and the erosion of Peronism leading to the military coup of March 1976, the Third World Priest movement declined and returned to a pre-1968 stage of loose-knit, individualized ministries at a local level, bound together only by a common dedication to the poor. Today many Third World Priests are in hiding or in exile, and the Argentine Church is a muted voice of resistance to authoritarian rule.

Like the Third World Priests, the Christians for Socialism became closely identified with one segment of a much broader political spectrum and overestimated the popular appeal and political efficacy of that segment. In their early phase they identified strongly with UP policies, then gradually moved to the left of the regime and toward closer identification with the position of the MIR on the extreme left. This precluded any influence they might have had with the government (just as the Third World Priests lost influence with Perón's government in early 1974), and also drove a further wedge between them and the hierarchy. Had the coup not intervened, it is likely that pressure from the Church hierarchy would have had the same effect of breaking up the Christians for Socialism movement in Chile that government pressure had in disrupting the Argentine Third World Priest movement.

Two final weaknesses of the Christian for Socialism attempt at living out a "prophetic" Christianity may be mentioned and compared briefly to the Argentine case. It has been suggested already that the membership of MAPU was largely middle-class in origin and outlook. The Christians for Socialism were also middle-class people whose backgrounds tended to be university oriented rather than popularly based. Although the Third World Priest movement had its share of middle-class professors, it seemed also to have a much higher proportion of active members who were working in "villas miserias," who had lengthy backgrounds as worker-priests, and whose political contacts were strongly rooted in the working class. By comparison, the Christians for Socialism were a more elitist group in the sense that they lacked these *direct* ties with the masses whom they sought to help. They did not create opportunities to build practical alliances with working class groups either within or without the Church. By their own admission, they failed to tap into the strong base of popular religiosity in Chile where the base communities are functioning today. The Third World Priests were less elitist and more successful at uniting popular religious and political expression through Peronism.

The other point of comparison involves the extent to which each movement pursued a strategy which promoted unity or division within the Church as a whole. Obviously, both movements had their detractors within the Church. But, on balance, the Christians for Socialism promoted far greater discord within the Church than did the Third World

Priests. While alienating a few of the most reactionary bishops, the latter managed to promote considerable unity and a closing of ranks *against* an unpopular government. Although some tension between movement and hierarchy always existed, far better rapport, mutual understanding, and restraint characterized their relationship than that of the Chilean hierarchy and Christians for Socialism. While part of the disparity can be attributed to differing political contexts as described above, part of the reason also lies with the separate political strategies chosen by the two movements.

Conclusions

Clearly, the Christian left does not conform very closely to the description implicit in development analyses. The Third World Priests in Argentina were less radical theologically and politically than Vallier (1972) imagined, and were more successful in uniting the Church around a program calling for social change and the return of democratic politics. On the other hand, the Christian Democratic experience in Chile was hardly the nonpartisan, socially integrating movement that development theory expected it to be. Nor can the political and religious fragmentation of the late 1960s and early 1970s be blamed only on the left. All political sectors were "partisan" and the extensively documented record of the efforts by the center and the right to prevent the left from achieving victory *within* the boundaries of the electoral process belie claims of the developmentalists to the contrary. In this respect a major accomplishment of the Christians for Socialism, in terms of liberation norms, was the forceful way in which they dispelled the illusion that the Church was neutral in politics if only it avoided *direct* partisan commitments. It can be argued, of course, that in making their own political choice to move toward the extreme left of the political spectrum, they made the *wrong* political choice.

It is also important to bear in mind the place of these movements within the institutional Church and their relation to its perceived needs. The Argentine case is instructive here. It shows that when it is in the Church's corporate interests (as seen by the hierarchy, not the left) to disassociate itself from the regime, an alliance between the left (which gives the Church linkages at the grass roots), and the hierarchy, however informal, can be effective in mounting a powerful campaign of denunciation. Clearly, both elements of the Church are pursuing a political strategy in such a case. Vallier saw the importance of disassociating Church and regime, but he denied that it was a political option and his theory prevented him from seeing the possibility which developed in Argentina of a radical left movement providing the energy to bring about such disassociation and making the Church a prominent voice for social change.

Let us close by returning to the developmentalist critique of the Christian left. On the basis of the data presented here, I would argue the following points. First, the distinction between pastoral and clerical radicals breaks down in the actual experience of any church attempting to bring about social change. The cases of Argentina and Chile bear this out, the latter quite dramatically with Christian Democracy spawning a plethora of politically activist Christian groups. On the other hand, Christians for Socialism did tend in practice to make their particular interpretation of the historically correct political option the only one acceptable for the entire church, as Vallier had feared they would. I do not find that the Third World Priests did this, and on Vallier's analysis they would have been more likely to than the Christians for Socialism because of the "undeveloped" character of the Argentine Church. Second, clerical radicalism does not lead to demands by clergy that the laity defend the Church's corporate interests. The hierarchy will look after the Church's institutional interests in any case. This is one important reason why the bishops came to support the Third World Priests in Argentina and to oppose the Christians for Socialism in Chile.

NOTES

1. Of the five writers who see the Church as a dynamic force for social change three had worked in Chile during the 1960s. Of those who see the Church as a moderate force for change, one (Smith) had looked at the Chilean case in 1974 after the fall of Allende. Levine and Wilde studied Colombia in the 1970s. Writers who focused on the Church as an obstacle to social change had studied the Brazilian case, where Catholic radicals were crushed after the military coup of 1964 (de Kadt), or they studied the Church from a frame of reference in which radicalism was institutionally (Mutchler) or ideologically (Vekemans) precluded.

2. The structure and evolving nature of the development paradigm can best be seen in the essay by Huntington (1971). Very recent writings on the Church have avoided the simplistic adaptation of a development model, and therefore do not come under the

criticisms presented in this article. See Bruneau (1974), Levine and Wilde (1977), and B. Smith (1976, 1977). However, in the newer literature there is not yet any comparative study of the Christian left, which was ignored or deprecated in the earlier literature.

3. Other writers who have made a similar argument include de Kadt (1970) and Sanders (1973). Much of the difficulty with this approach lies in the narrow understanding of politics which characterizes it. Levine and Wilde (1977) provide a good critical discussion of this issue.

4. There are two brief studies of the Christian left in Peru, neither of which has been published. They are Macauly (1972) and Mooney (1976). Two very recent studies of the Christian left in Chile are by Rojas and Vanderschueren (1977) and B. Smith (1978). None of these studies attempt systematic comparison of the Christian left across countries.

5. The political theory of liberation theology is treated at much greater length in Dodson (1974a). See especially Chapter Three.

6. Major works in the dependency literature are summarized and criticized in two recent essays: James and Bath (1976) and Fagen (1977). Dependency theory is a "given" in liberation theology.

REFERENCES

ALMOND, G. and B. POWELL (1966) Comparative Politics: A Developmental Approach. Boston: Little, Brown.

BERLIN, I. (1967) "Two concepts of liberty," pp. 141-152 in A. Quinton [ed.] Political Philosophy. Oxford Eng.: Oxford Univ. Press.

BRUNEAU, T. C. (1974) The Political Transformation of the Brazilian Catholic Church. London: Cambridge Univ. Press.

de KADT, E. (1971) "Church, society and development in Latin America." J. of Development Studies (October): 23-41.

――― (1970) Catholic Radicals in Brazil. Oxford: Oxford Univ. Press.

――― (1967) "Paternalism and populism: Catholicism in Latin America." J. of Contemporary History 2: 89-106.

DODSON, M. (1974a) "Religious innovation and the politics of Argentina: a study of the movement of priests for the third world." Ph.D. dissertation. Indiana University.

――― (1974b) "Priests and Peronism: radical clergy in Argentine politics." Latin American Perspectives 1: 63-67.

――― (1972) "The Catholic Church in contemporary Argentina," pp. 57-67 in A. Ciria [ed.] New Perspectives on Modern Argentina. Bloomington, IN: Latin American Studies Program, Indiana University.

DREKONJA, G. (1971) "Religion and social change in Latin America." Latin American Research Rev. 6: 53-72.

EINAUDI, L. et al. (1969) Latin American Institutional Development: The Changing Catholic Church. Santa Monica, CA: Rand Corporation.

Epica (1973) "Christians for socialism." (September): 4-8.

FAGEN, R. (1977) "Studying Latin American politics: some implications of a 'dependencia' approach." Latin American Research Rev. 12, 2: 3-26.

HUNTINGTON, S. (1971) "The change to change: modernization, revolution and politics." Comparative Politics 3: 283-322.

——— (1968) Political Order in Changing Societies. New Haven, CT: Yale Univ. Press.

JAMES, D. and C. R. BATH (1976) "Dependency analysis of Latin America." Latin American Research Rev. 11, 3: 3-54.

LEVINE, D. and A. WILDE (1977) "The Catholic Church, 'politics,' and violence: the Colombian case." The Rev. of Politics 39: 220-249.

MACAULY, M. G. (1972) "Ideological change and internal cleavages in the Peruvian Church: change, status quo and the priest: the case of ONIS." Ph.D. dissertation. University of Notre Dame.

MacPHERSON, C. B. (1964) The Theory of Possessive Individualism. Oxford Eng.: Oxford University Press.

MIGUEZ-BONINO, J. (1976) Christians and Marxists. Grand Rapids: Eerdmans.

MOONEY, M. H. (1976) "The role of the church in Peruvian political development." M. A. thesis. University of Windsor.

MUTCHLER, D. (1969) "Adaptations of the Roman Catholic Church to Latin American development: the meaning of internal church conflict." Social Research 36: 231-252.

PYE, L. (1966) Aspects of Political Development. Boston: Little, Brown.

ROJAS, J. and F. VANDERSCHUEREN (1977) "The Catholic Church of Chile: from 'social Christianity' to 'Christians for socialism' " LARU Studies 2, 14-59.

SABINE, G. (1952) "The two democratic traditions." The Philosophical Rev. 61: 451-474.

SANDERS, T. (1973) "The theology of liberation: Christian utopianism." Christianity and Crisis. 33: 167-173.

——— (1970) "The church in Latin America." Foreign Affairs (Spring): 289-299.

SCHILLEBEECKX, E. (1970) "El majisterio y el mundo politico." Enlace 13: 27.

SIGMUND, P. (1973) "Latin American Catholicism's opening to the left." The Rev. of Politics. 35: 61-77.

SILVERT, K. (1967) Churches and States: The Religious Institution and Modernization. New York: American Universities Field Staff.

SMITH, B. (1979) "The Catholic church and political change in Chile, 1925-1978." Ph.D. dissertation. Yale University.

——— (1975) "Religion and social change: classical theories and new formulations in the content of recent developments in Latin America." Latin American Research Rev. 10: 3-34.

——— and T. SANDERS (1976) "The Chilean Catholic church during the Allende and Pinochet regimes." American Universities Field Staff 23: 1-25.

——— and T. SANKS (1977) "Liberation ecclesiology: praxis, theory, praxis." Theological Studies 38: 3-38.

SMITH, D. (1970) Religion and Political Development. Boston: Little, Brown.

TURNER, S. (1971) Catholicism and Political Development in Latin America. Chapel Hill: Univ. of North Carolina Press.

VALLIER, I. (1972) "Radical priests and the revolution," pp. 15-26 in D. Chalmers [ed.] Changing Latin America: New Interpretations of its Politics and Society. Montpelier, VT.: Capital City Press.

——— (1970) Catholicism, Social Control and Modernization in Latin America. Engle-

wood Cliffs, NJ: Prentice-Hall.
——— (1967) "Church Development in Latin America: a five-country comparison." J. of Developing Areas 1: 461-476.
VEKEMANS, R. (1964) "Economic development, social change, and cultural mutation in Latin America," pp. 129-142 in W. d'Antonio and F. Pike [eds.] Religion, Revolution and Reform: New Forces for Change in Latin America. New York: Praeger.
WILLIAMS, E. (1973) "The emergence of the secular nation-state and Latin American Catholicism." Comparative Politics 5: 261-277.
——— (1969) "Latin American Catholicism and political integration." Comparative Political Studies 2: 327-348.

6

THE CHURCH AND THE DOCTRINE OF NATIONAL SECURITY

ROBERT CALVO

In a book which has circulated rather widely in Latin America (Lieuwen, 1960), it was stated that, with the passage of time, Latin American military men would intervene less and less in politics. This was not an altogether mistaken belief, considering that in 1961 Paraguay was a "military island" in a sea of Latin American civilian governments. Today the situation has radically changed in many ways. On the one hand, more than half the population of Latin America lives under military regimes; on the other, military domination has a different cast: it is no longer a caudillo who takes over, but the armed forces, which have institutionalized their access to the government. Linked to the foregoing is the emergence of an authoritarian ideological platform— the military call it a doctrine of national security—which provides the armed forces with the necessary rationale for their political activities.

This new form of gaining political power has not been free of tensions or conflicts with institutions dedicated to a democratic concept of political life. At the present time, the strained and difficult relationship between the Church and the military state is of major concern in Latin America. In the context of this concern, this paper will present an analysis embracing three aspects. The first describes the historical-sociological-political background of the military-regime problem in order to help explain it. The second summarizes the most important features of the doctrine of national security. The third discusses certain elements of the doctrine, beginning with the criticisms leveled by the Church.

I. The Historical-Sociological-Political Background Of The Military Phenomenon in Latin America

For purposes of analysis, it seems necessary to distinguish between two types of problems related to present military governments and the doctrine of national security. There is not only the problem of explaining the background of military intervention, but also the problem of defining the characteristics assumed by the military regimes which base themselves on national security.[1]

The first type of problem presents two aspects: the objective situation of the politicoinstitutional crisis (nation-state crisis) which detonates the political intervention of the military; and the perception by the military of the crisis and the role played by this perception in the doctrine of national security.

The second type of problem deals with the behavior of the military in power. It has any number of aspects, all of them associated with the nature of the military institution (the "total" professional socialization of military institutes, and the like) and the so-called contextual characteristics (the economy, culture, and the like).[2] Owing to lack of space, only the first type of problem in this complex situation will be discussed.

One of the most popular interpretations of the nation-state crisis (Germani, 1969) declares that because the processes of change are unsynchronized and conflictive, they make interventions more likely. Using the same approach (Cuellar, 1971), the Great Depression of the 1930s and the Second World War are linked with the rupture of the "oligarchical pact" in Latin America and the emergence of populist forms derived from the breakdown of traditional patterns of legitimacy or from the hegemonic crisis. The economic scheme of "inward development" based on import-substituting industrialization, which emerged with these new forms of domination, was nearly exhausted by the 1960s and had a negative impact on the rest of the social system. Frustrated aspirations and expectations, problems of capital accumulation, and widespread use of ideologies were elements of this crisis which has led to military intervention.

Although this interpretation has some diagnostic validity, it is rather one-sided in giving major importance to infrastructural factors, which are assumed to be closely linked to external factors—for example, imperialism and dependency—in the structural origin of the crisis. The problem has much deeper, historicocultural roots, which can by no means be reduced to simply an economic stage in Latin American history and which cannot be ignored in any attempt at interpretation. Two kinds of historical events are related to the present Latin American crisis and to "suspension" of this crisis by the military.

There is, first, the objective fact that military participation in politics is a constant found throughout Latin American history.[3] The military presence is simultaneous with and even predates the birth of Latin American states, which achieved political independence in the early part of the nineteenth century. "In those times," writes Beltrán (1970), "there was a mingling of political and military roles. The revolutionary sectors had few professional military men, and often the same people were simultaneously political leaders and soldiers."

During periods which varied from country to country, the military appeared on the national political scene—playing a "moderating" role—at times when the politicoideological battles of the civilians (or in some cases, of the military) threatened the stability of the national state.[4] This is precisely the type of evidence adduced by some authors (Cuellar, 1971) for their argument that the "directive" participation of the military in politics takes place in moments of hegemonic crisis, which may occur at any time in the development of a society.

No less important in the problem under study is the professionalization of the armed forces which, along with the state, seem to be relatively consolidated. "Military professionalization—that is, the existence of people who make war their sole occupation—is in keeping with rationalization of the state and the consequent specialization of functions" (Beltrán, 1970). The findings of authors like Putnam (1967) and Needler (1966) furnish some evidence for belief that the appearance of an ideological platform like the doctrine of national security is associated with the degree of professionalization and/or institutionalization of the armed forces.

The second kind of events refers to the continuous failure of the Latin American societies—that is, all the social conglomerates: classes, groups, institutions, ideologies, and so on—to constitute themselves as nation-states, in order to create a viable political system leading to formation of a broad and participatory social base.[5] Historically, this failure is connected, on the one hand, with the economic, cultural, and political characteristics of Iberian colonization and, on the other, with the sociocultural characteristics of the preexisting Indian populations. Both elements fused to create a rigidly dualist society, dominated by an exclusivist and predatory oligarchy. As is pointed out by Jaguaribe (1972: 49), Latin American societies remained underdeveloped until the early part of the twentieth century because they had become dualist societies in which the top priority given to the goals of the elite was not compatible with the interests of the masses. These countries were thus prevented from integrating, with the result that a social system unfit for development was established.

National development, spurred by industrialization through the import substitution which began with the depression of the 1930s, accelerated from the end of the Second World War until the early 1950s. Afterward, however, the structural limitations of Latin America's internal markets did not permit self-sustained growth of the economy.

In political terms, the economic scheme of import-substituting industrialization was stimulated and reinforced by the so-called populist plan, under which the progressive forces promoted political modernization by mobilizing the masses. Briefly, populism gave rise to pressing political questions which focused on the need for social participation and for power structure in accord with the mobilization and democratization of the masses. As Huntington (1972: 16) has stated, the changes implied in these questions tend "to undermine traditional foundations, and they complicate the problems of creating new bases of political association and institutions that combine legitimacy and effectiveness. The rates of social mobilization and political participation are high; the rates of political organization are low." Countries which have experienced this process have a history of instability, disorder, social insecurity, economic deterioration, and political polarization and violence, ranging from the armed left of Maoists and Castristas to traditional conservatism, whose factions also arm themselves, and spanning all the centrist parties.[6]

Within this sociopolitical framework, obviously very simplified, the military turn out to be the only social group with a broad national organization and perspective and which is sufficiently unified and powerful to impose its regime.

II. The Doctrine of National Security

The systematic elaboration of this doctrine has been centered essentially in Brazil and Chile, where it was followed by military takeovers.

General Carlos de Meira Mattos (1975) eloquently explains the genesis of the doctrine and its influence on the politicoadministrative action of Brazil:

> In the fourteen years from 1949 to 1964, the National War College had little influence on government decisions. During this period, it formulated its doctrine of national security and thoroughly researched the field of development. It trained civilian and military elites qualified to think objectively about Brazil as a whole, to draft a policy of using national power for purposes of security and to further explore attempts to choose development strategies. At the time of the 1964 revolution, the doctrine of the National War College was already formulated and had been discussed in workshops and classrooms. The leader of the revolution, President Castelo Branco, and his chief advisors Golbery do Couto e Silva, Ernesto Geisel, Juárez Távora, and Cordeiro de Farias—who were all ex-military men and had actively shared in drawing up this doctrine when they were members of the cadres of the National War College— found it easy to transform into government policy this doctrine that was the result of fourteen years of preparation in the São Jóao Fortress.

Some time later than Brazil, the Chilean military had attempted a systematic elaboration of the doctrine of national security. The military takeover of September 11, 1973 launched a production of literature about this doctrine comparable only to that of Brazil (Calvo, 1977: 51).[7]

An analysis of what has been written on this doctrine reveals it rigorously systematized presentation. Like an institutional organization chart, its constituent parts are ordered in a relatively logical and coherent whole. Some see in the doctrine an expression of the technical specialization and educational curriculum received by the military during their training.[8] It becomes clear with analysis that the doctrine reflects a predominantly military vision of society, the economy, and culture. The basic elements of society are seen through the world view of the professional soldier.

The doctrine contains concepts derived from the social sciences, especially from political science and geopolitics, which the military believe make it scientific, technical, and therefore neutral.[9] Some military men (Medina, 1976) claim that it is not ideological because it deals with a government function encompassing almost all national activities.

The military divide their doctrine into two major parts: its conceptual elements, and the security system it proposes.

BASIC CONCEPTS OF THE DOCTRINE

The doctrine rests on five key concepts: national security, the state, war, national goals, and national power.

The Concept of National Security

Various definitions of national security are provided by Brazilians, Chileans, and Argentines. They are all similar in content and do not differ appreciably in their bases. Perhaps the most widespread definition is that of the Brazilian Amaral Gurgel (1976): "National security is the guarantee given by the state to achieve or defend national goals against existing hostilities and pressures."[10]

The following characteristics of national security can be deduced from this definition: it is the ability of sovereign states to maintain themselves and survive; its existence is subject to the "weight" of national power; it is expressed in permanent political, economic, pyschological, social, military, and diplomatic actions; its purpose is to stabilize and strengthen the vital interests of the nation; it is aimed at guarding against and overcoming the effects of internal disturbances, natural catastrophes, and outside aggression; and it must ensure the national goals set by the government.

This concept of national security is novel to the uninitiated, for it goes beyond the traditional concept of national defense. According to advocates of the doctrine, national defense is part of national security, inasmuch as the latter acts in the national sphere and the former only in the field of warfare. National security acts through national power, whether in domestic or foreign affairs, and it is administered by the head of the state. National defense, however, acts through military power and is directed by the armed forces.

The State and National Security

The state is the legal manifestation of the nation, and it is dedicated to the common good of all members of society.[11] Social order requires that the state, by virtue of its authority, guarantee obedience of the law to all members of society. The state is the broadest legal grouping and it contains in itself all the means necessary for maximum fulfillment of the human being. To be stable, it requires a population settled in a specific and exclusive territory with precise borders, within which authority can be exercised independently of other states and which also delimits the areas of competence among them. Pinochet (1974), drawing an analogy with the organic, defines the state "as an organic component, produced by a combination of a part of humanity settled on a portion of territory, both of which are united under the idea of a state. Like any existing reality, the state had a structure and a goal."

The state is the agent which has national survival as its essential and ultimate goal. This means that it maintains public order, both legal and institutional, and ensures the free exercise of sovereignty and socio-economic development; in other words, it provides security and development. Security consists in protecting the nation from threats of any kind—war, internal disturbances, natural catastrophes, and so on. In the theoretical schema of the national security doctrine of the Latin American military regimes, the first two threats are given special importance.

War and Subversion

According to the military, national defense was initially intended only to prevent or cope with external threats. This concept had to be revised and linked with internal security because of a new form of aggression which appeared in several countries—the so-called subversion, or warfare, waged by guerrillas and irregulars.

This new form of war was the expression not only of conflicts in those countries which sought independence of the great powers and/or a change of government, but also of the conflict between the United States and the Soviet Union. Regarding the latter, General Castelo Branco says that "with the impossibility of a direct nuclear confrontation, hostilities between the great powers were channeled into peripheral wars like a 'war of liberation,' a 'revolutionary war,' or a 'local war' " (Mattos, 1975: 64).[12]

"As a general rule—states Chilean General Alejandro Medina (1976), "It was evident that the Marxist countries provided funds, training, and political orientation, as well as a concerted attack in the international organizations and the media, even using front agencies with the same ideological inspiration."[13] Faced with this threat, the state must mobilize all its natural power to resist it.

National Goals

National goals, as guideposts in the life of a nation, result from the balance existing between the means available to the country and the obstacles standing in the way of realizing aspirations and natural interests. Therefore, because only the government can assess the national situation, it has to set the goals.

The military use various criteria to classify goals. The most usual is one which distinguishes between permanent natural goals and eventual goals. The first category represents a living and very real tradition of natural interests, combining the aspirations of the nation in three basic aspects—self-determination, greater integration, and prosperity—which are manifested in the exercise of sovereignty, economic independence, and socioeconomic development. The second category of goals is that of unsatisfied aspirations and needs, but it is believed that their attainment is within the scope of national power, and that eventually they will become available within a given period of time.[14]

National Power

To exist fully, the state requires two elements: national power and national security. There is no national security without national power.

According to General Pinochet in his *Geopolítica,* national power "is a social factor capable of influencing the sentiment, thought, and will of the human masses in both the internal and external spheres" (1974). In the internal sphere, there is no power similar to that of the state; but this is not true in the external sphere, for the power of the state may be subjugated by another, greater, power.

Several factors increase national power. Since they are numerous, we mention only those significant in geopolitics.

National power is constituted by the territory, population, national character of the population, national spirit, renewable and nonrenewable natural resources, industrial capacity, capacity for scientific and technological development, military might, form of government, popular support, economic policy, quality of diplomacy, education and culture, communications systems, internal legislation, and sovereignty. Essentially, they are the same elements which make up the state.

National power is very dynamic as a consequence of the variations always affecting the elements which constitute it. It may therefore be increased or dangerously diminished to the benefit or detriment of the sovereignty of the state.

THE NATIONAL SECURITY SYSTEM

The security of a nation depends basically on the existence and execution of a national security system, both in a doctrinal and operational sense. This system is a harmonious whole, organized and functional, which should comprise the following basic elements: national goals, the national security doctrine, national security policies, the organic structure of the system, and a national security strategy. Some of these elements will be discussed in further detail.

The security system should encompass, channel, and direct all national activities: those directly related to internal policies, including the activities of political parties and pressure groups; those related to external policies; those related to the economic-financial complex; those related to the psychosocial field; and those activities specifically of the armed forces.

The system also has the following characteristics: it is unified and national; it is totally shared by the "living forces" of the nation, as consistent with national security; it is above politics ("national security is a lofty activity that pursues the supreme goals of the fatherland. For this reason, neither its direction nor execution should be subject to the pressures of organized political groups in special situations, since only the vital and higher interests of the nation should be taken into account"); and it changes and grows according to the variability of the nation's potential.

National Security Policy

National security policy consists of the lines of action, orientation, and programming established by the government and guided by the national security doctrine. National security policy is conditioned by internal and external factors. The most important of the internal factors is present economic and social development. Whereas the cultural aspect gives vitality to the national security policy, economic development is the sine qua non of this security. "There can be no security without development, just as there can be no development without security," says Villegas (1968), an Argentine general who has been interested in the relationship between development and security. On the one hand, insufficient development cannot provide the minimum resources needed for an adequate degree of security; on the other, development without security cannot be successful in the long run, since insecurity will eventually jeopardize prospective development.

Social development influences the national security policy because social and economic disparities create internal tensions which result in increased domestic security measures to prevent possible threats.

The basic external factor in the national security policy is the evolution of the international situation in terms of changes in the balance of power between the great powers and the consequent influence of the latter on other countries.

Given these features, the national security policy can be characterized as follows: it is based wholly on the spirit and letter of the national security doctrine; it is directed toward attaining the political goal of national security; it is national in that it covers all areas and agencies of the state; it is flexible, for it depends on external and internal variables; and it is closely influenced by development in all its aspects—political, economic, social, and cultural.

The Organic Structure of the System

This refers to the group of agencies which are organized in a harmonious and hierarchical way to be responsible for carrying out national security. Its constituent principles are the same as those which characterize the system as a whole. The functions of these agencies are to direct, advise, plan, and implement in the various fields of action—internal (economic, defense, psychosocial, and so on) and external (diplomatic).

National Strategy

Strategy is the science and art in using all national resources, including the armed forces, in order to provide effectively for the attainment of the nation's vital goals, safeguarding against any kind of potential or presumed enemy.

The strategy, therefore, consists in applying national power—political, economic, psychosocial, and military—to attainment of the national goals determined by policy when these goals are confronted with hostilities from the national power of other states. It is as important in peacetime as in war. It conditions, coordinates, and directs the sectors in charge of the resources and activities of the state in their implementation of the various strategies derived from the national strategy. Furthermore, the formulation and execution of national strategy are the responsibilities of the government. There are as many strategies—political, economic, psychosocial, and military—as there are spheres of action.

III. The Church and the Doctrine of National Security

The previous section attempted to present an objective synthesis of the doctrine without injecting value judgments and/or interpretations. We thereby hoped to avoid the mistakes of some critical studies which, owing to their complete lack of objectivity, have distorted the doctrine, transforming it into an "entelechy" and attributing to it every event in countries under military governments. We do not, however, wish to conceal the fact that the excesses of this doctrine have been the object of valid criticism which has come mainly from the Church and which will be broadly discussed in this section.

The Church reacts strongly against established political power when it becomes evident that there is a violation of human rights and persecution of both civilians and the clergy. There are several kinds of Church documents which cast serious doubts on the Christian character of the national security doctrine. One type of Church document presents philosophical, economic, and political reasons. This category includes for example, "La Seguridad Nacional, condición del bien común" (National Security as a condition of the common good) by Msgr. J.M. Santos (1976), Bishop of Valdivia (Chile), and "Doctrina de la Seguridad Nacional a la luz de la doctrina de la Iglesia" (The National Security Doctrine in the light of Church doctrine) by Msgr. C. Padin (1968), Bishop of Bauru (Brazil). A second type of criticism, supplemented by elements of the first type, presents religious and theological reasons. Such documents as "Comunicacão pastoral au povo de Deus" (A pastoral message to God's people) of the Episcopal Conference of

Brazil (1977), "Nuestra Convivencia Nacional" (Our National Coexistence) of the Episcopal Conference of Chile (1977), and "Reflexion Cristiana para el Pueblo de la Patria" (Christian Reflections for the People of the Fatherland) of the Episcopal Conference of Argentina (1977) belong to this category.

The content of these documents centers on some key concepts about man, society, and history. Let us examine some of the criticisms they raise.

CRITICISMS OF THE NATIONALISM AND AUTHORITARIANISM OF THE DOCTRINE

One of the principle criticisms contained in the above-mentioned documents is aimed at the nationalist bias of the national security doctrine. It is a fact that this doctrine makes loyalty to the nation an imperative for all its citizens, which requires that the real interests of a nationality be placed above all other interests. Understood in this way, nationalism inspires, motivates, and influences all policy formulation and strategy conception of these regimes.

In this respect, Msgr. Jorge Hourton, Auxiliary Bishop of Santiago, recalls the teachings of Pius XII on nationalism just at the time when the national security doctrine burst on the Chilean scene with unprecedented force.

It has been too quickly forgotten that the nationalist state has been responsible for the sacrifice of an enormous number of lives and property and that it has imposed oppressive economic and spiritual burdens. The substance of the error consists in confusing national life as such with nationalist policies. The former is the right and glory of a people, and it should be fostered; the latter is the germ of infinite evils, and it can never be sufficiently rejected. National life is, by itself, the operating whole of all those values of civilization that are peculiar to and characteristic of a given group and that serve as the link spiritually uniting this group. At the same time, this life enriches, through its own contribution, the culture of all humanity. In essence then, national life is not political. This reality is so true that, as history and experience demonstrate, national life can develop alongside others, within the same state, just as it can also transcend the political confines of the state. National life did not become a starting point for the dissolution of the community of man until it began to be used as a tool for political ends—that is, when the ruling and centralized state made nationality the basis of its expansionist drive. Then the nationalist state—seed of rivalries and incentive for discord—was born [Hourton, 1976].

This criticism of nationalism has led to criticism of another aspect which, according to Chilean and Brazilian bishops, is central to the present formulation of military nationalism: the triple identification of "nation, state, and military government" and its corrolary, the subservience of individual to state. The Brazilian bishops write:

> In the humanist and Christian vision, the nation is the sum of all the forms of association of its people. The right of free association should be recognized, respected, and encouraged by the state—that is, by the government. To be nationalist, therefore, does not mean sacrificing a faith, a belief, ideas, or values that may appear to be harmful to or incompatible with the interests and attitudes of the prevailing political system.
>
> Also, from a humanist and Christian standpoint, the nation is not synonymous with the state. It is not the state that grants liberties and human rights, which existed long before the nation itself. It does, however, behoove the state to recognize, defend, and foster the human rights of each and every one of its citizens.
>
> Those holding power are also tempted to confuse the people's duty to be loyal to the nation with their duty to be loyal to the state—that is, the government. To place the state, the government, above the nation, means that the security of the state is overvalued and individual security is debased. This is to reduce the people to silence and a climate of fear [Episcopal Conference of Brazil, 1977].

The nation-state identification denounced by the Brazilian bishops becomes even more reprehensible when the military sector assumes the right to be the only depository of the interests and values of the nation.[15] As has been pointed out in a recent study, "the idealized vision of military groups that they are above ideological, political, economic, and social disputes has logically resulted in reaffirmation of their claim to be the most suitable interpreters of national goals." From this perspective, those in power regard all dissenting voices, criticisms, and denunciations of the military regimes as attacks on the nation itself (Vicaria de la Solidaridad, 1977).[16]

The Chilean, Brazilian, and Argentine bishops have not overlooked the basic inconsistency between theoretical formulation of the national security doctrine and political practice of the military regimes. The military say they hold to a Christian concept of the individual, society, and state. Nonetheless, by their extreme concentration of power, violation of human rights, and restraint of freedom, they contradict this concept. Thus, Chilean and Brazilian episcopates have constantly stressed the social teachings of the Church in this matter.

The subservience of individual to state and his reduction to the role of nothing but citizen, violate the Christian concept of person and state. Man as man—that is, endowed with intelligence and will—has certain inalienable rights. In this anthropophilosophical concept of man as a person, as having a spiritual nature, as a center of freedom and knowledge, man himself is more a whole than a part, more an end than a means. But, as one writer comments, "the human person—if he is defined in terms of himself, if he is a being—cannot become complete and final except in intimate fulfillment with another person" (Moreno, 1977). Man, as a person, requires society *per abundantiam*; as an individual, he requires it *per indigentiam*. The Second Vatican Council states that "the social disposition of a man shows that the development of the human person and the development of society itself condition one another, because the beginning, the subject, and the end of social institutions are and should be the human person who, by his very nature, absolutely requires social life." Society appears, therefore, not only as a means, providing the person with the conditions of existence and development he needs, but also as an instrument of personalization. The Thomist doctrine declares that "each person is to the community as the part is to the whole," but at the same time, "man in his totality and in all his characteristics is not structured for the sake of political society." The national security doctrine would seem to contradict this principle in asserting "all in the state, nothing against the state, nothing outside the state."

"National interest" in the Brazilian military, "common good" in the Chilean, are two widely used concepts. In its Declaration of Principles, the Government of Chile states unequivocally that "the goal of the state is the general common good, defined . . . as the ensemble of social conditions that permits each and every Chilean to reach full personal fulfillment."

This definition would appear to be objectionable not for what it expresses, but for what it does not express. In correct doctrine, the common good is the goal and task of society. It is not the simple sum of private individual good; rather, it encompasses all the good that society can transmit and that reverts to the person through justice. In order to be vitiated, the common good entails and requires recognition of the fundamental rights of the person. It therefore embraces right, justice, liberty, and material prosperity.

It can again be demonstrated, as has the Church in Chile and Brazil, that the military declarations are a dead letter. There is no common good in Brazil (Episcopal Conference of Brazil, 1977: 12), where the power of the state is indifferent to the persecution of laymen, priests, and bishops, where it tolerates terrorist attacks on those who have raised their voices for innocent people in prison, and where there is no justice for the poor. Nor is there a common good in Chile (Episcopal Conference of Chile, 1977), where the state of siege has become a permanent situation, where certain human rights are systematically violated, and where economic recovery is being accomplished at an intolerable cost to the impoverished majorities.

CRITIQUE OF THE CONCEPT OF SECURITY

Another of the biases found in the national security doctrine is the exaggerated importance given to the concept of security, to the point of turning it into an end in itself. The Brazilian bishops are very clear in their denunciation of this attitude: "The ideology of national security placed above personal security is spreading throughout the Latin American continent, as has happened in the Soviet countries . . . this doctrine leads regimes that rule by force to incur the characteristics and practices of the communist regimes—the abuse of power by the state, arbitrary imprisonment, torture and suppression of freedom of thought" (Episcopal Conference of Brazil, 1977). In this regard, the doctrinal reflections of Msgr. Santos are relevant. He writes that national security does not constitute an end in itself. It is intended to be a means by which the person can fully realize himself, a means which contributes to attainment of the common good of society. This is its norm, its unit of measurement, and its standard of evaluation; this must be used to judge its procedures. "Everyone," says John XXIII, must act according to his own decision, conviction, and responsibility, and not be moved by coercion or pressures that almost always derive from force, because a society that is based solely on force has to be characterized as inhumane. In such a society, man is, in fact, deprived of his freedom, rather than feeling encouraged to improve his life and perfect himself."

The more cohesive a community is internally, the less need there is to use force to unite it. "It would be foolish to think that a nation does not need to protect its existence by means of the instruments appropriate to national security, but it would be equally foolish to think that national security can be placed above the human person without safeguarding the legitimacy of its procedures and consideration of the common good."

Another pernicious effect of overvaluing security is its manipulation by certain social groups. Frequently, protecting essential rules is confused with maintaining the status quo, chiefly by the action of interested groups who view any change or tendency to change as a threat to basic rules, even calling these changes subversive. Since national security regimes have generally lost touch with a large part of their social base, they easily become victims of such a confusion.

The consequences of this confusion are reflected in what one critic (Orrego, 1976; CISEC, 1977) has referred to as "the logic of total security": the security doctrine is founded on the belief that conflict is a real possibility and that it must be prevented. Because there are numerous causes which may generate a conflict, security tends to be all-embracing, seeking to control all foreseeable situations. At the beginning, the military fought armed extremists, but since this was not sufficient to achieve "total security," not only are the Marxist political parties proscribed, but also those parties which are "easy prey" for the Marxists—in the case of Chile, the radical parties and the Christian Democrats. This, however, is still not enough. Total security becomes like a snowball rolling downhill, continually growing in size with those who are "infiltrated" by Marxism. Union, members and professionals are added to the proscribed parties, and finally the Church itself. In their search for total security, national security regimes end by marginalizing the majority of a society which will never be secure enough for those in power.

In this connection, Brazilian bishops have protested that "inspired (by the national security doctrine), the military regimes, in the name of their battle against communism and for economic development, declare an 'anti-subversion war' against all those who do not agree with the authoritarian vision of the organization of society" (Episcopal Conference of Brazil, 1977).

NOTES

1. It is hardly necessary to stress that the national security doctrine does not appear in a monolithic form in all Latin American countries. The countries can provisionally be classified according to the degree to which this doctrine has been systematized and conceptualized and according to the prevailing national security system. In first place are the countries under military regimes with a high degree of doctrinal systematization and conceptualization (Brazil and Chile); next are the countries under military regimes with doctrines that are not very systematized (Argentina, Bolivia, and Uruguay) and those with governments controlled by the military (Ecuador, Peru, and some Central American countries); and finally, there are a few countries with formal democracies where their military groups possess the doctrine but without the objective and subjective conditions which exist in the preceding countries.

It should be made clear that this is an elementary classification which does not pretend to cover all the different versions of the national security doctrine. There are other equally relevant variables and criteria, such as the various national goals set by countries and the various forms of alliances, and of social influence entered into by military and civilian groups.

2. It should be mentioned here that this study is based on a theoretical-methodological premise. The social reality of the countries of the region, their different and contradictory political experiences, and the speed of their sociopolitical changes are usually beyond the interpretive scope of theoretical schemes. As Aron says, "there is no primary cause, no principal cause. The different orders of events constantly act and react on one another, and there is no evidence that a given order of events will exercise the same action in all societies" (1956: 170).

3. At present, as Lowenthal (1976) points out, the Latin American military institutions exercise their political influence either directly or openly as rulers or indirectly as a specially privileged pressure group. In no country of Latin America—with the possible exception of Costa Rica, where the officers' corps is almost completely disbanded with every presidential election—do the armed forces play a minor political role or even one limited to policing and national defense.

4. The socialization of the military takes into account the central role played by this group in the development of Latin American societies.

5. Deutsch and Foltz (1966) have pointed out that the nation is characterized by: (1) its independence—that is, the fact that its affairs are not directed from abroad; (2) its relatively secure and stable cohesiveness; (3) its political organization, in the sense that the "nation" provides the administrative, legal, and enforcement means to enable the government to effectively control public affairs; (4) its autonomy—that is, the ability of the government to generate the necessary support and consensus to maintain its control; and (5) its legitimacy, which is the mechanism that helps maintain a high level of loyalty to the nation.

6. The periods of President Goulart in Brazil, Perón in Argentina, and Allende in Chile are almost paradigms of the situation described.

7. In 1974 General Pinochet republished his *Geopolítica*, which he had written in 1968 when he was still an army colonel, a specialist on the general staff, and professor of geopolitics in the army's War Academy. A year earlier, in 1973, a collection of essays had appeared under the title "Fuerzas Armadas y Seguridad Nacional" (The Armed Forces

and National Security), edited by the Institute of General Studies and published three weeks after the September 1973 takeover. (These essays had been written and were already available some time earlier.) In September 1975, Colonel Gerardo Cortés Rencoret gave a lecture on this subject to the faculty and students of the Austral University of Valdivia. This lecture was reprinted in the newspaper *Mercurio* of Santiago, in the *Cuadernos* of the Political Science Institute of the Catholic University of Chile, and in the collected work "Nuestro Camino" (Our Path), distributed by the Government Information Office.

In December, 1975, the Economics Department of the University of Chile organized a seminar on the "Strategy of Economic Development for Chile," in which one of the participants was General Agustín Toro Davilá, rector of that university and director of the National Security Academy.

In addition, other actions were taken to systematize study of the doctrine and make it better known. The National Security Academy was established as an advanced institute of the branches of the armed forces. Courses were offered in the army's War Academy to specialized journalists and in the Catholic University of Chile, while they were made compulsory in the Catholic University of Valparaíso and in the fourth year of the social science programs of secondary schools.

July 1976 marked the first appearance of a journal called "Seguridad Nacional" (National Security) in Latin America (Calvo, 1977: 51-52).

8. In the case of Brazil, the worship of technology by the military elite is rooted in the positivism of Saint-Simon, influential during the early years of the Republic (Ríos, 1970: 151).

9. An illustration of this is the comment of General De Meira Mattos: "The national security policy is formulated under a rigorous process of scientific reasoning: it is divided into a system, a structure, and a technique that constitute the instruments of an ordered and consistent rationale leading to policies and strategies that will efficiently achieve the desired goals" (1975).

10. The Chilean military have formulated the following definition: National security is the structuring of the potential of a country so that the latter can carry out its development in complete control of its sovereignty and independence, both internal and external.

11. A concept widely used by the Chilean military.

12. The Latin American military have adopted the North American geopolitical concept of a world divided into two opposing blocs of power: "communist world" and "free world." The Latin American countries are members of the so-called free world, which is threatened both within and without by "international communism."

Under the ideological division of labor during the cold war, the United States had the task of discouraging and generally counteracting the military force of international communism. The Latin Americans' mission was to prevent subversive activities in their countries. Whereas North American leaders have significantly modified this concept, the Latin American military have stubbornly insisted on maintaining it unchanged.

13. One of the most striking features of the right-wing authoritarian regime is its militant anticommunism. Where does it come from? The answer, which is a complicated one, can be only partial and therefore provisional. Literature on the subject indicates that it lies in the almost total politicomilitary dependency of the Latin American armies on the U.S. army. This dependency stems from the latter's provision of not only arms and technicomilitary training, but also, to a considerable extent, of continual ideological indoctrination.

14. Brazil and Chile, it would seem, do not differ substantially in their national goals as may be appreciated in the available literature. General Golbery Do Couto e Silva states that for Brazil, the goals are "national integration, self-determination and sovereignty, well-being, and progress" (1967). The Chileans have the same framework of reference.

15. This position, in the case of Chile, is clearcut. Decrees one and two of the constituent act of the governing junta state "(1) that the public force which under the constitution is composed of the Army, Navy, Air Force, and Police, has been organized by the state to safeguard and defend its moral and physical integrity and its historical and cultural identity, and (2) that, therefore, its supreme mission is to ensure above all else the survival of the superior and permanent realities and values of the Chilean nationality. . ."

16. Again, the case of Chile is dramatically paradigmatic, as is evidenced by the controversy surrounding the letter sent to the OAS by five Chilean lawyers protesting the violation of human rights in Chile (Calvo, 1977: 63).

REFERENCES

AMARAL GURGEL, J. A. (1976) Segurança e democracia. Rio de Janeiro: José Olympio.

ARON, R. (1956) Recherches et débats. Paris: Centre catholique des intelectuels français.

BELTRÁN, V. R. (1970) "Estrategia, armas y cambio social en America latina," pp. 27-51 in V. R. Beltrán [ed.] El papel político y social de las Fuerzas Armadas en América latina. Caracas: Monte Avila.

CALVO, R. (1977) "Seguridad nacional y temas conexos." Tierra Nueva 23: 47-70.

CISEC (1977) Hacia un estatuto para la paz en Chile. Santiago: CISEC.

CUELLAR, O. (1971) "La participación política de lost militares en América latina," pp. 13-69 in L. M. Vega et al Fuerzas Armadas, poder y cambio. Caracas: Tiempo Nuevo.

DEUTSCH, K. and W. J. FOLTZ [eds.] (1966) Nation-Building. New York: Atherton.

Episcopal Conference of Argentina (1977) "Reflexión cristiana para el pueblo de la patria." Criterio 1764: 267-269.

Episcopal Conference of Brazil (1977) "Comunicacao pastoral au povo de Deus." Cadernos de CEAS 47: 5-14.

Episcopal Conference of Chile (1977) "Nuestra convivencia nacional." Solidaridad 15.

GERMANI, G. (1969) Sociología de la modernización. Buenos Aires: Paidós.

HOURTON, J. (1976) Iglesia y democracia: La ensenanza de Pío XII. Santiago: Ediciones Aconcagua.

HUNTINGTON, S. (1972) El orden político en las sociedales en cambio. Buenos Aires: Paidós.

JAGUARIBE, H. (1972) Crisis y alternativas de América latina: reforma o revolución. Buenos Aires: Paidós.

LIEUWEN, E. (1960) Armas y política en América latina. Buenos Aires: Sur.

LOWENTHAL, A. (1976) "Ejercitos y política en América latina." Estudios Internacionales 35: 38-64.

MATTOS, C. de Meira (1975) Brasil: Geopolítica e destino. Rio de Janeiro: José Olympio.

MEDINA, A. (1976) "Teoria de la Seguridad Nacional—Su orientacíon en Chile." Seguridad Nacional 2 (Septiembre): 99-108.

MORENO, F. (1977) Democracia y desarrollo. Santiago. (mimeografiado)

NEEDLER, M. (1966) "Political Development and Military Intervention in Latin America." American Political Science Review 60: 616-626.

ORREGO, F. (1976) "Libertad y seguridad nacional," pp. 123-150 in G. Arriagada, Seguridad nacional y bien común. Santiago: Corporación.

PADIN, C. (1968) "La doctrine de la sécurité nationale à la lumière de la doctrine de l'Eglise." SEDOC 431: 432-444.

PINOCHET, A. (1974) Geopolítica. Santiago: Andrés Bello.

PUTNAM, R. (1967) "Toward explaining military intervention in Latin American Politics." World Politics 20: 83-110.

RIOS, J. A. (1970) "Los militares y el poder en Brasil," pp. 147-160 in V. R. Beltrán [ed.] El papel político y social de las Fuerzas Armadas en América latina. Caracas: Monte Avila.

SANTOS, J. M. (1976) "La seguridad nacional, condición del bien común," pp. 87-119 in G. Arriagada et al. Seguridad Nacional y bien común. Santiago: Corporación.

SILVA, Do Couto e, G. (1967) Geopolítica do Brasil. Rio de Janeiro: José Olympio.

Vicaria de la Solidaridad del Arzobispado de Santiago (1977) Estudio sobre la doctrina de la seguridad nacional y régimen militar. Santiago (mimeografiado)

VILLEGAS, O. G. (1968) "Seguridad, política, estrategia." Temas Militares 4.

7

CHURCHES AND HUMAN RIGHTS IN LATIN AMERICA
Recent Trends on the Subcontinent

BRIAN SMITH

Over the past fifteen years the military have seized power in most major South American countries, leaving only Colombia and Venezuela with democratic regimes. The armed forces claim that only they are capable of controlling the domestic violence and social disruptions which accompanied the rapid political and economic changes of the 1960s. This process of social conflict and subsequent military intervention has been especially notable in the countries of the subcontinent region—Brazil, Bolivia, Chile, Argentina, Peru, and Uruguay.

Military rule, however, has not led to a decline in violence; indeed, most of these governments have resorted to extremely repressive measures in pursuing their objectives. In responding to the problems which brought them to power (labor unrest, inflation, societal polarization, and the growth of Marxist parties or guerrilla movements), the military have employed severe measures to restore order and promote more stable economic growth. These efforts have involved placing strict controls on organized labor, student groups, and political parties, suspending constitutional guarantees and processes, and offering generous incentives to domestic producers and foreign investors. Power has been consolidated by effective mobilization of the forces of physical coercion (the armed forces and the police) and by the appeal to traditional emotion-laden symbols such as anticommunism, nationalism, and protection of private property (Comblin, 1977; Methol Ferré, 1977).[1] Although guerrilla activity has declined and inflation rates have slowed in some places, these military regimes, in the process of promoting stability, have systematically violated a whole gamut of human rights as guaranteed by the two United Nations covenants— the International Covenant on Civil and Political Rights and the

155

International Covenant on Economic, Social, and Cultural Rights (Amnesty International, 1975-1976a: 84).[2]

Amidst this atmosphere of repression, churches have become important actors in the struggle to counter these abuses of state power in the subcontinent. At the international level, church networks have become one of the most reliable sources of information to the outside world on the extent of rights violations inside these countries. In turn, the international network of the churches has provided considerable financial and material support to groups working to defend and promote human rights in the southern tier of Latin America.

At the national level, the Catholic bishops of these Latin churches have increased their public condemnations of abuses of power. In so doing, they not only have denounced such crimes as murder, torture, and denial of habeas corpus and fair trial, but also have pointed to what they believe are the deeper underlying causes precipitating the rapid increase of such systematic violations of human rights—unjust economic structures, maldistribution of land and wealth, lack of effective social participation by the poor, and the pervasiveness of an ideology of national security which subjugates all rights of the person to the expediency of the State (Mitchell, 1977).[3]

Several of the most recent pastoral letters of the bishops of Brazil, Chile, and Argentina, for example, have clearly emphasized that there is a connection between violation of classic civil rights and the desire upon the part of wealthy elites to preserve their economic power. They point to a clear relationship between abuse of persons (especially the poor) and a refusal to respect basic economic and social rights in society by those who benefit from military rule (USCC, 1977a, 1977b, 1976d). They also call upon existing governments as well as landed and industrial elites to make profound changes in the economic and social systems as a necessary step to guarantee the full panoply of human rights as defined by the international covenants of the United Nations.

Most of these episcopal letters have urged secular leaders to make such changes as greater distribution of land and other economic resources, respect for independent labor unions, effective social participation by the poor in decisions affecting their lives, and fair application of law to limit government power. In these documents, the bishops also commit the organizational network of the Church to a vigorous defense of those whose rights are being violated and to a more profound identification with the plight of the poor (CELAM, 1970).[4] This general concern for human rights and new commitment to the oppressed have legitimized the setting up of a whole new series of social and pastoral programs in Latin American churches over the past decade, including new Church-sponsored organizations concerned with the promotion of human rights. Since the early 1970s, churches in Chile, Brazil, Paraguay, Bolivia, and Argentina (Lernoux, 1977; Culhane, 1975; Latinamerica Press, 1975, 1977b)[5] have created new religious and social structures to respond to the needs of the poor who have borne the brunt of repression in these respective countries.

While the documents of the hierarchies in these countries have been widely publicized both in South America as well as in Western Europe and North America, to date there has been little research done on these newly emerging human rights commissions and lay leadership programs functioning at lower levels of the churches. The activities of these new organizations have expanded rapidly in the last several years, and they not only have provided substantial assistance to those suffering human rights violations, but also have precipitated serious conflict between Church and state and at times tension within the respective churches themselves.

It is, therefore, important to study these new organizations in greater detail in order to assess the Church's real capacity to promote the structural changes the bishops see as a necessary basis for the observance of all human rights. Such information is also important to assess what contradictions are emerging for churches as a whole in this work and whether they can continue to make an active promotion of human rights an essential part of their religious mission.

This paper will focus on the learning experiences and accomplishments of Church-sponsored human rights commissions and other pastoral programs which have emerged since the early 1970s in Chile, Brazil, Paraguay, Bolivia, and Argentina. I shall analyze (1) under what conditions, and with what type of support, these programs have emerged, (2) what range of activities they have undertaken to promote civil, political, social, and economic rights, and (3) what impact they have had both on the political system and on the respective national churches themselves.

I shall give brief descriptive overviews of the activities of each of these churches in the area of human rights using the three above questions as organizing components for the available empirical data. In a concluding section I will offer a comparative analysis of all five cases as to what they reveal regarding the capacities and limitations of churches as complex organizations in protecting and promoting the full gamut of human rights.

I. Chile: The Committee of Co-operation for Peace, the Vicariate of Solidarity, and the Base Communities

Within three weeks of Chile's military coup of September 11, 1973, Catholic, Protestant, and Jewish leaders moved to establish emergency committees to assist refugees and also families of those who had been killed or jailed or who had disappeared. There are several reasons why church leaders acted so quickly and with government acquiescence. In previous years, all church leaders had been forced to take the social concerns of the poor more seriously due to the steady movement to the left in the political system since the early 1960s. During both Frei's and Allende's presidencies, many church groups focused more efforts on identifying with problems of the poor, and the Catholics had begun to establish small basic communities in working class areas to evangelize the poor more effectively. The churches also maintained fairly cordial relations with the Marxist government, and established closer communication with one another in the process. When the coup occurred, by and large major church leaders publicly remained neutral. The Permanent Committee of the Catholic Conference even issued a mildly critical declaration two days after the coup, lamenting the bloodshed and calling upon the military to respect all gains made by the working classes during the last decade (Oviedo Cavada, 1974: 174).

In the aftermath of the coup, when thousands were being tortured, murdered, or put in large concentration camps, the persecuted turned in droves to the churches for help. All other major social and political organizations were placed under strict controls, and the past performance, current neutrality, and existing organizational network of the churches (especially the Catholic Church) made them ready channels of assistance. Furthermore, the particularly brutal nature of the repression shocked international public opinion, and Protestant and Catholic Church groups in Western Europe and North America were most willing to provide immediate financial and material assistance to Chilean Church leaders attempting to help those in need. The new military regime acquiesced reluctantly to church efforts to assist those being persecuted, seeking religious legitimation for having overturned the longstanding democratic traditions of the country, and because it had no effective mechanism to handle the human casualties of its own brutality.

Finally, due to the long and vigorous history of political participation and multiparty competition in the country, many civilian leaders were anxious and willing to do something to counter the repression and assist those being persecuted. Many, especially in parties associated with the Christian left—MAPU and "Izquierda Cristiana"— had formerly been active in church-sponsored educational or social programs in the 1960s and found no difficulty in moving back into church structures to carry out humanitarian programs.

All of these political and religious factors in the context of sudden and brutal repression led to the formation of the Committee of Cooperation for Peace by seven major religious denominations in the country.[6] Over the next two years, the Committee established a whole range of services for Chileans suffering the effects of the coup—legal aid, assistance to workers arbitrarily dismissed from their jobs, medical programs in areas where public health clinics had been suspended, small self-help projects for the unemployed, and soup kitchens in urban working-class areas for starving children. The Committee also established regional offices in 15 of the 25 provinces where similar projects were begun. By 1975 over 300 full-time lawyers, social workers, and medical personnel were working in various parts of the country, and the annual budget (over $2 million) was provided mainly by Protestant and Catholic sources in North America and Western Europe and some nonconfessional agencies (U.S. Congress, House, 1976: 59).[7]

In December 1975, General Pinochet demanded the churches disband the Committee of Peace for having assisted many Chileans sought by the secret police (DINA) to leave the country. The government also argued that many civilians formerly associated with the Allende government were using the Committee to continue their political activities under Church auspices. Thus, under severe pressure both from Pinochet and the government-controlled press, church leaders agreed to close the Committee in late December. However, Cardinal Silva immediately moved to incorporate many of the activities and personnel of the former Committee of Peace into a new organization under Catholic auspices—the Vicariate of Solidarity—established in late January 1976. Over the past two years this Vicariate has established offices in the majority of Chile's 25 dioceses. These offices provide legal and health services, manage between 40 and 50 farm cooperatives in rural areas, and support soup kitchens for hungry children and adults in major urban areas. The Vicariate also issues a biweekly bulletin ("Solidaridad") from its Santiago headquarters which publishes accounts of its various projects as well as data on malnutrition, unemployment, and disappeared persons. Its budget is somewhat larger than that of the Committee for Peace, though funds are drawn mainly from the same foreign sources as supported that group. The Protestant churches have also continued to support, on their own, self-help worker enterprises with assistance from West European sources (Vicaría de la Solidaridad, 1977).

In addition to the work of the Committee for Peace and its successor, the Vicariate, the small base communities established in most of the 25 Catholic dioceses of the country have taken on new vitality and importance since the coup. During the Frei and Allende years these groups did not attract significant numbers of people due to the expanding activities of social and political organizations associated with parties. But since 1973, these neighborhood groups have become the only opportunities for Chileans (especially in working-class areas) to meet and discuss their problems. These communities are subdivided into three or four sectors, each focusing on different religious or social issues—bible study, catechetical training, prayer, and self-help social services. Thus far there has been no systematic study of these groups, but it was estimated in 1975 that there were approximately 20,000 active leaders of these communities and 10,000 more (almost exclusively women) who have received extensive training as catechists (Gilfeather, 1976).[8]

Taken together, the activities of all of these programs and structures operating under Church auspices in contemporary Chile have dealt with the effects of violations of a broad range of civil, social, and economic rights. So far, their impact on changing the political and economic structures which cause such violations has, however, been minimal. Official repression continues, with almost no opportunity for effective participation or distribution of resources in favor of the poor. In fact, the policies of the junta have rolled back most of the working-class gains made under Frei and Allende—labor unions are under government surveillance, wages are limited, agrarian reform organizations are being dismantled, and speculators are permitted to amass wealth and buy up enterprises formerly owned by the government. Arrests and tortures have subsided since 1974 and 1975, but the courts only very recently have begun to act with any independence and accept the Vicariate's legal requests to investigate lists of disappeared persons.

Despite their inability to affect direct change, the work of the Committee for Peace and the Vicariate have had an impact in other important ways. These committees have amassed well-documented evidence on civil rights violations. Based upon these reports and other sources (e.g., early on-site inspections and some newspaper stories in Chile), international organizations have been able to publicize continuing rights violations in the country. The Committee for Peace and the Vicariate have also provided survival assistance to thousands who would have perished or despaired, and thus have kept alive a spirit of hope. In addition, the small base communities have nourished a sense of solidarity and critical awareness among working classes, while serving as surrogate training grounds for future political leaders if and when the military relinquishes control of the country.

The impact of these activities on the Church has been considerable, but also not without tensions for the Church itself. For the first time in its history, the Chilean Catholic Church is beginning to penetrate the culture of the poor, and urban workers and slum dwellers are identifying with the Church now much more than ever before. But both the upper class and the military are disillusioned with the Church and view it as naive or as an obstacle to their current plans for the country. Right wing Catholics have also publicly attacked the Church for being infiltrated by Communists (Sociedad Chilena de Defensa de la Tradición, Familia y Propiedad, 1976). Since the coup, nearly 200 priests (mainly foreigners) have been expelled or urged to leave the country. Criticisms of foreign sources of support for church programs have also appeared in the press, such as the attempt to discredit the Inter-American Foundation by *El Mercurio* in January 1978 (El Mercurio, 1978).

Although the hierarchy has occasionally criticized the government for its general economic and political policies, their public documents have been very cautious and usually include some concessions to the government. For example, in their 1975 pastoral letter, "Gospel and Peace," the bishops thanked the military for having saved the country from Marxism, and praised the actions of the wives of the military for helping the poor (Comité Permanente del Episcopado de Chile, 1975). In their document, "Our Life as a Nation," they said that some abuses of power or unwarranted actions are inevitable and that there is an international campaign to discredit Chile's reputation organized by Marxists abroad (USCC, 1977b). Furthermore, in the four and one-half years since the coup, the bishops have seldom critized the government publicly for torture, and have only expressed sharp criticisms (or threatened excommunication) when the authority or person of bishops themselves have been attacked.

This ambiguous stance and selective public criticisms are due to divisions of opinion within the hierarchy as to the merits of the government, to their desire to maintain communication with the military, to an unwillingness to precipitate an all-out war with the state, and to a fear of affecting a more serious public division than already exists among the bishops and faithful alike. As a result, the prophetic role of the bishops has been exercised with extreme caution. But, while at times they have acquiesced to government demands regarding Church-sponsored programs, on the whole their cautious stance has made it possible for the whole new network of human rights activities at lower levels of the church to continue with some degree of effectiveness, under implicit Church protection.

II. Brazil: Small Base Communities, Justice and Peace Commissions, and Land Commissions

The reaction of the churches to the Brazilian military coup of March 1964 was not as swift or dramatic as in Chile. Moreover, new church structures to promote human rights in Brazil have not been able, so far, to mobilize with the same degree of effectiveness and coordination as in Chile. Nevertheless, some new programs have begun to operate in the past few years affecting civil, social and economic rights, and small base communities are now mushrooming in many rural areas of the country and perform similar critical roles as in Chile.

There are many reasons for this relatively slow reaction to an authoritarian regime by the Brazilian Church. First, when the coup occurred, the great majority of the hierarchy acquiesced in hopes that the new government would be able to control the social turmoil of the Goulart administration, and carry out its own announced plan for stable and effective economic development (Bruneau, 1974: 66, 93, 181).[9] Furthermore, the immediate aftermath of the Brazilian coup was not as brutal and repressive as in Chile. The military did not immediately resort to widespread torture or mass murder, nor did they close Congress and suppress all forms of social participation. In addition, although the Brazilian Church, like the Chilean, had begun to involve itself in social issues in the early 1960s (paralleling the new awakening of social consciousness in the universal Church reflected by Vatican II), neither the hierarchy as a whole nor the laity were strongly committed to this option. A small core of bishops centering around Dom Helder Camara were urging a more active social commitment by the Church, but, by 1964, they had lost influence in the National Conference of Brazilian Bishops [CNBB] (Bruneau, 1974: 124). Many Catholic Action lay leaders active in promoting social change in rural areas in the pre-1964 period moved away from the Church by 1965, when the bishops attempted to exercise stricter controls on their programs and eliminate all activities with political repercussions (Bruneau, 1974: 126). Hence, in the aftermath of the coup, the leadership of the CNBB favored cooperation with what seemed to be a moderate regime, and in any case the Church lacked the organizational capacity or network to oppose official policies.

In 1968, however, the government began to impose more repressive measures to curb escalating opposition and eliminate growing leftist guerrilla activities. Habeas corpus was suspended, all civilian control over security forces was eliminated, the Congress, the courts, and the press were severely curtailed, and the use of torture became systematic and widespread. These repressive policies also began to affect the Church itself, as church publications, radio stations and pastoral programs in rural areas were placed under close surveillance and some church personnel (especially in rural areas) harassed, imprisoned or expelled.[10]

In such an atmosphere of controlled and systematic repression which also touched the institutional church itself, bishops as a group began to criticize the regime, and new church structures at the local level (base communities and self-help social programs) emerged as alternate forms of social participation and humanitarian assistance for the poor. In May 1970, the Episcopal Conference published its first major public criticism, denouncing the use of torture and lack of fair trials and expressing the need for greater social participation and respect for legitimate criticism of government policies (CNBB, 1970: 415).[11]

At this time several dioceses began to implement some of the new pastoral orientations of Medellín—formation of small base communities, lay leadership training, and social action favoring the poor. In the northeast of Brazil, for example, where the repressive political and economic policies of the regime have been the most severe (and where harassment of clergy first began), both base communities and social programs run by lay leaders began to take root by the late 1960s (Hope, 1975: 46).[12] Small base religious communities also sprang up in the early 1970s in the center-west and in several urban areas, such as São Paulo. They emerged in response to the elimination of other forms of social participation. Although these communities are in the beginning stages of development and face problems due to long-standing patterns of personalistic piety, the rootlessness of migrants, and lack of well-trained personnel, they have mushroomed throughout Brazil over the past five years.

No systematic study of these groups has yet been done, but it is estimated that about 50,000 such centers are operating at the present (Bono, 1977: 1). The Episcopal Conference in 1976 issued a document outlining the focus and purpose of such base communities. Included in the desired activities of these groups is the development of critical social and political awareness among the participants (Estudos de CNBB, 1976a). The political sensitivity of these orientations has led to increasing numbers of arrests of lay leaders and technical experts assisting these communities, and many have been tortured (Hope, 1975: 54; Bono, 1977: 20).

In addition to these new grassroots self-help programs and religious communities, the National Episcopal Conference in 1972 authorized the establishment of Justice and Peace Commissions, both at the national level as part of the CNBB itself and in several dioceses. The purpose of these commissions is to conduct study projects of socio-economic needs of various regions and provide assistance to prisoners and their families. Due to the lack of staff and the weak structural development of the Church in many areas of the country, these commissions have not yet begun to function effectively.

In the archdiocese of São Paulo, however, with the largest concentration of population in the country (over ten million people) and one of the most outspoken of the Brazilian bishops, Cardinal Evaristo Arns, the Justice and Peace Commission over the past few years has inaugurated several programs pertaining to violations of civil, social, and economic rights. In 1975 it published two books on the link between private death squads and security forces in the early days of the government and on the maldistribution of income and economic resources in the archdiocese (Szulc, 1977: 19). Lists of disappeared persons were also printed in the archdiocesan newspaper, *O São Paulo,* based on documented evidence brought to the Commission by private individuals and church personnel. In 1977 the Commission received grants from the Inter-American Foundation and from Catholic organizations in West Germany. With some additional local contributions, the Commission expanded its personnel to provide emergency relief for prisoners, ex-prisoners, and their families, offer legal and social services to the labor sector, disseminate information on the Commission activities, and assist other dioceses in the creation of similar Commissions.

In addition to Justice and Peace Commissions, the bishops of the Amazon region have started programs for Indians and small landholders who are being displaced by government development projects and large national and international agrobusiness enterprises. Under the auspices of the National Justice and Peace Commission and the CNBB's Commission of Missionary Action, meetings were held in June 1975 by prelates and technicians in these areas to discuss the dispossession of peasants and to begin legal aid and educational programs to help protect their land claims (Estudos de CNBB, 1976b).[13] Since then, similar programs have been inaugurated by several Amazon dioceses but, as with the base communities, large numbers of participants have been harassed, arrested, or murdered.

While not as well organized or funded as the Chilean Church's activities for human rights, these new programs in Brazil have attempted to promote and defend a whole range of civil, social, and economic rights of the oppressed. Their impact so far on government and business policy has not been dramatic. While the number of cases of torture and disappearances has decreased since 1974 and the Congress has been reopened and censorship bans have been lifted on several publications, no effective political participation exists for the vast number of citizens. Nor has the government changed its economic strategy of development which allows industrialists and agricultural enterprises to amass great wealth and land at the expense of workers, peasants, and Indians.[14]

As in the Chilean case, one of the most effective but limited contributions of these new programs has been the provision of alternate forms of social participation for the poor and powerless. While not affecting significant changes in economic and political structures, these at least have provided opportunities for some self-help and for the nurturing of a critical awareness and sense of dignity among them.

The impact of these structures on the Church, however, has been very notable since 1970, for the government has increased its surveillance and harassment of participants in these small base communities, self-help projects, Justice and Peace Commissions, and land commissions. In addition, paramilitary death squads and security forces have murdered several priests, and even kidnapped a bishop for a short period of time in 1976. More persecution of church personnel is occurring in Brazil than in Chile. This not only has solidified church identity with the oppressed, but also has stimulated the hierarchy as a group to issue more decisive denunciations of the government. In this way, the equilibrium of the institutional Church is now clearly on the side of the lower classes. Thus, in November 1976, and again in February 1977, the National Conference of Brazilian Bishops issued strongly worded documents condemning the murder of priests and Indians, attacking policies which absolutize national security, and bluntly stating that the present model of Brazilian development is characterized by injustice and promotes institutionalized violence (USCC, 1977c, 1976d). Both of these documents are far more consistent and critical of the government than comparable statements by the Chilean hierarchy. It is also clear that a consensus now exists among higher and lower leaders in the Brazilian Church that opposition to the government is necessary, since the state itself has singled out the Church for special repression as a subversive organization (Barbosa, 1978: 27).[15]

The Church has suffered both external limitation and increasing internal tensions as a result of its human rights programs and the prophetic stance of its bishops. For example, the Church is heavily dependent on the state for maintaining its schools, universities, radio stations, and hospitals, and since the late 1960s the government has curtailed funding for these operations and levied taxes on church properties. Increasing numbers of foreign priests are being expelled from the country, and the archdiocesan newspaper of São Paulo is one of the few remaining newspapers subject to censorship prior to publication. In late 1976 the Church was also ordered to withdraw some of its personnel from mission territories where murder and dispossession of Indians and peasants are occurring, although later the order was reversed.

Right-wing Catholics belonging to the "Tradition, Fatherland and Family" movement also have increased their public attacks on the Church as being infiltrated by communists. One bishop who belongs to this organization (and who owns a considerable amount of land),

Archbishop Geraldo Sigaud of Diamantina, in February 1977, publicly accused two fellow bishops of being communists—Bishop Pedro Casaldáliga of São Felix and Bishop Tomáz Balduino of Goias Velho (USCC, 1978b: 15). Both of the accused have been active in defending the land claims of peasants and Indians in rural areas. The government mounted a major public campaign to discredit these two prelates and gave Archbishop Sigaud's accusation widespread circulation in the government-controlled media. Only strong pressure by the Vatican and the Episcopal Conference kept the Minister of the Interior from expelling Casaldáliga (a Spaniard) from the country. All of these events, however, point to continual Church-state conflicts in the near future and further external pressures by the government to circumscribe human rights activities by Catholic religious and lay leaders.

Unlike the Chilean Church, the Brazilian Church's official concern with human rights originated from a direct attack on the Church itself, and as this attack has intensified so have the efforts of many bishops, priests, and lay leaders to promote civil, social, and economic rights of the poor. The institutional infrastructure of the Brazilian Church and the amount of foreign support for its human rights programs are both far less developed than is the case in Chile. The bishops attempt to offset this institutional weakness through more aggressive public denunciations than the Chilean bishops, but this in turn precipitates stronger official repression of local action programs. The institutional power of the Church to blunt the authoritarian policies of the regime is therefore limited, but as repression continues the whole character of the Church is gradually changing and its mission to the poor more consciously felt and affirmed.

III. Paraguay: Peasant Leagues, Small Base Communities, and the Committee of Churches for Emergency Assistance

The oldest continuous dictatorship in South America exists in Paraguay, where Alfredo Stroessner has held power since 1954. In this highly personalistic regime, almost all social institutions in the country (unions, professional associations, courts, universities, business organizations) are controlled or infiltrated by Stroessner sympathizers. A powerful police force (operating under continuous state-of-siege conditions) maintains "order," and the system as a whole is held together by a highly pervasive pattern of corruption supported by profits from institutionalized smuggling (Dominguez, 1975: 95-96).

Between 1958 and 1975 there were five brief but intense waves of arrests and torture involving political opponents to the regime— students, labor leaders, dissident members of the Colorado Party (Stroessner's official group), suspected members of a small communist party. In April and May 1976, however, a new and more widespread wave of repression occurred aimed particularly at members of the Protestant and Catholic clergy and peasant and Indian leaders associated with church programs, especially in rural areas. Over 1,000 men and women were arrested at this time and many were subjected to torture and other forms of cruel and inhuman treatment in 13 detention centers in various parts of the country. In addition, 32 of Paraguay's 34 foreign Jesuit priests were expelled from the country (Stephansky and Alexander, 1976: 161).

Although the government claimed that these programs were supporting guerrillas and planning violent revolution, no substantial proof was provided to justify these claims, nor is there any significant terrorist activity in the country (Stephansky and Alexander, 1976: 174). The real reason for the repression of church personnel was the fact that both Catholic and Protestant Church organizations have set up independent structures for both social and religious participation outside government control. In the aftermath of Vatican II (1962-1965) and Medellín (1968), the Catholic Church began to concentrate more effort on evangelizing hitherto neglected groups in Paraguay—peasants and Indians in the interior of the country who constitute two-thirds of the population. Foreign missionaries (especially Spanish Jesuits) have been most active since the mid-1960s in establishing peasant leagues in rural areas which include credit unions and small agricultural cooperatives. Money for these projects has been provided by foreign church agencies (such as Catholic Relief Services in the United States, and Adveniat and Misereor in West Germany). Some of the activities of these leagues have included teaching peasants and Indians their legal rights and helping them pressure the government to apply its own agrarian reform and labor laws more fairly. Parallel to these Catholic peasant leagues have been similar organizations sponsored by the Disciples of Christ from the U.S. These also provide credit to small landholders and train peasants in the rudiments of government and law as these effect their interests (Stephansky and Alexander, 1976: 180).

Such organizations have enabled peasants and Indians to be more aware of their civil and economic rights under existing law, while stimulating them to become spokespersons to represent directly their own interests without reliance upon any of the organizations asociated with the government. Even though most of the leagues purposely chose peasants publicly known as members of the ruling Colorado Party, the government was most concerned that they were being trained in independent organizations outside its control. Furthermore, since these cooperatives and credit unions were able to bypass intermediary agents in marketing their produce, they were able to receive fairer prices for their goods. Large landholders and financial and commercial institutions saw their socioeconomic dominance threatened, and therefore actively opposed these new programs. All of these factors led to the harsh crackdown of mid-1976 with massive arrests, torture, and deportations of clergy and laity active in the leagues.

The reaction of the churches to this repression has occurred on several fronts. First, small base communities and deacon training programs for the laity have taken on new vitality now that the leagues are more circumscribed. These pastoral programs have begun to flourish in almost all major regions in the interior. They involve small groups of 40 to 50 people (mostly men) and combine bible study and catechetical training with frank discussions of agrarian and social problems, such as the legal right of peasants and Indians to seek redress of grievances and form self-help organizations. These new base communities have also been subject to similar harassment by police forces, but lay leaders are determined to continue their activities despite risk to their lives.[16]

The Catholic hierarchy reacted swiftly and strongly to the mid-1976 wave of arrests which also was accompanied by a press campaign charging communist infiltration in the Church. On June 15, 1976, all eleven Catholic bishops in Paraguay issued a pastoral letter that was read in churches at Sunday Mass. They unequivocally denounced the use of violence and torture to eliminate subversion (even terrorism) and demanded an end to arbitrary procedures, massive arrests, intimidation of entire peasant villages, confiscation of goods, and prolonged holding of people incommunicado. They also emphasized the need for an efficient and respectable judiciary to administer justice fairly (USCC 1976b: 7, 9, 10, 11). The bishops condemned the government's campaign of defamation and persecution against the Church, emphasizing that only church leaders can judge what truly conforms to the Gospel.

Finally, they affirmed the "inalienable responsibility of the Church in the promotion of activities which are inherent to it," and renewed their "decision to carry them forward at whatever cost in terms of sacrifice" (USCC 1976b: 14; Stephansky and Alexander, 1976: 209).[17]

The third and final effort to promote and defend human rights by churches in the aftermath of the most recent wave of repression has been the formation of the Committee of Churches for Emergency Assistance. On June 28, 1976, representatives of the Catholic and Lutheran Churches and the Disciples of Christ announced the establishment of a new ecumenical organization to help prisoners and their families (USCC, 1976c: 19). The Committee operates out of the chancery office of the Episcopal Conference of Paraguay and provides food and medicines to prisoners, economic and rehabilitation assistance to families of prisoners, ex-prisoners, or the disappeared, runs a documentation and information service, and offers legal aid to those charged with crimes (Stephansky and Helfield, 1977: 4). The Committee has received financial and material support from the World Council of Churches, Catholic Relief Services (U.S.), Misereor (West Germany), Christian Aid (England), Christian Church (U.S.), and the Catholic Justice and Peace Commission in Holland. Catholic and Protestant leaders in human rights working in other parts of Latin America, North America, and Western Europe have also visited the Committee on several occasions over the past two years to give it moral support and international visibility (Wilde, 1977, 301; Comité de la Iglesias, 1977b, 6; 1977c, 6).[18]

The Committee has achieved some important results over the past two years. It has been given daily visiting rights to Emboscada prison (where most of the prisoners are now incarcerated), and the living conditions there have improved significantly due to food and medicines the Committee has brought in. Literacy training programs and artisan cooperatives have been set up in the prison under the Committee's direction. The sale of artisan products, such as woodcarvings and woven baskets, serves not only to raise additional relief funds, but also circulates public reminders in society at large that there are people in prison.

Lists of prisoners also have been prepared and presented to the International League of Human Rights during its two visits to Paraguay in 1976 and 1977. The government has allowed 45 of these prisoners to be processed in civilian courts, and the Committee has provided lawyers for the defense of 40 of them. The government has also released over 200 prisoners since September 1976, so that by December 1977 there were only 179 remaining in Emboscada. (The whereabouts of many who have disappeared, however, is still not known and many people are now imprisoned for shorter periods, thus maintaining a climate of fear.) The bulk of the Committee's budget (more than one-half of its funds) is spent on relief programs for families of prisoners or persons who have disappeared in the countryside. To date 177 projects (assisting 224 families) have been set up. These include not only food and clothing, but also help to establish or continue self-help projects in farming, artisan work, or husbandry (Comité de las Iglesias, 1977a: 3-4).

In this way, the work of the new ecumenical committee has contributed to some significant changes on behalf of legal rights and care of prisoners and survival aid for their families. Furthermore, self-help projects similar to cooperatives begun by Catholic and Protestant churches ten years ago are being reformed with aid from this Committee. But the basic structures of political and economic power of the country have not changed significantly. Stroessner is still in complete control and in early February 1978 was given yet another term in office in a controlled election. The economy has been bolstered by recent financial agreements allowing both Brazil and Argentina to build hydroelectric dams in Paraguayan territory (Vidal, 1978), and no major changes have occurred in the concentration of land and wealth in the country.

The government has made concessions by releasing some prisoners, allowing civil trials for others, and permitting various social and economic improvement programs by the Committee of Churches. These concessions, however, have been due not only to Church denunciations, but more importantly to pressure from various international human rights organizations and from the U.S. government, to which General Stroessner is particularly sensitive. There is no major internal threat to Stroessner's power at present and he can afford, under prodding by Washington, Amnesty International, and the International League of Human Rights, to loosen the repression a bit in order to maintain U.S. economic and military aid (Barbosa, 1977: 302; Stephansky and Helfeld, 1977: 12).[19]

Both the peasant leagues and the small base communities which have been badly crippled but still function, and the Committee of Churches (moving cautiously but swiftly with strong international support during this latest period of decompression), have all had much more impact on the churches themselves than on the political and economic system. Church leaders and personnel now sense the impact of the repressive nature of the Stroessner regime more than in previous periods, since the most recent attacks have been directed primarily at their own institutions and at clerical and lay personnel. The Catholic hierarchy has clearly committed itself to continue these new social and religious programs as integral parts of the mission of the church, and in so doing are making the institution more credible than before in the eyes of the vast majority of poor in the country.

The peasant leagues and cooperatives may be smashed, and this fate could also await the new Committee of Churches if Stroessner feels it is getting out of hand and when the recent focus of international attention on Paraguay subsides. The small base communities, bible study groups, and catechetical and deacon training programs, however, will probably be defended more vigorously by the churches since they are easier to justify on specifically religious grounds, and also receive very little foreign financial support compared to the other social projects. As in Chile and Brazil, these small groups are breeding grounds for future local leaders who learn to exercise their rights of social participation in surrogate fashion under church auspices. The sense of dignity and critical awareness of poor people is being kept alive, and in the long run this is far more deleterious to Stroessner's totalitarian regime than food, clothing, medicines, or legal aid programs sponsored by foreigners.

IV. Bolivia: Justice and Peace Commission and Permanent Assembly of Human Rights

Official Church opposition to the military regime in Bolivia since 1971, as in the case of Brazil, has been slow in developing. In many ways religious opposition to the Bolivian government is similar to the Chilean case, where far more significant action on behalf of human rights has occurred at lower levels of the Church and in an ecumenical context.

When General Hugo Banzer overthrew the populist-leftist military government of General Juan José Torres in August 1971, the Catholic bishops accepted the new regime with relative calm. They lamented the killing, arrests, and deportations which occurred, but expressed hope that the new government would restore order, and affirmed that church buildings were rightful places of asylum for politically persecuted persons (CEP, 1976: 22). But throughout 1972 the military did not respect this ancient right of asylum in churches, and on several occasions houses of bishops, priests, and nuns were searched, and persons there seeking help were arrested. In addition, 18 foreign priests and three Protestant pastors were expelled from the country. Several bishops on their own expressed public criticism of the government for raiding church buildings, but the 22-man Episcopal Conference (half of whom are foreigners themselves[20]) said nothing.

Although political parties, labor unions, and the press were not as severely repressed in Bolivia in the immediate aftermath of the coup as they were in Chile, during 1972 there were countless number of arrests (especially in mining, working-class, and union organizations), and torture and detentions without charge were widespread. After a Jesuit priest was arrested in January 1973, a public letter was signed by 99 priests, nuns, and Protestant pastors strongly attacking the government for these abuses of power, and also criticizing the Catholic hierarchy for their silence as a group in regard to these violations (CEP, 1976: 53). At about the same time, a group of Catholic laity and priests convinced the bishops to set up a Justice and Peace Commission (similar to the one begun in Brazil in 1972). This organization was endorsed by the Bolivian Episcopal Conference, but not constituted as an official organ of the Church. Rather, it was to be primarily the work of the laity. Dr. Luis Aldolfo Salinas, the last civilian to hold the office of president of the country in 1969, was named its first president (CEP, 1976: 67).[21]

Although originally established primarily as a reflection group to study social and economic questions in the light of the Church's social teachings, this group quickly moved into human rights work as a result of popular needs and pressures. It was soon inundated with petitions for legal aid by families seeking the whereabouts of kin who had been arrested or had disappeared. As a result, over the next two years the Justice and Peace Commission expanded its activities to include habeas corpus petitions to the courts for missing persons and material relief for their families. It also established offices in five regions outside La Paz and received financial assistance from Church-sponsored organizations in the U.S. and Western Europe. In turn it became the most reliable source of information on violations occurring within Bolivia upon which international human rights groups (such as Amnesty International) have based their reports.

In addition, it also engaged in other activities affecting sensitive political issues embarrassing to the government. It published over 301 articles in the press on human rights and pressured the government to issue a general amnesty for political prisoners. Public prayer vigils and fasts in criticism of government policies were also organized (CEP, 1976: 150). Furthermore, in February 1975, the Commission published a book recounting a massacre of 100 peasants near Cochabamba perpetrated by the military one year before.

This occurred three months after a major new wave of repression. In November 1974, the government issued a decree outlawing all public political activities and strikes, placing parties in recess, removing current leaders of all labor, professional and student organizations, postponing elections scheduled for 1975, and imposing mandatory public service on all citizens over 21 years of age. In the face of this repression, the Justice and Peace Commission stood out as the last remaining critical public voice against the government. The military expelled two foreign priests working closely with the Commission and threatened the bishops with possible expulsion of 14 more foreign clerics if they did not reorganize the Justice and Peace Commission to stop its involvement in political affairs. Although a committee of the Episcopal Conference had criticized the November decrees as "totalitarian" and contrary to the social principles of the church regarding basic human rights (CEP, 1976: 132), as a group the bishops acquiesced to official demands. The government had closed down a church-operated radio station in the mining region in January, and had also conducted further raids on bishops' houses in La Paz and Santa Cruz. In the context of this mounting attack on Church-affiliated organizations and personnel and in light of the heavy dependence of the Church on foreign clergy, the bishops opted for a strategy of conciliation with the military and placed the Justice and Peace Commission in a state of recess (CEP, 1976: 161).[22]

Throughout 1975 mounting student and labor unrest and mining strikes occurred despite the government ban on political activities. The Conference of Religious Orders of Men and Women in Bolivia petitioned the bishops to assist the striking miners who had been fired, and in April in their monthly bulletin published an analysis of the loss of purchasing power and real income by miners, workers and peasants due to currency devaluation, inflation, and controls on wages (CEP, 1976: 95, 186). In late July three foreign nuns were expelled from the country for purportedly engaging in subversive political activity.

Finally, in December 1976, the Episcopal Conference issued its first collective public criticism of the Banzer government. It criticized the very skewed distribution of wealth and unfair wage policies of the regime which made the poor bear a disproportionate part of the cost of development. The bishops also attacked the model of the state being constructed by the military which prolonged economic injustices by not allowing for adequate social participation by miners, peasants, and workers (Centro de Proyección Cristiana, 1977: 22).

In the same month, representatives of the Lutheran and Methodist Churches and a priest from the Conference of Religious Orders of Men and Women met with several lay persons to form the Permanent Assembly of Human Rights in Bolivia. This ecumenical organization included in its stated goals the sensitizing of public opinion regarding human rights, the circulation of documents of reflection on statism and national security, and the defense of structures of participation (parties, unions, workers' and peasants' organizations) (Asamblea Permanente, 1976; USCC, 1978a). The Assembly received the blessing of both Cardinal Maurer of Sucre and Archbishop Manrique of La Paz, although it was not formally tied to Catholic and Protestant church structures. It immediately moved to establish financial ties with Protestant funding agencies in Europe, and by August 1977, had set up legal aid service for prisoners and their families, as well as for miners fired from their jobs for striking and union activities. Similar to the former Justice and Peace Commission, it established regional offices in several other cities of the country, but with more financial assistance and staff than its predecessor. In its publications it listed names of those killed in the last six years and has cited documented evidence of violations of such basic rights as the right to work, the right to education, the right to organize unions, the right to habeas corpus, and a fair trial (Asamblea Permanente de los Derechos Humanos de Bolivia, 1977). It also has urged general amnesty for all political prisoners and those in exile.

One major reason the Permanent Assembly has been able to continue its activities is that General Banzer in late 1977 announced that there would be general elections in July 1978. Banzer has been conscious of U.S. interest and pressure to see democratic procedures reestablished in the country. This has made it harder for the government to repress dissent with the same amount of force as in 1975. In addition to the Permanent Assembly, many political, labor, and professional organizations have been active recently in pressuring the government to allow political exiles to return to the country for the election campaign. In late December six miners' wives, whose husbands are among this group (which numbers over 15,000), began a hunger strike in the Chancery of the Archdiocese of La Paz. The strike soon spread to student, professional, and labor organizations in more than nine cities of the country totaling more than 1,000 people (Latin America Political Report, 1978d: 12; Lucha, 1978: 21).

The Permanent Assembly provided material support for the strikers and publicized their demands in newspaper ads (Asamblea Permanente de los Derechos Humanos de Bolivia, 1978).[23] Many of the participants gathered in churches in various dioceses. When troops invaded several of these buildings in La Paz and arrested clerical and lay participants of the movement, Archbishop Manrique threatened to place the archdiocese under a three-day interdict and excommunicate those conducting the attacks (Latin America Political Report, 1978c: 29). On January 18th General Banzer gave in to the demands of the hunger strike. He announced amnesty for all political exiles and prisoners. He also said he would make no reprisals against hunger strikers or their supporters, would release the 200 people already under arrest for having taken part in the movement, and lift the ban on trade union activities. Public attention focused on preparing for the July elections and the hope for a civilian victory at the polls.[24]

Thus, church activities for human rights since 1971 in Bolivia have been variegated and at times less than consistent. Only when the property or religious personnel of the institution have been under direct attack have the bishops been willing to confront the state openly, and then only on certain occasions. The traditional conservative orientation of the bishops, the lack of strong social commitment before the military coup and the heavy dependence on foreign clergy have all made the hierarchy rather cautious in their defense of civil, social, and economic rights.

However, the clerics and religious at lower levels of the Catholic Church, especially in combination with lay Catholic and Protestant groups, have been able to mount some effective opposition to repression. Precisely because there is significant international pressure (particularly from the United States) on the regime (Latin America Political Report, 1978a),[25] as well as some effective domestic secular opposition to the government, the strategies of the Permanent Assembly and other church leaders have been able to make some gains for civil and social rights.

The impact of those activities of the former Justice and Peace Commission and the current Permanent Assembly has perhaps been as problematic for the churches as for the government. Some Catholic bishops supported the efforts of the Permanent Assembly in the hunger strike, but these involved direct attacks on the churches themselves, and the government was in a much weaker position than before due to domestic and international pressures. The past record of the bishops, however, provides little evidence to believe the hierarchy will now become a consistent defender of civil, social, and economic rights of oppressed miners and peasants.

Furthermore, the actions of both the Justice and Peace Commission and the Permanent Assembly have precipitated some public divisions in the Catholic Church. In 1974, in 1977, and most recently during the 1978 hunger strike, a small group of diocesan clergy (predominantly Bolivians) issued public criticisms of religious order priests (overwhelmingly of foreign origin) for becoming involved in politics and importing foreign ideology into the country. In addition, after the hunger strike a representative of the Latin American Anti-Communist Confederation (a right-wing Catholic organization headquartered in Mexico) visited Bolivia. In a press conference he accused Archbishop Manrique of being responsible for communist infiltration in the Bolivian Catholic Church. The government media gave considerable attention to these incidents, although the number of both diocesan clergy and conservative laity ready to assist in this campaign against church leaders and foreign priests involved in human rights activities in the country is relatively small (El Diario, 1978a, b).

Finally, unlike the churches in Chile, Brazil, and Paraguay, the Bolivian Church does not yet enjoy a significant network of small base communities which can act as training grounds for indigenous lay leaders. This means that the church must still depend heavily on foreign clergy to run its pastoral programs in the near future. This makes it particularly vulnerable to government attack. It also means that it cannot serve as an instrument for social participation and consciousness-raising at the local level with the same effectiveness as do several other national churches in the subcontinent.

For all of these reasons, although some significant changes have occurred (especially in recent years), chronic structural weaknesses and contradictions persist in the Bolivian Church. These severely limit its capacity to act as a consistent force promoting human rights, except in certain crisis situations.

V. Argentina: The Ecumenical Movement for Human Rights and the Permanent Assembly for Human Rights

Church responses to human rights violations in Argentina since the military coup in 1976 have been somewhat different from other countries in the southern region. Although church leaders have spoken out against abuse of power and formed or participated in ecumenical organizations to promote human rights, their actions to date have been more circumscribed and their effectiveness more limited than that of their counterparts in neighboring countries. This is due mainly to the distinctive political situation and climate of insecurity which still prevails in the country.

In the late 1960s and early 1970s armed leftist movements emerged to oppose the military regime which took power in 1966—for example, the Montoneros and the People's Revolutionary Army (ERP). Through ransom from kidnappings, money stolen from banks, and assistance from abroad, these organizations formed the best equipped and most effective guerrilla movement in Latin America by 1973. The withdrawal of the military from power in March 1973, and the subseque⁻ᵗ return of Juan Perón, proved a disillusionment for the left. Two months after his death they resumed their armed struggle in September 1974. During the year-and-a-half rule of Isabel Perón, the country experienced severe economic difficulties, with inflation reaching an annual rate of 700% by March 1976. After 1974, however, a state of siege was also imposed with more than 3,000 persons placed in preventive detention. Private death squads, some of which were financed or assisted by the government itself, began to operate with impunity and were responsible for a large proportion of the 1,500 assassinations which occurred during the eighteen months following Perón's death. The most infamous of these groups is the Argentine Anti-Communist Alliance (AAA), which has very close ties to the police and is responsible for over 300 murders in 1974 alone (Amnesty International, 1976b: 7).

Given this climate of terror, insecurity, and economic disruption, many Catholic bishops publicly welcomed and promised support to the government which took power in March 1976 (CELADEC, 1977: 40). The Church itself had suffered serious internal divisions during the late 1960s and early 1970s, when a group of several hundred priests actively opposed the former military regime and publicly urged major structural changes in the direction of a socialist economy. This movement had some positive impact on several bishops, but clashed with others (Dodson, 1973).[26] By 1974 the organization had disbanded (itself suffering some of the attacks by the right wing death squads), and the leadership of the Episcopal Conference was under the control of conservatives who welcomed the return of the military.

In the months following the March coup, however, several events precipitated action by church leaders on behalf of civil and political rights. The waves of killings and disappearances continued, and by November 1976 the deaths totaled over 1,200 (CELADEC, 1977: 34). These were perpetuated by both the left and the right. Many of those being persecuted and fired from their jobs flocked to churches for assistance and provided clear evidence to church personnel of systematic use of torture by the military to extract information. By the end of the year at least 25 Catholic and Protestant clergy had been arrested and ten others assassinated by right-wing death squads (Argentina Outreach, 1977: 16). Bishop Enrique Angelelli of La Rioja was killed mysteriously while collecting evidence concerning the deaths of two priests in his diocese who had been active in programs assisting the poor (Catholic Institute for International Relations, 1976: 5).[27]

Amidst this continuing violence and persecution of the churches themselves, the Catholic hierarchy issued a pastoral letter in May 1976 condemning abuses of power. The bishops denied that the welfare of the state was above the rights of individuals, and criticized the government for prolonged detentions, torture, denial of habeas corpus, and firing of workers for political reasons. They also stated that forcing others to go hungry "in order to gain unreasonable profit" was wrong, and that halting inflation too hurriedly at the expense of workers was a cardinal sin. The bishops, however, gave recognition to the delicate situation of the country and also condemned revolutionary uprising and "Marxist solutions to our problems" (USCC, 1976a: 18-19).

Two months later representatives of Catholic and Protestant churches formed the Ecumenical Movement for Human Rights (MEDH), an organization established to aid families of kidnapped persons and assist all those suffering the effects of "political and economic terrorism and indiscriminate repression." It included in its stated goals the preparation of documents concerning human rights violations, the formation of a body of lawyers to provide legal aid to those arrested and families of the disappeared, and the communication with prisoners and other detainees (Movimiento Ecuménico por los

Derechos Humanos, 1976). It also has sought some financial assistance from international Catholic and Protestant organizations, but not to the extent as similar committees in Bolivia, Paraguay, and Chile. In Argentina, any group with large amounts of outside funding is suspected of being a siphon for guerrilla support.

In addition to this ecumenical group, another organization to defend human rights was established in late 1975 by some Protestant and Catholic leaders along with intellectuals, professionals, and party representatives. This committee, known as the Permanent Assembly for Human Rights (APDH), documents cases of disappearances, presents legal petitions to the courts on behalf of those detained, and writes public letters to General Videla seeking investigations as to the whereabouts of those who are missing (Brewin et al., 1976).[28] It has neither sought, nor received, substantial amounts of international funding for its activities.

To date, the accomplishments of these two Church-related organizations have not been nearly as effective or publicized as the activities of ecumenical committees in Chile, Paraguay, and Bolivia. The Permanent Assembly has gathered well-documented evidence on cases of disappeared persons and the use of torture, and has sought redress for victims of repression in the courts and from Videla himself (Buenos Aires Herald, 1977: a, b; Latinamerica Press, 1977a). The Ecumenical Movement has, in addition to offering legal aid, provided access to emergency relief for families of prisoners and the disappeared. There has been, however, very little response on the part of the courts and the government to legal petitions or requests by church leaders for investigations (Latin America Political Report, 1978b: 38).[29] There is good reason to believe that Videla himself does not wield effective control of the military and that strong right-wing elements in the armed forces and police act independently to perpetrate murder and torture. Conservative business groups seem to support these elements, and very repressive economic measures continue against workers and unions.

Furthermore, guerrilla activities also continue and Videla uses this argument to justify further repression. In addition, over 60 lawyers have been assassinated since 1974, along with countless union and party leaders and those engaged in social programs assisting the poor. This in turn has forced Church-sponsored human rights organizations to act with extreme caution and keep a relatively low profile.

The impact of these new Church-sponsored organizations has sensitized church leaders to the chronic problem of repression, and has provided them with substantial documentation that kidnapping, murder, and torture originate more from government security forces than from guerrilla action. The hierarchy issued a second pastoral letter in May 1977, partly as a result of this information, condemning these abuses by the government and criticizing violations of workers' rights to work, to health care, and to education. While reaffirming their rejection of Marxism, the bishops also stated that this does not justify branding as Marxists all who work for justice on behalf of the poor (USCC, 1977a: 26, 27, 29).

Work for civil and political rights or for basic social assistance to the poor has precipitated continued attacks on church personnel. By December 1977 some 30 priests were in jail in Argentina, and at least 17 have been murdered by security forces (Latin America Political Report, 1977). In this sense, the Argentine situation resembles the Brazilian case of direct frontal attack on the churches themselves. The Argentine bishops, however, have been far more willing to communicate with the government and try to exercise influence behind the scenes than have their Brazilian counterparts. They still have hopes for Videla (a devout Catholic), they fear further reprisals from right-wing security forces, and are aware of the continued presence of guerrilla activities in the country. The Catholic Church in Argentina has not yet established a firm network of small base communities for evangelization and social participation which characterize the Chilean, Brazilian, and Paraguayan churches.

For all these political and religious reasons, the impact to date on human rights activities by Argentine churches has been the least effective of all other church groups in the subcontinent. The Catholic Church remains a weak and underdeveloped institution, with no past history of strong social commitment by the hierarchy. While it is slowly becoming sensitized to human rights issues as these directly affect its clergy and laity, the present prospects for the Church promoting civil, social, and economic rights are modest at best.

VI. Conclusions

Although there are characteristics peculiar to each of these new church pastoral and social organizations in the five countries, some common patterns can be identified. These pertain to the three issues raised in the introduction to this paper: (1) how and why churches have become involved in human rights activities in the subcontinent; (2) the scope and extent of their work; and (3) the impact of these new structures both on society and the churches themselves.

All five cases indicate that church programs for human rights are basically reactive strategies, responding to unforeseen crises in secular society. The policy of promoting human rights (although legitimized in the Medellín documents of 1968) did not become a conscious priority of any of the national hierarchies until they were stimulated to act by pressures from below in their own churches or from outside the ecclesiastical institutions. In some cases the killing of clergy moved the bishops to set up emergency programs; in others, direct attacks on already existing church programs benefiting the poor moved them. In many situations, however, the response came from general public pressure, as many people had nowhere else to go for help and the churches were the last remaining organizations with any relative degree of freedom to act.

In all these countries the international linkages of the churches gave them an important capacity for action. Access to finances and material support in both Western Europe and the United States enabled them to begin humanitarian projects to assist the persecuted. In turn, the information on rights violations to which religious personnel had access by direct experience could be effectively and swiftly communicated through the international network of the churches themselves. Without such ability to transfer money, material, and information across national borders, these new Church-sponsored programs could not have been begun nor sustained.

Some of these churches are clearly learning from one another and making efforts to share experiences and strategies within the southern tier region itself. This process is facilitated by the growing network of communication and exchange of religious and lay personnel across national borders, which makes churches one of the few effective private transnational actors in the region capable of counteracting the international reach of the military. The growing ecumenical cooperation between Catholics and Protestants in Latin America also enhances the structural capacities of all Christian denominations to combine efforts and promote rights activities. In fact, much of the financing for these new human rights committees in Catholic countries comes from Protestant sources in Western Europe and North America.

Regarding the scope and extent of activities of these new programs, it is clear that most of the aid they provide goes for the defense of classic civil rights—the right of habeas corpus, the right to a fair trial, the right to be protected against torture. A broad consensus exists on the legitimacy of these individual rights—especially among funding agencies in Europe and the United States. The programs are also able to perform humanitarian functions, such as allowing prison visits, improving the living situation in jails, enhancing communication between those detained and their families, and providing food, clothing, and health care for families. In some instances (such as the Chilean, Brazilian, and Paraguayan cases), churches have been able to promote some social and economic rights; for example, the right to work or the right to participate in social organizations of one's own choice.

In no case, however, have churches been able by themselves to affect major changes in the political and economic structures underlying or causing the violations of civil, social, and economic rights. Where changes have occurred in patterns of repression (e.g., in Paraguay), they have been due primarily to pressures by foreign governments, or in conjunction with foreign pressure and activity by both religious and secular domestic forces within the countries themselves (e.g., in Bolivia). Even in such cases, it is too soon to predict whether a fundamental reorientation of political and economic institutions will occur, or whether this "decompression" is merely a transitory concession. Furthermore, where military regimes are strongly entrenched and unyielding to foreign and domestic opposition to their policies (e.g., in Chile and Brazil), not even momentary amelioration has been achieved by the churches.

What these human rights committees and other new pastoral programs of the churches among the poor have accomplished over the past several years, however, is to sensitize many bishops, clergy, and religious to the close relationship between the existing unequal arrangement of economic and political power and the systematic violation of civil rights of individuals and groups. In almost all of the major episcopal documents on human rights originating from the subcontinent recently, there has been a strong appeal for changes in basic institutional structures and more equitable distribution of wealth and resources in order to remove the causes of murder, torture, and kidnapping.

The bishops see very clearly that those being persecuted are predominantly spokespersons for the poor or working-class leaders themselves. A major reason for their being attacked, claim the bishops, is their demand that society meet the basic human needs of their people in a more just fashion—employment, housing, education, and health care. Now that guerrilla activity has subsided significantly throughout the region, the primary reason for repression is that the poor are demanding social and economic rights. The hierarchies, therefore, emphasize the necessity to affect changes in economic development models based on national security ideology and manipulated by elites toward other strategies of development, which include more equitable distribution of land and income as they proceed. They also stress the importance of allowing intermediary structures of social and political participation (e.g., labor unions, political parties, civic and professional associations or neighborhood groups) between the state and the individual, both to affect such changes and to provide accountability of power.

Despite these arguments on the close interrelationship of defense of civil rights, fulfillment of human needs, and responsible uses of power, there is no indication that the bishops' words are, or will be, taken seriously in the near future by those controlling economic resources or wielding coercive authority. But such pronouncements nevertheless are important because they provide an alternative moral perspective and force which challenges the legitimacy and pervasiveness of national security ideology underlying all of these rights violations. An important power of the Church, therefore, lies at the deeper ideological and spiritual level. The influence is potentially very great, since Christianity is deeply embedded in Latin American culture, and people, even if they do not practice their religion regularly, still have emotional ties to the Church. This is particularly true for middle class groups and the poor themselves. Not only have the hierarchies refused to give complete legitimation to national security regimes (as they often did to earlier authoritarian or oligarchic governments in Latin America), but the latent moral force of the church (which is most notable in crisis situations) is helping to prevent the values and symbols of this new secular ideology from gaining complete public acceptance.

In addition to this moral contribution to the defense of human rights in the subcontinent, the other most significant accomplishment by the Church at the domestic level has been to provide alternate forms of participation which can nourish a critical consciousness as well as a spirit of resistance among Indians, peasants, and workers. The new small communities and other lay training programs in the churches are acting as social incubators for future generations of leaders of the poor, and are providing them with a sense of hope and solidarity. These organizations are counterproductive to the efforts by dictatorial regimes attempting to construct a new model of society and new type of person completely dominated by state power and terror. In the long run, these are probably the most significant contributions Latin American churches are making to affect eventual structural transformations and return to democratic procedures. At the very least, they are blunting the impact of repression generated both by the military and economic elites to maintain their power.

In an immediate sense, the impact of these new programs on the churches themselves has been profound. In some instances the programs have precipitated outright persecution which reaches the highest level of church leadership. This has helped to sensitize many bishops to the plight of the lower clergy, religious, and working-class laity in a way that otherwise would not have been possible. Further, these experiences are making them aware, for the first time, that the real threat to the institutional interests of the Church comes from the right and not the left. It is shifting the priorities of the Church to a closer identification with the poor, since these people make the most pressing demands on the Church's time and resources, while showing the greatest willingness to participate in its new evangelical efforts.

Serious internal tensions and contradictions have resulted from these new directions in the Church which place important limits on how far efforts to defend human rights can go. Upper-middle-class groups, reactionary Catholics, and military officers are by and large outraged at this betrayal by church leaders of their interests. These groups wield considerable influence not only in secular society but within the church itself, since they still provide significant financial support for other Church-sponsored activities—schools, hospitals, charity funds, and the like. They can also mount effective terror campaigns against church personnel (as witnessed by TFP activities in Chile, Brazil, and Argentina), while exploiting internal divisions in the hierarchy and clergy.

A primary Catholic concern (reinforced strongly by the Vatican) is to maintain the public unity of the institution at all possible costs, while remaining open to minister to the spiritual needs of all classes of people. The Catholic Church has traditionally opted for a church rather than sect model of religious development, and this places theological limitations on its prophetic capacities as well as on its ability

to represent the interests of any one social group forcefully and consistently. Both political and religious factors, therefore, influence the
official policies of churches as articulated by bishops. They do not
want to alienate elite groups any more than necessary, and are not
likely to write them off on behalf of human rights programs which bring
an all-out conflict between the Church and secular power.

Furthermore, as was seen in the case of Bolivia in relation to the
clergy, and in Chile and Argentina in regard to money, international
sources of support for human rights programs create some problems
for the Church at the domestic level. Not only are some indigenous
groups within the local churches suspicious of those with access to
resources (and therefore, power) from abroad, but the military governments of these countries are sensitive to foreign influences due to their
exaggerated sense of nationalism. While this dependency of the
churches has not yet become a major limitation on church programs,
it certainly has caused tension. It is also probable that this vulnerability
in terms of foreign personnel and finances will be another factor keeping
bishops from allowing an all-out confrontation between Church and
state on behalf of human rights.

Finally, despite recent commitments to the interests of the poor and
new working-class receptiveness to church activities and participation,
all of the churches in the southern region have only begun the process
of penetrating and understanding lower-class culture. Small base
communities are just beginning to take root, and the vast majority of
poor still have very little formal contact with the churches. Churches
are, on the whole, very underdeveloped institutions in this area. It will
be some time before new communities can function effectively and
autonomously sufficient to withstand sustained frontal attacks on
their personnel by repressive governments.

The important factor, however, is that these new programs have
started to operate. Moreover, given the clear intentions of the military
to stay in power for a long time, the programs analyzed here are more
than short-term emergency efforts. If both international pressure and
cautious diplomacy by the bishops can prevent prolonged Church-
state confrontations, they may very well grow stronger. Such new
grassroots structures could be important instruments for bringing
about long-term change in both Church and society. The Church,
therefore, while not a consistent or strong defender of rights, provider
of needs, or instrument of power, does wield some crucial moral and

structural influence in this region of the continent—influence which may be quite significant for the future direction of these societies.

NOTES

1. The protection of national security has been emphasized by these military regimes in their attempts to provide themselves with a sense of legitimacy and justification for systematic repression. National security ideology includes among its major components anti-Marxism, patriotism, technocratic value-free planning, and the subordination of personal rights to the interests of the state.

2. Several international organizations have documented these violations on the basis of on-site fact-finding investigations and personal testimonies of individuals or groups within these Latin American countries. Included are Amnesty International, the International League of Human Rights, the International Commission of Jurists, the Commission on Human Rights of the United Nations Economic and Social Council, and the Inter-American Commission on Human Rights. Amnesty International, for example, it its 1975-1976 annual report, indicated that 80% of all reported incidents of serious torture to date have occurred in Latin America.

3. Two very useful collections of 14 of these documents have recently been published in English by the Latin American Documentation Service of the U.S. Catholic Conference. See references for individual citations in the LADOC "Keyhole" Series.

Mitchell (1977) provides an excellent summary of the general analysis and principles laid out in these documents regarding the interrelationship of human rights, human needs, and political and economic power.

4. This new emphasis in the Church towards service of the world, especially the poor, was officially endorsed in the documents of the Second Vatican Council (1962-1965), as well as by the Latin American bishops themselves in their second General Conference held in Medellín, Colombia, in August 1968. At this meeting, representatives of every episcopal conference in Latin America committed the Church to act as a "catalyst in the temporal realm in an authentic attitude of service." As pastors they dedicated themselves "to denounce everything which, opposing justice destroys peace," "to defend the rights of the poor and oppressed," and "to encourage and favor efforts of the people to create and develop their own grass-roots organizations for the consolidation of their rights and the search for justice."

5. Although Paraguay has not recently come under military rule, the twenty-four-year-old military government of General Stroessner in the last two years has escalated its repressive measures considerably against *campesino* leaders. The Paraguayan churches responded to this recent increase in terror by setting up an Emergency Committee on Human Rights.

Despite systematic violation of human rights by the Uruguayan government since the 1973 civil-military coup, religious groups have not been able to establish programs to promote human rights comparable to those in sister churches in other areas of the Southern Cone. The reasons for this are due to the long-standing weakness of the Uruguayan Church, the heavily secularized culture in Uruguay, and the effective neutralization of the Church by an alliance among conservative Catholics, the press, and the military.

In Peru, the military have not been guilty of violations of human rights (especially civil rights) to the same degree as their counterparts in Brazil, Chile, Argentina, Paraguay, Bolivia, and Uruguay. In the last two years, however, very repressive social and economic measures (particularly against workers in the form of wage controls and restrictions of union activities) have occurred. While the Church has not felt it necessary to establish human rights committees specifically to meet the needs of prisoners or families of disappeared persons, the bishops have begun to criticize severely the economic policies of the government along the same lines as the hierarchies in Brazil, Chile, and Argentina.

6. Two bishops were responsible for inaugurating this commission—Auxiliary Bishop Fernando Ariztía of the Western Zone of the Catholic Archdiocese of Santiago and Bishop Helmut Frenz of the Lutheran Church of Chile. Both men had been particularly active in programs helping poor before the coup and had been exposed to many cases of cruelty against their people in the days immediately following September 11th. Frenz was also a German and had direct access to immediate funding from Western Europe, including the World Council of Churches in Geneva. Both of these men urged other Catholic, Protestant, and Jewish leaders to join them (including Cardinal Silva), and together they formally established the Committee of Cooperation for Peace on October 6, 1973. Ariztía and Frenz served as cochairpersons.

7. Between October 1973 and December 1975, the various projects sponsored or assisted by funds coming through the Committee for Peace reached over 100,000 persons needing legal, medical, or economic assitance in addition to those workers assisted by 126 small enterprises set up in various parts of the country (U.S. Congress, House, 1976: 59).

8. Many of the self-help projects in these local communities (e.g., soup kitchens) are also assisted by the Vicariate of Solidarity.

9. Not only did high inflation, corruption, and incompetence characterize the democratic regime of Joaõ Goulart between 1961 and 1964, but many in the country felt that communists had a strong possibility of taking over the country as a result of this turmoil. With the exception of Chile and Cuba, the Brazilian left was the best organized Marxist movement in Latin America in the early 1960s, especially in rural areas of the northeast.

10. Between 1966 and 1971 several conflicts between the government and some bishops and priests occurred when the latter began to criticize publicly the economic policies of the government, which favored industrial development at the expense of social programs to assist the poor in interior regions. By 1969 eleven foreign priests had been expelled (of over 5,000 in the country) and one priest closely associated with Dom Helder Camara had been assassinated.

11. An English translation of the section dealing with repression and torture appears in LADOC Volume I, No. 13 (June, 1970).

12. "Operation Hope," begun by Dom Helder Camara, is one of the best-known examples of grassroots self-help programs in Northeastern Brazil. Begun in 1967, it has sponsored projects in literacy training, housing, health, and recreation in 13 urban and rural communities in the Recife-Olinda diocese. Materials and salaries for specialists are provided by the West German bishops, but most of the participants are volunteers. In addition to basic humanitarian aid, there has been a consistent emphasis on raising the social consciousness of the people. Small group discussions of community problems, identification of desirable social and economic objectives, and petitions to local authorities for better services have all become integral parts of this program.

13. Thousands of Indians and peasants have been living on these lands for years and therefore qualify by law for ownership. Nevertheless, they have never obtained legal titles from the government and now are being evicted, and in some cases murdered, by both security forces and private land developers.

14. This situation of "decompression," begun after President Ernesto Geisel took office in 1974, was only in part due to urging by the Church. The accumulated effects of rapid economic growth (primarily favoring the upper- and middle-income sectors) and organized terrorism since 1968 have solidified the power of the government. The present administration could easily afford to ease up on some of the repression and make concessions, as none of these changes would create a serious threat to military power, and tight control is still maintained over the major decision-making centers of society.

15. Security dossiers are now prepared on bishops and priests identified with these new Church-sponsored communities and programs. Among the questions included in the two-page questionnaire to be completed by police agents are: Does the bishop or priest try to disfigure the person of Christ? Does he try to disfigure the person of God? Does he talk about *comunidades de base?*

16. A priest with first-hand knowledge of deacon programs told me of his admiration for the men training to be deacons who return to groups time and time again even after being arrested and tortured.

17. One of the key government strategies used to discredit the churches is to accuse priests and ministers of betraying their ministry and acting as guerilla priests and ministers of betraying their ministry and acting as guerilla agents. The chief of the security police, Pastor Coronel, made a report to the Colorado Party in 1976 naming several missionaries as conspirators in a clandestine movement known as the OPM (Organización Político Militar). In addition, the government has produced a number of popular pamphlets and catechisms to be used in religious classes in public schools in which communism is presented as the cardinal sin for Christians, and images and activities of "bad priests" are sketched and rejected as being against true religion (Ministerio de Educación y Culto, 1977a, b).

18. In February, 1977, Cardinal Evaristo Arns of São Paulo, Brazil, personally visited the office of the Committee of Churches for Emergency Aid in a spirit of fraternal solidarity, only the third Roman Catholic Cardinal ever to visit the country. He held a press conference with Archbishop Rolon of Asunción, and both praised the committee publicly for its important work.

Other Protestant and Catholic church persons from Western Europe and North America have also visited the committee over the past two years, and thus have added to its reputation as being internationally supported in the eyes of the Paraguayan government.

19. Stephansky and Helfield in their latest report for the International League of Human Rights conclude that:

Notwithstanding the indications of amelioration, we found no compelling evidence of change either in the overall gravity of the human rights crisis or in the character of the basic institutions underlying that crisis.

Most importantly, the institutions that are at the root of the repressions of last year remain unchanged.

What our mission encountered was an interlude of amelioration, a welcome one to be sure, but nevertheless an interlude to an uncertain future. There have been interludes before, of the kind we encountered, for example, in the periods that preceded episodes of repression of 1958-1959, of 1965 and of 1969, as well as the period that preceded the most recent repressions of 1975-1976. Whether the present interlude will end with another repressive episode in a continuing cycle of repression and alleviation, or whether it can mark the beginning of an era of more durable government, will depend on governmental decisions yet to be taken [1977: 12, 17, 18].

20. Bolivia has one of the highest percentages of foreign-born priests of all Latin American churches, with 80% of the clergy coming from abroad.

21. I am most grateful to Rev. Eric de Wasseige, O.P., for much of this information on the Justice and Peace Commission of Bolivia. He worked on this commission for two years before being expelled from Bolivia in March 1975, and is now with the Washington Office on Latin America (WOLA), a Church-sponsored organization in Washington, D.C., set up by Protestant denominations in the United States to monitor human rights violations in Latin America.

22. The Commission was later reopened but placed under the direct control of the hierarchy and was constituted by a more conservative group of laity and clerics than its predecessor.

23. As the hunger strike spread, so did the demands of the participating groups. These included a withdrawal of military personnel from mining villages, restoration of union rights, and the rehiring of miners fired for strike activities.

24. Several civilian candidates competed in the July 1978 elections against the hand-picked candidate of Banzer, General Pareda Asbún. The latter won the election, but, according to reports by international observer teams, only with the help of massive fraud. Amidst mounting domestic and international pressures for a new election, a week later General Pareda Asbún engineered a counter-coup (very possibly at Banzer's suggestion). Hence, once more democratic procedures were thwarted, despite strong efforts by both domestic and international groups to the contrary.

25. Some observers in Bolivia believe that the really effective check on Banzer in early 1978 was a public remark made by the U.S. AID Director in Bolivia at that time: "President Carter believes that the Bolivian electoral process in 1978 is very important, not only for Bolivia, but for the whole of Latin America."

26. The best account of the origins and development of this organization, known as "Movement of Priests for the Third World," has been written by Dodson (1973).

27. The deaths occurred in an area of the country where the right-wing Catholic organization, "Tradition, Family and Fatherland," is active, and after Bishop Angelelli had spoken against the military coup.

28. Bishop Carlos Gattinoni of the Methodist Church was chosen as the first president of the Permanent Assembly, and Monsignors Jaime de Nevares and Enrique Angelelli (died 1976) also became members of the coordinating committee when the Assembly was formed.

29. In January 1978, the government did acknowledge that it was holding 3,700 persons and began to release some of their names. This concession, however, seems to have been the result of international pressure by the governments of France and the United States more than domestic church appeals. The French government increased diplomatic pressure in Argentina after two French nuns were kidnapped in December 1977. U.S. Secretary of State Vance made a trip to Argentina in late 1977 and also expressed this country's extreme concern over the human rights situation in Argentina. President Carter, during his visit to France in December 1977, stated publicly: "The Argentine situation is the most serious in our continent."

REFERENCES

Amnesty International (1976a) The Amnesty International Report, 1975-1976. London: Amnesty International Publications.

————— (1976b) "Report of an Amnesty International mission to Argentina." Amnesty International Publications 6 (November 15): 7-10.

Argentina Outreach (1977) "Church members under attack." No. 2 (January-February): 16.

Asamblea Permanente de los Derechos Humanos de Bolivia (1978) "20 días de huelga de hambre!" Presencia (January 15). La Paz.

————— (1977) La declaración universal de los derechos humanos y la represión en Bolivia (October). La Paz.

————— (1976) Primera reunión de la Asamblea Permanente de los derechos humanos en Bolivia 22 (Deciembre). La Paz.

BARBOSA, R. (1978) "Issue of communism in church-state relations in Brazil." LADOC 8 (January-February): 24-27.

————— (1977) "New hope for Paraguay's prisoners." Christian Century 94 (March 30): 301-302.

BONO, A. (1977) "Cross vs. sword: Catholic aid to poor in Brazil is worsening conflict with military." Wall Street Journal (June 2): 1, 20.

BREWIN, A., L. DUCLOS and D. McDONALD (1976) "One gigantic prison." Inter-Church Committee on Chile (November). Toronto. (mimeo)

BRUNEAU, T. C. (1974) The Political Transformation of the Brazilian Catholic Church. London: Cambridge Univ. Press.

Buenos Aires Herald (1977a) "APDH seeks disappearance probe." (August 12).

————— (1977b) "Human rights assembly petitions the president." (March 23).

Catholic Institute for International Relations (1976) Death and Violence in Argentina. London: Catholic Institute for International Relations.

CELADEC [Comisión Evangélica Latinoamérica de Educación Cristiana] (1977) Iglesia Argentina: Fidelidad al evangelio? Lima: CELADEC.

CELAM [Council of Latin American Bishops] (1970) "Peace," p. 80 in Vol. 2 of The Church in the Present Day Transformation of Latin America in the Light of the Council. Bogotá: General Secretariat of CELAM.

Centro de Proyección Cristiana (1977) "Documento del episcopado Boliviano sobre la misión de la Iglesia ante la sociedad histórica del país," in Los Derechos Humanos hoy en Latinoámerica: las declaraciones y documentos de la Iglesia universal y las Naciones Unidas. Lima: Centro de Proyección Cristiana.

CEP [Centro de Estudios y Publicaciones] (1976) Bolivia: 1971-1976; Pueblo, Estado, Iglesia. Lima: CEP.

COMBLIN, J. (1977) "La doctrina de la seguridad nacional," in Dos ensayos sobre seguridad nacional. Two volumes. Santiago: Vicaría de la Solidaridad.

Comité de las Iglesias (1977a) Boletín Informativo (Asunción) (Septiembre): 1-6.

————— (1977b) Boletín Informativo (Julio): 1-6.

————— (1977c) Boletín Informativo (Mayo): 1-6.

Comité Permanente del Episcopado de Chile (1975) "Evangelio y paz." Mensaje Volume 24 (Octubre): 462-473. Santiago.

CNBB [Conferencia Nacional dos Bispos do Brasil] (1970) "Documento pastoral do

Brasilia." Revista Eclesiastica Brasiliera Volume 30 (Junho): 415-425. Brasilia.

CULHANE, E. K. (1975) "Strange alliance in Uruguay." America 17 (May).

El Diario (1978a) "Clero diocesano pronuncia sobre la misión de la Iglesia." 29 (Enero). La Paz.

—— (1978b) "Relaciones sobre la infiltración comunista en la Iglesia Boliviana." 7 (Febrero).

DODSON, M. (1973) "Religious innovation and the politics of Argentina: a study of the movement of priests for the Third World." Ph.D. dissertation. Indiana University.

DOMINGUEZ, J. (1975) "Smuggling." Foreign Policy No. 20 (Fall): 87-96, 161-164.

Estudos de CNBB (1976a) Pastoral Social, No. 10 São Paulo: Ediçaoes Paulinas.

GILFEATHER, K. (1976) "Women in ministry." America 2 (October): 191-194.

HOPE, M. (1975) "The people's priest." Lithopinion [New York] (Spring): 46-55.

Latin America Political Report (1978a) "Bolivia: delaying tactics." (February 10): 46.

—— (1978b) "Argentina: whose balloon?" 12 (February 3): 37-38.

—— (1978c) "Bolivia: the will of the people." 12 (January 27): 29-30.

—— (1978d) "Bolivia: heavens above." 12 (January 13): 12-13.

—— (1977) "Argentina: war of words." 11 (December 3): 397-399.

Latinamerica Press (1977a) "Armed band seizes members of Argentina multichurch group." 9 (December 22): 1-2.

—— (1977b) "Bishops challenge Peru's economic policies." 9 (July 21): 3, 4, 8.

—— (1975) "Government bars bishops' letter on violence in Uruguay." 7 (October 16): 1.

LERNOUX, P. (1977) "Church cowed by Uruguayan military." Report to Alicia Patterson Foundation (January 18): 8-page memo.

Lucha (1978) "Bolivian hunger strike." (January-February): 21-24. South Bend, In.

El Mercurio (1978) "La Inter-American Foundation y sus programas en Chile." 25 (Enero): 24. Santiago.

METHOL FERRE, A. (1977) "Sobre la actual ideología de la seguridad nacional," in Dos Ensayos Sobre Seguridad Nacional. Two volumes. Santiago: Vicaría de la Solidaridad.

Ministerio de educación y Culto (1977a) "Estudiano felices sin comunismo." Asunción: Ministerio de educación y culto. (mimeo)

—— (1977b) "Las verdades anticomunistas de hoy." Asunción: Ministerio de educación y Culto. (mimeo)

MITCHELL, R. A. (1977) "Latin American bishops speak: human rights, needs and power." Washington D.C.: Woodstock Theological Center. (unpublished)

Movimiento Ecuménico por los Derechos Humanos (1976) "Documento Base." 9 (Junio). Buenos Aires. (mimeo)

OVIEDO CAVADA, C. [ed.] (1974) "Declaración de comité permanente del episcopado sobre la situación del país," p. 174 in Documentos de Episcopado Chile, 1970-1973. Santiago: Ediciones Mundo.

Sociedad Chilena de Defensa de la Tradición, Familia y Propiedad (1976) La Iglesia del Silencio en Chile. Santiago: Edunsa.

STEPHANSKY, B. S. and R. J. ALEXANDER (1976) "Report of the Commission of Enquiry into human rights in Paraguay of the International League for Human Rights, July 6-15, 1976." U.S. Congress, House Subcommittee on International Organizations of the Committee on International Relations, Human Rights in Uruguay and Paraguay, 94th Congress, 2nd session: 161-218.

STEPHANSKY, B. S. and D. M. HELFELD (1977) "Denial of human rights in Paraguay: report of the second commission of enquiry of the international league for human rights." (December): 4-5. New York.

SZULC, T. (1977) "'Recompression' in Brazil." New Republic 7 (May): 19-21.

USCC [United States Catholic Conference] (1978a) "Bolivians seek democracy and freedom." LADOC (Washington, D.C.) 8, 3 (January-February): 44-47.

——— (1978b) "Sigaud versus Casaldaliga and Balduino." LADOC Volume 8, 3 (January-February): 15-23.

——— (1977a) "The Common Good and the Present Situation." Argentina Episcopal Conference. LADOC Keyhole Series 16: 23-29.

——— (1977b) "Our life as a nation." Chilean Episcopal Conference. LADOC Keyhole Series 15: 41-54.

——— (1977c) "Christian requirements of a political order." National Conference of Brazilian Bishops. LADOC Keyhole Series 16: 54-67.

——— (1976a) "A Christian reflection for the people of Argentina." LADOC Keyhole Series 15: 16-20.

——— (1976b) "Amidst persecutions and consolations." Episcopal Conference of Paraguay. LADOC Keyhole Series 15: 6-15.

——— (1976c) "Paraguay churches unite their efforts." LADOC 6, 65 (July-August): 19.

——— (1976d) "Pastoral message to the people of God." National Conference of Brazilian Bishops. LADOC Keyhole Series 15: 21-35.

U.S. Congress, House Subcommittee on International Organizations of the Committee on International Relations (1976) "Prepared statement of Jose Zalaquett Daher, chief legal council, committee of cooperation for peace in Chile," p. 59 in Chile: The Status of Human Rights and Its Relationship to U.S. Economic Assistance Programs. 94th Congress, second session.

Vicaría de la Solidaridad (1977) "Vicaría de la solidaridad: un año de labor." (Santiago) (Enero). Santiago. (mimeo)

VIDAL, D. (1978) "Paraguay enjoys old siestas and the new boom." New York Times 18 (February): 6.

WILDE, M. D. (1977) "Paraguayans savor Christian solidarity." The Christian Century 94 (March 30): 302.

Part III

PATTERNS OF INNOVATION

Introduction

It is difficult to disentangle the impact of new ideas and new experiences in the process of change in the Latin American churches. In some cases, innovations have grown out of new understandings of religion and/or politics which have led to the development of new organizational structures and goals. In others, the experience of new ways of acting—both within the churches and in society at large—have played a major role in transforming outlooks. In any case, it is probably unwise to draw too sharp a separation between ideas and experience. These are *dialectical* processes: ideas, structures, and experiences all move and change together in a continuous flow of mutual impact.

In this overall process, several key elements stand out, most notably a renewed commitment to the poor and a general concern for building structures of community. Consider first the issue of the poor. Of course, the Church has always been concerned to help the poor, but the commitment at issue here goes far beyond conventional charity to enjoin on religious people a positive obligation to share lives and experiences of the poor. The depth of this commitment and the enormous implications it holds for the Church are the subject of Katherine Gilfeather's contribution. Gilfeather's analysis of the experiences of religious women living in marginal areas in Chile brings out very sharply the impact of experience on these sisters, particularly with respect to the content of their religious life and to the nature of their role within the institutional church. Her work suggests the great potential such new experiences have for transforming the inner life of the Church as a community. But she documents as well the high degree of frustration these women find in the Church as their new experiences generate modes of perception, belief, and action which find little or no place within the formal structures of the ecclesiastical institution.

A stress on experience means a concern for ways of living together and sharing the joys and troubles, the pleasures and distress of life. At Puebla, a major effort was made to reassert the values of fraternity, sharing, and participation, and to stimulate Latin American Catholics as they build new structures of community. A centrally important expression of these goals has been the widespread development of small, homogeneous groups of committed Christians—known variously as "basic Christian communities," "base communities," or "ecclesial base communities."

Thomas C. Bruneau examines the origins and implications of the rapid growth of base communities both in general and in the important case of Brazil. Such communities provide alternatives to the traditional structures of the Church. They are more flexible than the large and typically understaffed parishes, and moreover provide an atmosphere of open, democratic participation which is a new element in the life of the Church. Bruneau considers in detail the way the experience of democratic participation in these communities may spill over into other areas of social and political life. At the very least, they are a source of new experiences and new orientations—a surrogate for the participation Brazilian society as a whole denies. At the most, they stimulate commitments to activism and change with vast implications for the Church and society alike.

What is the response of churches to drastic social change? We have already seen elements of a response to changes of a conservative kind, but what of revolutionary change? In contemporary Latin America, Cuba since 1959 offers a fascinating laboratory of change, and Margaret Crahan provides a synthetic view of the impact of the Cuban Revolution on the nation's weak and backward churches, both Catholic and Protestant. Her analysis sheds considerable light on the way in which institutional transformation and changes in the sheer volume and meaning of religious affiliation and practice go together.

The final article in this volume, by Alexander Wilde, reflects in general terms on the processes explored in these pages. He notes the emergence of a common *Latin American* perspective among the once fragmented churches of the region, as they develop common organizational structures and experience similar political pressures in various nations. Wilde highlights the way in which new ideas and experiences in Latin American Catholicism have taken on deeper and broader significance because of the impact of authoritarian military regimes. At issue is not a choice between theology, experience, or political context as the single key to understanding the process of change. Rather, it is the interaction and mutual impact of these elements which makes the recent development of religion and politics in Latin America so uniquely fascinating. Looking at the years since Medellín and projecting for the future, Wilde notes the extent to which Puebla provides grounds for continued growth, change, and openness. Ironically, it seems that as political structures have grown more closed and authoritarian throughout the region, the churches (once models of hierarchical rigidity themselves) have moved in the opposite direction: praising the values of participation and democracy while in practice defending and preserving an open space for hope and change.

8

WOMEN RELIGIOUS, THE POOR, AND THE INSTITUTIONAL CHURCH IN CHILE

Sister KATHERINE ANNE GILFEATHER, M.M.

The Church in Chile, in its efforts to reach and evangelize the poor, crippled by a gradually diminishing clergy, has over more than a decade come to place extraordinary emphasis on the presence of religious personnel in marginal urban and rural areas. This pastoral priority has induced considerable numbers of religious women to leave their original works (especially education) to take part in the direct apostolate in marginal areas, while the majority of foreign religious women who have recently arrived have opted to follow their example.

The style of life chosen by these women is simple, often in the extreme, but is in all cases a brusque change from their previous standard of living. Though these changes were necessary to achieve the desired identification with the poor, nevertheless, there have been secondary effects of this pastoral approach which require consideration and some form of evaluation at this moment in the history of the Chilean Church. It is our opinion that these women present a microcosmic reflection of the Church itself and its sincere struggle to remain faithful to its interior dynamism, which is the Spirit working through human history.

The New Testament itself gives proof that the first Christian women were proficient scholars of sacred scripture and that they assumed roles of considerable leadership; it was not, however, a participation without problems. Although the New Testament reflects a Judaic theological and sociological frame of reference with respect to women, the Pauline theology of "equality in Christ" offered a new religioussocial framework for man-woman relations in the Christian community—a truly revolutionary approach whose implications were not then understood.

Perhaps the major source of information on the status of women in the first Christian communities is found in the Acts of the Apostles. The first clue we find which throws light on the status of women in these communities is contained in the story of Paul's conversion. He had asked and was given permission to arrest members of the new Church, women as well as men (Acts 9: 1-2). If women had been secure, under the dominion of their husbands in private and silenced in the churches in public, there would have been no need to persecute them. The punishment and confinement of men would have been sufficient. We see the same situation in Antiochia, Thyatira, and Beroea, where women enjoyed great influence in Christian communities. They were designated as prophets; others received authority to dedicate themselves to teaching and interpreting the central concepts of the faith. Acts abounds with data concerning the participation of early Christian women in the affairs of the community and its cultic life. There is no doubt that this participation was significant in attracting other women from every social class who became active at all levels of the institutional life of the Church.

However, the concept of "equality in Christ" was obscured in the later writings of St. Paul; what he understood as a temporal ethic of the status quo in the context of the "last days" became, two generations later, moral orientations to conserve the same status quo. Having lost the vision of an imminent kingdom, the Church was deprived also of the theology which had helped it to live in that Spirit. As a consequence, we have inherited two diverse messages: the theology of our "equality in Christ," and the day-to-day practice of the subordination of women. Efforts at reconciling these opposing concepts have brought the Church to an ambiguous position of maintaining the status quo on the one hand by a subordination of women on the social level, and an affirmation of the concept of equality as functional in the "world to come" on the other. The effect of this almost Gnostic dualism has been confusion, distortion, and the consequent elimination of feminine influence from the Church's public sphere. She might aspire to sainthood, to martyrdom, to being a teacher in the community, but could never intrude beyond the clerical pale. Women have thus been excluded from roles of equal responsibility with men in the institutional, theological, and spiritual lives of the Church, thereby impoverishing it and debilitating its pastoral action.

With the above as a statement of the situation to date, we focused our research precisely on the pastoral action of the Church in Chile and upon the most numerous sector of pastoral personnel—religious women (Catholic sisters). We chose what we felt to be a particularly creative group of these women, those living and working in marginal areas, in order to evaluate the consequences of their identification with the poor for their own lives and for the Chilean Church as a whole. Our choice created, in turn, a need to face the frustrations of these women in many areas and at all levels, and to relate this to "structures" operative in their institutional-Church relations, congregational ties, previous formation, vocational commitment, doctrinal stance, planning, schedules, and even in their attitudes toward work and play. Having described the basic content of this paper, we would now like to explore the historical evolution of the problem.

The Problem in its Historical Dimension

When we speak of the dynamic of history, whether with respect to the Church or to humanity in general, we are speaking in sociological terms of social change. We would like to stress four dimensions of change—individualization, innovation, concern with power, and secularization—(Nisbet, 1970: 370-394) which we feel are basic to any discussion of social change, but seem particularly applicable to the area under discussion. The first of these is "emergence of the individual" as a focus and concern, thereby replacing the restrictive social codes and traditional communities of long duration. This poses serious challenges to the individual's relationship to religion, and to the institution of the Church, which has traditionally offered a buffer in man's relations with the larger world. The person seeking refuge against a loss of identity in that world has several options: (a) a position which affirms the world and sustains dialogue with the environment, offering the possibility of a redemptive experience; (b) a sectarian stance in search of a group whose philosophy contradicts the actual values of society in a dramatic form (Marty, 1960: 125-132); and (c) the "community" solution, which offers support rather than isolation. Experience proves that the first position is difficult; religious energies tend to be dissipated and identify with the very upheaval the individual seeks to escape. The second stance is attractive but ultimately dangerous in the light of its tendency to escapism. Only the third option offers its members mutual support, helping them achieve the goal of the first position without falling into its inherent traps. It appears to offer the shock absorber absent in the traditional institutionalized bureaucratic Church.

This option is found within the Church in Basic Christian Communities, in numerous orientation and formation groups grounded structurally on small homogeneous communities of mutual support, and also among religious communities. In great part these have rejected traditional concepts and the restrictions of antiquated and dysfunctional structures in order to search for new forms of community life in circumstances more in accord with their Gospel values. A graphic example is the case of religious women working in apostolates among marginal groups, particularly those living in urban *poblaciónes* or "shanty-towns." Their rejection of traditional structures is apparently rooted in their search for something more radical, more authentic—a simple life style in an atmosphere of mutual support. Their search has led them to ongoing innovation, which is our second dimension of change.

Over the centuries, the Church, like all institutions, has repeatedly faced the need to change in order to carry out its divine-human role and function. This need of functioning in a world in flux among men and women whose needs are profound and diverse has brought the Church to innovation, not as a *structure*, but rather through the brotherhood of its members. These people, moved by a genuine desire to make the message of Christ known and understood and, in part, by a rebellion against the dysfunctionality of Church structures and the alienation of its hierarchy from contemporary reality, have begun a voyage toward the future in search of something better. They have made new discoveries along the way simply because they were looking for "something." The place of "luck" or coincidence in the development of new concepts—that is to say, "innovation"—has been called "serendipity" among sociologists and the action of the Spirit among Christians. It is the discovery of valid results not deliberately sought, a happy surprise.

Acceptance of the essential concepts of Vatican II and of the Medellín Documents is the acceptance of the necessity of getting used to "change" as a constant in our lives. It requires a certain elasticity which would make possible the acceptance of changing circumstances without losing the sense of continuity and essential integrity. The effort to achieve this balance has been costly for the Church and its personnel. Faced with the necessity of making the Good News understandable, above all to the poor and marginal, it became obvious that many structures and methods had lost their meaning in the light of actual circumstances, and it is the responsibility of pastoral agents, religious women and priests, to confront and solve pastoral dilemmas. The investigation under consideration was begun to observe the innovations of a group of religious women who aspire to reach the marginal sectors of society through a close identification with all aspects of that lifestyle. The changes which this determination brought about in their lives, their spirituality, and their general attitude toward the Church and its structures, are the focus of this study. One such change in attitude can be observed with respect to power/authority structures in the Church.

Although Christian authority has always been based on "service," there does exist an ecclesiastical power structure which has been, up to the present, carefully limited. We have spoken for centuries of "clergy" and "laity," of "pastors" and their "flocks" which follow the voice of the Church. Vatican II restored the dignity of the lay role in a definitive form and, although implementation has been uneven throughout the Church, the importance of this role is growing steadily. Historic circumstances have placed the Church in a pastoral dilemma. Lacking clergy, she has sought among laity and religious replacements in various aspects of the priestly office. Religious women (sisters), above all in Latin American countries, carry immense responsibilities in pastoral work without enjoying even the most minimal participation in the ecclesistical power structure.

There is an ever-growing movement in the Church which insists on a more profound study of the concept of "power," which is seen as coming from God and not from the institution. Thus, the "extension of power" as a dominant consideration, the third dimension of change, has now come to be a reality in the Catholic Church. Religious personnel in close contact with pastoral problems and in charge of actual "innovations" to make the Good News vibrant can perhaps best understand and describe the ecclesiastical power structure in practice, as they are the ones who live out the consequences and feel the limitations which this structure engenders. The religious women under consideration, by their very style of life and identification with the most marginal social groups, offer a particularly interesting case study for our observation.

The last aspect of social change, secularization, is the best known. I prefer to use the Weberian concept of secularization as rationalization for the purpose of this analysis, with emphasis on the influence of rationality over the merely traditional. Above all, "secularization" is seen as the source of those values and attitudes which lead to (1) the rejection of old norms of submission, (2) a heightened esteem for the earth and matter in the context of a future life, (3) respect for the individual and for the individual and collective well-being, (4) control of the environment rather than a passive submission before it, and (5) most important, a preoccupation with the welfare of men and women here and now and not only in their transcendental dimension.

These characteristics of secularization are amply demonstrated in the pastoral action of the Chilean Church. Through the exercise of its prophetic role, in confrontation with an environment hostile to the exercise of human rights, the Church has been "the voice of those without a voice" and the hope of the masses who live in misery and hunger. The hundreds of "dining rooms" for children, only one example of the Church's social action, are in the hands of religious and other dedicated lay women. However, this preoccupation with the human condition, with suffering and despair, has its repercussions among individuals who live and work in constant contact with these groups. These are the repercussions which we probe in the lives of those religious dedicated to the marginal groups in our society—the economically deprived.

The Problem in its
Historical-Ecclesiastical Dimension

Even before the Vatican Council II (1961-1962), the Chilean Episcopate had begun to meet with experts and technicians in the elaboration of a Pastoral Plan for the country. This plan initiated a series of changes which even the Bishops themselves could not have foreseen.

Lamenting the lack of a global pastoral plan, the document underscored the ignorance and divorce from reality which existed within the Church, declaring that

> There is an even greater ignorance of the mission of the Church to a world in the process of rapid changes. Our generation feels called to the construction of a new temporal world and the Church is not sufficiently aware of or present to this great labor. It is ignorant of it for the most part and frequently assumes a hostile attitude toward it. The great problems of vital interest to men today do not appear to preoccupy the Church at all [Centro Bellarmino, 1962].

Nevertheless, the document insisted that "the objective of the apostolate of the Church is man and that this man lives in the world by the will of

God and for this reason must dedicate himself to the world." In the section "Guideline for Action" the document affirms:

> The most fundamental aspect of a reorganization of the apostolate in accord with actual conditions is not primarily the elaboration of a plan for the convenient management of available resources, but rather a cultural mutation, a change of attitude and of spirituality which would be directed toward a continuous theological revision based on a sociological understanding of the reality. Only in this way could rational planning be given a soul [Centro Bellarmino, 1962].

The document stressed the need for penetrating the world, above all the most abandoned sectors. This penetration was seen to require a direct confrontation with socioeconomic problems, if they were serious about giving preference to the laboring class.

Among the priorities mentioned, the plan included a general mission for the entire country during 1963. It was called the "Gran Misión" and it reached the most distant corners of the land and the most abandoned of its people through the recruiting of hundreds of religious women, seminarians, priests, and dedicated laymen and women. An unanticipated consequence of this process was the conscientization of great numbers of religious for whom a hitherto unknown world had been opened. The majority, who had been dedicated to education and were largely unaware of the problems of pastoral work among the poor, now found themselves enriched by their experience, and many were convinced of a new direction in their lives.

At the same time, the Second Vatican Council had a major impact. In the third session, beginning in 1964, the Council had stated firmly that in the Gospel and in the traditional doctrine of the Church "the poor" occupied a place of preference with respect to the announcement of the message of Salvation. The texts considered at this time were among those most discussed, "The Church and the Modern World," "The Missions," "The Religious Life," and so on. These texts were received with enthusiasm and widely promulgated. Study of and reflection on these texts was very common during those years; the great majority of religious had their own copies of the Council Documents and used them for private meditation and reading.

In our opinion it was the conjunction of the Chilean Episcopal concern expressed in the Pastoral Plan (Centro Bellarmino, 1962), the experience of the Gran Misión of 1963, and the strong impact of the results of the Vatican Council II, which prepared the way for the first "experiments" with small communities of religious in the marginal areas of Santiago. Later the Medellín Documents (CELAM, 1969) would lend further support to this new innovation.

With time it was possible to perceive a growing consciousness of the poverty and misery oppressing the masses, of the structural factors perpetuating that situation, and of the urgent need for change. One could observe clear indications of a growing tendency among many religious congregations to commit themselves and their individual members to the interests of the poor, of urban and rural laborers, and to reject former commitments to the dominant and favored minorities of society. This was only a beginning, but the profound significance of this beginning would be apparent only with the passage of time and the accumulation of human experience. It was, nevertheless, a response to the challenge of Medellín directed to religious communities with respect to their mode of service:

> The particular mandate of the Lord to evangelize the poor should bring us to a distribution of our resources and apostolic personnel in such a way that effective preference is given to those sectors that are most in need, economically poor and segregated for whatever cause [CELAM, 1969; author's translation].

Women Living on the Margin of the Institutional Framework

I. WHO SHALL BE INCLUDED?

Our initial desire was to investigate only a sample of those religious working in *poblaciónes* and in rural apostolates throughout the country (Gilfeather, 1978). However, early in the preparations it was decided to include all of these religious with only one condition—that they live as well as work in these marginal areas. This would, of course, greatly limit the numbers involved and keep the study focused on its prime objective. A list was drawn up of 45 small communities in the Santiago area. Personal visits to each group resulted in the elimination of 13 communities whose style of living did not coincide with our criteria for a marginal situation. Thus, 32 small communities became the basis of our investigation in Santiago. Following the same procedure, 58 small communities in 18 dioceses throughout the country were contacted and the purpose of the study explained. Of this number, 50% coincided with our objectives, bringing the total number of small communities under investigation to 61. "Small communities" consisted of, on the average, three persons per house. The total number of individuals involved was 136.

II. THE INSTRUMENT

Initially, our plan included private interviews with each religious woman, but preliminary visits to *poblaciónes* led us to abandon this approach. The varied schedules of these women would have meant three or four visits to each small community in order to interview each member. Time and expense factors led us to choose a more functional approach in a questionnaire which, along with two personal trips to each house for the purpose of coming to know the women, their works, and their situations, became the basis of our study.

It may be well at this point to clarify the meaning of "marginal." As used here, marginal refers to those areas inhabited by the very poor who do not enjoy the normal conveniences of those living in better neighborhoods (light, water, gas, and so on). The situation would be similar to the worst slum areas. The term has also been used to describe works or apostolates outside the normal institutional framework of the Church. As used in Chilean ministerial documents, "marginal" has been reserved for those *poblaciónes* or slum areas without any conveniences (light, water, and so on). We have been less strict here, since we feel that the concept of marginality is very relative. We refer to the effects of an all-pervasive environment, rather than to the absence or presence of certain commodities. (Anyone with first-hand knowledge of life in a *población* is well aware that one can theoretically have water but not be able to get a drop throughout the major part of a day.) In the case of rural Chile, not only are normal commodities and conveniences absent, but most cultural and recreational facilities are also lacking.

In order to determine the real level of poverty of the women in our study, it is necessary to keep in mind that we are looking at the situation from their point of view and most of them come from middle- or upper-middle classes; thus the environment of any *población* would be a serious and drastic change from their normal life situation.

III. THE WOMEN AND THEIR ENVIRONMENT

Sixty two percent of these religious lived in small groups of from two to four persons, with three being the more usual size of a community. Seventy-one percent were from 30 to 50 years of age, a relatively young group except when one considers the rigors of this style of life. Education levels were especially high, as almost 70% had university degrees or at least Normal School diplomas. The majority were foreigners and 67% of them had spent less than 10 years in the country.

The largest portion of responses came from those in urban marginal sectors (69.2%), while 30.8% lived in rural areas. Over 60% had lived in a marginal sector from one to six years, while only 30% had been there longer. It is interesting to compare the years in which the majority of religious began to live in marginal areas with possible factors of influence. These coincide with the publication of the first reflections on the Medellín Documents (CELAM, 1969) and the letters and Pastoral Plan of the Chilean hierarchy (Centro Bellarmino, 1962). These last designated work among marginal sectors as top priority in the allocation of pastoral resources (1970-1974). The years of greatest influx into the marginal areas coincide with a political period which gave emphasis to the promotion of the laborer and the marginal in general, penetrating society with the mystique of the "New Man." After 1974 there is a notable decline in the number of religious women going to live in marginal areas.

It was rather more complex to identify the principal work of these women. The majority worked at more than one type of job, often combining a profession with part-time pastoral activities. Financial factors are responsible for a good part of this complexity; many religious are forced to take on remunerative work to defray the expenses which the small allotment from the diocese cannot begin to cover.

Together with the size, placement, and activities of the community, we should consider the history of the group—the path followed by each member as they came together. Only 8.8% were assigned to their present situation by superiors, while 91.2% were living in marginal areas by their own choice. It is clear that religious women are particularly sensitive to the voice of the hierarchy in Chile in the selection of apostolic activities, and ecclesiastical priorities as expressed in letters and pastoral plans had a major impact in their decisions.

This is extremely positive from the position of the institutional Church, but it is important to remember that new priorities may have unanticipated consequences, such as unwittingly damaging other works which also have their place in the pastoral life of the Church. An overly simplistic type of focus can give exaggerated emphasis to one area, making others appear old-fashioned and unworthy of approval. This seems to have been the case with the marginal apostolate: many religious decided to go out to marginal areas to be in accord with the stated pastoral priorities of the Church, without any real calling or capacity for this style of life. What better setting for later frustration?

Along with a strong desire to identify with the poor and abandoned, almost a third of our sample specified that they were led by a desire to live a more radically evangelical lifestyle in a small supportive community. This stated desire convinced us of the importance of investigating the type of spirituality present in these small groups and the potential they offer in creative planning for the religious life of the future.

What exactly is a marginal area like? Here we draw on our experiences in Santiago, Concepción, and Talca. Most houses are similar, mainly constructed of wood (very few of concrete) and quite small, with combined livingroom-dining areas, and a kitchen which is often visible as one enters. Bedrooms are extremely small, but in most cases private. In many small houses we saw the efforts of religious to keep a small room apart for meetings or visitors so that the occupants of the house might enjoy some privacy. However, this was not always possible, due to the lack of space. Furniture is extremely simple and sparse, usually of cane or cheap wood of the type found in lower-middle-class or laborers' homes. The presence of small touches of color, rag rugs or knitted cushions, plants, and colorful posters gave evidence of the interest taken in raising the morale of family members and refusal to be dominated by the depressing effect of extreme poverty. Since the houses in marginal areas are placed close together, there are no real gardens, trees, or shade; only the everpresent flower boxes in the windows and a few plants at the front gate offer a touch of green to an otherwise bleak atmosphere. For this reason, most religious women try to spend at least one day a week away from their marginal areas, seeking the recreation, fresh air, and green grass they must live without all week. The streets are unpaved and become a morass of mud and puddles during the winter season and a sea of fine dirt that fills the air and the houses in summer. Many women assured us that the daily struggle to keep themselves, the house, and the washing clean took far more time than ever before. The obvious lack of privacy was even more astounding after conversing with these women. Accustomed to a life which had contained periods of silence and tranquility, they had had to resign themselves to the noise of the *población,* the radios playing incessantly at high volumes, the crying and screams of children, the ever-present *cantinas* (bars) and their clientele; in short, to number less inconveniences which come from having to live on top of each other in conditions of extreme poverty.

Tensions and Frustrations

A search for the source of tensions and frustrations in the lives of these religious women constituted one of the essential dimensions of the investigation. It was our conviction that these women were among the most highly frustrated of Church personnel. We further hypothesized that this frustration would have its roots in the misery of their environment (above all in urban settings), in their style of life, in the absence or presence of structures in their community life, in their congregational ties, and, of most interest to us here, in their relations with the institutional Church.

Our data show that the urban-rural factor is of great importance in determining the level and quality of frustration. Three Frustration Indexes showed that religious in urban marginal areas suffered a much more exaggerated form of frustration than their rural sisters in all of the following areas: the environment and all its aspects, congregational ties and interpersonal relations, the Church (its treatment of women and the lack of sufficient financial help) the lack of structures in all aspects of life (privacy, rest, recreation, prayer, and so on), and, finally, from the rigidity of their previous spiritual formation. These women were both more conscious of and more anxious for solutions to these problems than religious women in rural areas. They felt more confronted by their environment and more obliged to give an adequate response to that confrontation. As a result, this confrontation with abject misery, unjust structures in operation, and personal impotence produced tension and the tension engendered even more frustration. Not only was the frustration level higher, but its quality was distinct. Whereas both urban and rural groups suffer from ill health, physical and mental, deficiencies in formation and professional preparation, tiredness and lack of time, only the urban group had become more highly conscious of the necessity for structures in their lives and the consequences of their absence whether with respect to prayer, recreation, or rest, and the relation of all this to their own frustration. In the rural groups frustration appeared to be more diffuse in its origins.

The relationship between frustration and structures was one of the most revealing of the study. The immense importance of such factors as overworking, exhaustion, rest, recreation, and their effects on all areas of life was clearly demonstrated by the women's responses. All these factors either required structures for their protection, or were symptoms of the lack of these structures. The previous formation of these women often made life almost impossible and added to their already rising frustration level. Religious in urban settings felt themselves judged and confronted by their own environment; they felt forced to question all the elements of their consecrated life; their poverty appeared a sham in the face of such misery, their celibacy, as previously understood, an obstacle to healing friendship. The following is an expression of the feelings of a large group of urban religious:

> Unhappily, our formation does not offer a healthy policy that would enable us to enjoy recreation and rest. There are many who think that it is less agreeable to the Lord to give oneself free time, indeed, many look down upon a sister who takes a free day for herself. For this reason we live in anxiety and nervous tension [Gilfeather, 1978].

The lack of preparation was highly correlated with frustration, and we can see the cause rather clearly with respect to a group that is so highly educated but whose education has little or nothing to do with the exigencies of the environment. As we see the numbers of religious women going out to marginal areas seriously diminishing in the past few years, we need to ask if there has been sufficient reflection upon the experience of women in the field and if their experience has been used to enrich the preparation of new candidates. Only in this way can the original traumatic situations be avoided. Without serious reflection in this area, others will be condemned to repeat the mistakes of their sisters.

THE INSTITUTIONAL CHURCH
AND ITS CONTRIBUTION TO FRUSTRATION

The sources of frustration with the institutional Church are varied and multiple. Central is the economic factor which is intimately related to the quality of ties between religious women and the Church. This was expressed in the following hypothesis: "The lack of concrete interest and adequate financial support on the part of the institutional Church is an added source of tension and frustration for religious in marginal situations" (Gilfeather, 1978). The data show that 92% of these religious, both from urban as well as rural areas, stated categorically that they suffer from a lack of sufficient financial support.

In the pastoral action of the Church in Chile, women have many and profound responsibilities. Nevertheless, access to levels of real authority in the ecclesiastical pyramid remains closed to them. This will be discussed in a later section, but it suffices here to emphasize that this situation is, without doubt, one of the prime sources of frustration for these religious women and one which resists all rationalizations and arguments to the contrary. Women, both religious and lay, carry heavy pastoral burdens of great responsibility but the exercise of real authority, symbolized by the priesthood, is beyond their reach.

Based on responses to our questionnaire, an Index of Frustration with the Church was constructed. Upon joining the two highest levels of frustration, we found that 75.9% of these religious felt frustration with the institutional Church. Most lived in urban marginal areas, a fact which corresponds with our original hypothesis. We also found that the younger religious were more highly frustrated than their older sisters, while the level of frustration rose steadily with the level of education. Taking nationality into consideration, North American religious were the most highly frustrated (87.5%), followed closely by the Europeans. The Spanish and other Latin Americans felt relatively lower degrees of frustration (60%), while the Chilean religious occupied an intermediate position (78%).

We have noted some correlation between the frustration of the women and their relations with the institutional Church. Let us take a closer look at this relationship.

Religious and the Institutional Church: Responses

Experience is the key to human relations, and we see a clear expression of this fact in the relations between the religious women under observation and the Chilean hierarchy. Although we have already mentioned briefly some aspects of this relationship, there is one dimension not often taken into account: the indifference toward women, perhaps unconscious, but nonetheless notable in the official documents of the Church. For example, the Medellín Documents mention women only once as part of a multitude of groups seeking justice throughout the continent. In his well-known book *Theology of Liberation* (1973), Gustavo Gutiérrez writes that his work is based on the Gospel and the experiences of men and women in Latin America. But there is no mention of the intrinsically unjust position of women in Latin American society, and much less of their secondary position in the Catholic Church. Some argue that injustice affects so many dimensions of life in Latin America and is such a common component in all structures that it is not worthwhile stressing a mere symptom of a more pervasive problem. It is important to bear in mind that people respond to their environment in accord with their previous experience. If this experience has been liberating, responsible, and creative, the response will be a healthy one which should enrich personal fulfillment. But if this experience has been limited, restricted, bitter, and dependent, the response will be immature, irresponsible, and inconsequential for personal fulfillment. The latter has been the real experience of Latin American women. How can they be expected to contribute in a liberated, creative fashion to the development of a free continent?

The reader will recall that the actual pastoral priorities of the Catholic Church in Chile led to changes in structures and proceedings, which in turn led to new roles for women in pastoral action. Thus, women have been incorporated on a number of different levels of pastoral planning into roles of administrators of parishes in many dioceses of Chile. Many works traditionally reserved to priests are now in the hands of women. The importance of this work is such that not a few congregations have closed some of their schools in order to give their personnel the liberty to dedicate themselves to this new pastoral dimension. Despite the ample horizons offered in positions of leadership and responsibility, we still find that almost 76% of our sample felt frustrated with the institutional Church.

The pastoral experience offered to the Chilean women, particularly the religious women, is both varied and profoundly responsible. Nevertheless, this experience has proven itself to be a double-edged sword. Although her responsibility grows, this has the unanticipated consequence of making her more conscious of her secondary position in the Church, her lack of real authority in ecclesiastical structures, and her totally limited role in the area of cult. Our data show that more than 28% of these women felt abandoned by the institutional Church; 37% felt they had no way to give an accounting of their labors to the institutional Church, nor did they see any apparent desire on the part of the Church that they should do so; 56% felt that the pastoral work of the Church was highly inadequate in the areas of catechetics, sacramentalization, and youth, but likewise felt unable to communicate this to policy makers. The factors which caused the highest frustration are the following:

(1) Many positions of great responsibility are already in the hands of women but positions of ecclesiastical authority remain beyond their reach 79.4%
(2) The position of the hierarchical Church with regard to the ordination of women is both illogical and inadmissible........69.2%
(3) Financing on the part of the institutional Church is totally inadequate in the face of our needs........61% (A second "control" question revealed that 92% suffer from a "lack of financial support.")

In a recent study of women working in the Church in Chile, we find an interesting contrast to those data. Asked if they felt that lay and religious women were given works of lesser responsibility than men, 66% were emphatically negative. Their reasons can be summarized as follows:

Women are sharing at least equally with, if not outdistancing men with respect to burdens of responsibility in the Church's pastoral programs. We are likewise talking about real responsibility, not the possession of clerical titles or status [Galilea, et al., 1976].

There are substantial differences between that group and the present sample which help account for the contrary opinions. In the 1976 study the great majority of women involved lay women, not religious. Their educational level was far lower, and the extent of their dedication much more limited, ranging from two or three hours to a few days weekly of pastoral service. The present sample deals with highly educated women, completely dedicated to the ideal of service, identified by their very role with the institutional Church, and therefore highly vulnerable with respect to its policies and deficiencies. To put it succinctly, they have more to lose.

The religious woman engaged in pastoral action in Chile knows her own capacity, her professional preparation, and the success she has enjoyed in exercising responsibility for the People of God. At the same time she is becoming more and more conscious of the lack of theological and psychological bases for those restrictions which have reduced her to a secondary position in the Church. This gap between ecclesiastical structures and changing cultural mores continues to produce enormous tensions among these women, particularly those most dedicated to pastoral action who are more vulnerable to the experience of two coexisting realities in constant warfare.

I. THE FINANCIAL PROBLEM

We have already alluded to this problem in the discussion on frustration. Here we would like to analyze in greater detail what lies behind the statement by 92% of the sample that they are receiving inadequate financial support. Aside from the fact that many are already receiving help from their own congregations to supplement the monthly stipend received from the Chancery (Administrative offices of the Church), 42.2% feel obligated to work in some remunerative field which in many cases takes them out of the marginal area and seriously limits the time dedicated to pastoral work. We are here faced with the fact of "pastoral efficiency." If the Church is concerned with forming its personnel, helping them to renew their religious dedication, and orienting their pastoral labors, it seems somewhat myopic to destroy their efficiency by not providing the necessary means to do the job well. However, there is a strong possibility that many religious prefer to work in this fashion as a proof of their identification with the environment, or because they feel guilty if they do not face the same risks and sufferings of their neighbors. Reflecting on the questionnaire data and also on our conversations with these women, we are led to formulate several questions in this regard. Are these women being realistic with regard to their needs? Is there a frank and open dialogue with ecclesiastical superiors or, on the contrary, does there exist a tendency to "angelism" on the part of one side or both? Is it possible that they have adopted certain aspects of this style of life without having accomplished a total identification and, for this reason, feel themselves deprived of resources to which they had access in another context? In any case, is it really possible to give up one's standard of living entirely? Is it indeed even realistic to hope to do so? Are they aware of the effect which this factor might produce not only among those who already live in marginal areas, but also among those who are considering this possibility and are perhaps vacillating in the face of the effects of this financial problem?

If the Church continues to emphasize the same priorities in the future, it will have to confront the conditions in which many of its personnel in marginal areas are living, and they, in turn, will be forced to evaluate their style of life and work in the light of their own personal and community limitations.

II. IMAGE OF THE CHURCH

With respect to the Church model preferred by these women, they were presented with a selection in two different areas. The first included a type of "universal Church" to which all could aspire to belong, with different levels of commitment. Along with this was included an "elite Church" model which would exact a profound commitment from its members and would, for this reason, be a "minority Church." The majority 57.7%, chose the elite Church model, only 11.6% chose the universal model, while 22.2% chose a combination of both concepts in which the minority would influence the formation of the masses.

Taking into consideration the position of the Church in society, the sample was presented with a second selection. The first Church model offered was that of a "conformist Church" which would adapt to any type of society in order to protect its institution and its liberty of action. The second model was that of a "critical Church," one more prophetic in its approach to injustice despite any problems which this stance might occasion. Over 88% of the religious women chose a critical Church model. The 6.8% which chose "another model" were referring to a critical model based on charity and wisdom. None chose a conformist Church model.

III. THE RELATIVE IMPORTANCE OF PASTORAL PROBLEMS

With respect to opinions on the highest priority problems in the Church, we asked our sample to rank the problems they considered most urgent for the Church. With a total of nine choices, responses were scattered, but the most frequent choices were the following: primarily "the need to build strong effective primary communities" (Comunidades de Base)—38.3%; secondarily "the protection of human rights in society"—24.4%.

In the 1976 study, these same pastoral priorities were evaluated and compared with the responses of the Chilean bishops (Smith, 1979) to the same question. The results were extremely revealing. The most frequent first and second choices for these women was the need to build strong effective primary communities (Comunidades de Base), while the bishops chose as the most urgent problem the lack of vocations to the priesthood and, in second place, the need to augment pastoral personnel with well-prepared laymen. This emphasizes certain tendencies already detected among the bishops, most notably their strong preoccupation with personnel problems such as the rapidly disappearing clergy and how to fill in the gaps thus created—that is, a preoccupation with "means." The women in both samples face the pastoral problem itself—the "ends"—evangelization of society. Perhaps they are less concerned with means because they are so personally involved at the grass-roots level. The bishops, on the other hand, are limited by their very ecclesiastical role.

With respect to the religious women under study, their choice of evangelization through small communities of mutal support and their emphasis on the protection of human rights brings to mind those new values necessary for building a more humanized society. Even in the case of their pastoral priorities, these women are faithful to their humanizing vocation in the Church as well as in society.

IV. FORMS OF DOCTRINAL COMMITMENT

One of the principal hypotheses of our study was that "the experience of women working and living in marginal areas would make them more critical of the institutional Church and would lead them to a less literal position with respect to its teachings." The assessment of doctrinal positions, never an easy task, becomes extremely difficult through a questionnaire, for as an individual becomes less literal and rigid in religious perspectives, the structure of the questionnaire becomes less useful. It offers no other alternative but to present the individual as "less religious" because of low scores in scales of doctrinal affirmations and practices of traditional interpretation. A solution was sought and found in the use of a scale (Hunt, 1972) offering three possible positions:

(1) *A Literal interpretation*: the individual accepts the affirmation as true without questioning it in any form. This position seems to imply that the individual has not reflected upon the relationship of this affirmation to other areas of life.

(2) *An Antiliteral interpretation*: the individual rejects the Christian orientation as without value in itself. This attitude is based on an ingenuous, literal and pseudoscientific interpretation of religion, and seems to reflect a rebellion against the rigid teachings of childhood or against those who have presented onerous restrictions on personal life.

(3) *A Mythological interpretation*: the individual reinterprets the religious affirmation in order to find the profound symbolic meaning which exists beyond a literal interpretation. This type of person has a more complex religious frame of reference and is capable of assimilating both the intention of orthodox religion and the realities of the contemporary world. This level of commitment is considered the most mature.

The Hunt scale adapted for our study was composed of ten affirmations, with three possible responses for each—each alternative corresponding to one of the above interpretations. The sum of the individual responses and the resulting scale gave us an Index of Doctrinal Commitment Position. It is important to emphasize here that the Index represents only an orientation or tendency; nevertheless, the results seem valuable enough for careful reflection.

While more than 66% of the religious in our sample took a mythological stance with regard to doctrinal commitment, less than 23% possessed a literal interpretation and barely 10% could be classified as antiliteral. A literal interpretation was most frequent among older women, while the mythological interpretation was most common among younger religious. The higher the level of education, the more probable was the presence of a mythological position, while a literal interpretation was most common among religious with less education. In terms of nationality, North Americans were strongly mythological, Europeans (with the exception of the Spaniards) offered the only anti-literal position, while Latin Americans (with the exception of Chileans)

and Spaniards were most representative of the literal position. Interestingly enough, the group possessing a mythological position showed
itself most frustrated with the institutional Church.

The group was highly mature with respect to its doctrinal position,
having demonstrated a marked tendency to reinterpret religious
affirmations in search of a more profound symbolic meaning rather
than the absolutism of total blind acceptance or total rejection. This display of maturity in the area of doctrinal commitment can be evaluated
only adequately as part of the larger dimension of personal spirituality,
of which it is both an aspect and an indication. Thus, we are led to
expect a reflective spirituality on the part of these women, one which
goes beyond the surface, a personal freedom unfettered and creative in
its confrontation with the environment. The following section will
analyze their spirituality and its profound relationship to the marginal
experience.

Changes in Spirituality Patterns

The response of these women to the frustrations of life is rather
unique in its blend of rebellion with innovation *within* and continuing
commitment *to* institutional structures. They look for new ways to
achieve their goals; they question those goals institutionalized by society
and even by the Church. Their very style of life is counter to the material
goals of success and comfort of their own society. The values they
stress—compassion, mutual affirmation, respect for life, creativity,
dialogue, and the like—are in fact those most needed in our alienated
society which speaks incessantly of "community" without knowing
how to achieve it. It is our belief that religious women possess the
most adequate response to the present societal frustration. The very
apostolic experience which they have chosen demonstrates an openness
to the search for more functional means and methods; for this reason
we hoped to find the same search in the realm of spirituality, the same
"rebellion" and "innovation" we have come to expect in their day-to-day
living. We expressed this in the following hypothesis: "The experience
of these women has the potential to enrich and deepen their spirituality"
(Gilfeather, 1978). Due to the limitations of space, we will consider
only some of the traditional components of spirituality.

A. Prayer. One factor which must be considered in any discussion of prayer is the context in which it takes place. The presence or absence of a small chapel or oratory can enrich or impoverish that context and is an indication of the importance given to prayer in the community. The fact that 90% of the sample live in small communities where space is extremely limited but which possess a small chapel or oratory speaks eloquently of the priority given to prayer by these religious. Looking at the content of their prayer, we find three principal orientations: 53% pray the Divine Office in common (psalms and readings from Old and New Testament and the Fathers of the Church); 49% participate in free, shared prayer with others; while over 17% prepare paraliturgical ceremonies in the absence of a priest. These orientations are not exclusive but overlap in various combinations of activities. The importance of the Divine Office, which is the Church's official prayer, reveals the spirituality of these women. They seek bonds of union with the universal prayer of the Church. Their shared vocal prayer provides a firm basis for mutual support and understanding. The frequency of paraliturgical ceremonies, directed by the sisters themselves, clearly shows that they are learning to detach themselves from a total dependence upon the clergy for spiritual development and opening themselves to receive what is necessary from their sisters.

To what can we ascribe these orientations in their prayer life? Were these orientations always present? Over 90% declared that their prayer life had experienced great changes since their coming to live in a marginal area; thus their spirituality clearly has been affected by their marginal experience. A closer look at their responses indicated the extent and content of this change. The terms they use reveal that from a rational, theoretic, structured, private prayer, it has come to be "affective, evangelical, down to earth, communal, intimate, interiorized, and based on life." In this way the religious themselves evaluate the effect of the environment upon their prayer and the development of new modes of prayer and of being present to the Lord as well as to one's brother and sister.

B. Meditation. One of the classic activities of the spirituality of religious life is meditation, and despite what we would expect from a group which is often plagued with constant calls for service and little free time, over 90% dedicate time each day to this exercise. The terms used to describe changes in their meditation are very similar to those used for prayer: "done with more regularity, less theoretic, less structured, more profound, more effective, based more on daily life, done with greater pleasure and for longer periods."

C. Devotion to the Virgin Mary. Considered one of the oldest and dearest devotions in the Church and deeply related to the life of the religious, devotion to Mary has become a rather ambiguous aspect of the spirituality of many of these religious. A quarter of our women stated that their devotion to the Virgin Mary had either diminished or no longer existed. The majority, almost 60%, expressed their veneration on one or another level, but of that group, over 38% stated that their devotion had been enriched profoundly by their marginal experience. They spoke of the Virgin Mary as having become a "real person" to them, nearer and more of a woman like themselves. She was no longer the powerful Mother of God, but rather the "poor virgin," the "woman of faith" who accompanied them in their labors for a suffering people. It is possible that those who felt their devotion had diminished or disappeared were rejecting an image of Mary which no longer holds meaning in the face of their experience or the context of their lives.

D. Revision of Life. This refers to an evaluation of an individual's life in the light of the Gospel and in common with the members of his or her community. The purpose is to grow in Gospel values with the support of the entire primary group. Fully 68% of our sample take part weekly in this type of evaluation, and from their responses it is clear that their marginal experience has enriched and deepened this activity. The terms they use recall those mentioned for meditation and prayer. Thus, their revision of life has become "more demanding, it exacts more effort and commitment, it opens new horizons and areas before untouched, it is more down to earth, more evangelical, more sincere, more supportive, based on real life, I get much more out of it."

E. Spiritual Direction. Traditionally considered essential in the religious life, spiritual direction by a priest has become a luxury for most religious in areas with few priests. Only 28.7% of our sample enjoys some form of spiritual direction, "although unsatisfactory," while 50% feel the deprivation of direction keenly and hope to find help "someday." The most realistic attitude was expressed by over 23% of the sample, who found a substitute among friends or the members of their own primary community. This new form of spiritual orientation deserves our attention not only because it satisfies a need and offers a substitute for priestly direction, but also because it constitutes an integral form of human and spiritual growth that is at least as sound, if not sounder, than traditional forms of direction. A well-established group where sincerity, openness, and a desire to mature in the Lord are dominant provides the best context for personal growth. Interestingly, the great majority of those who had chosen this type of orientation in their lives live in urban marginal areas. Throughout our observation of these women it became obvious that those living in urban areas were more creative in their search for solutions. This creativity may be the fruit of a more deeply felt need than that experienced by their rural sisters.

F. Sharing the Faith Experience. From earliest times, the Christian community has been based on a sharing of the faith experience. Although such sharing is essential to the Christian commitment, Christians have for too long been formed in a contrary type of spirituality stressing independence and detachment from others. This has been particularly true in the religious life. It was all the more surprising, then, to find that over 95% of the sample expressed a strong desire to share their faith experience with their sisters and others. Almost 67% find it easy to do so, while a third complain of obstacles which are, in great part, difficulties in interpersonal relationships. The resulting lack of communication and the climate of conflict created make sharing impossible. What interests us here is the perception of need for mutual sharing of one's faith experience in Christ. If this conviction is strong enough solutions will be sought to problems, be they lack of time, exhaustion, or personal conflicts. Clear goals and strong motivation can help cut through the thick curtain of obstacles which can smother life in common, leaving only an attitude of tolerance in a boarding-house atmosphere.

G. The Vows. As these are so essential to the life of a religious, we wished to evaluate their relevance in the lives of our group. Over 85% of those living in urban marginal areas declared their vows to be more relevant today than ever; 72% of their rural sisters agreed. The reasons recall those given for changes in prayer, meditation, and revision of life. Those who feel most "questioned" by their environment (the urban sisters) are those whose vows are more relevant than ever. Their vows have opened up a new liberating dimension which supports rather than limits their commitment.

The vow receiving the greatest coverage in writings on the religious life today is poverty; it was, likewise, of most interest to our group. In speaking of changes in their living out of the vow, the sisters used terms which express the values they prize most highly: "the vow (poverty) gives me greater liberty, it permits real solidarity with my people, it frees me for service, I feel it is a source of liberation for me, it helps me to be more open to others, I am drawn to share more of what I am, I feel that it leads me to question myself and my motives, through it I am learning to accept myself as I am." If, as we suggested previously, one's participation in human affairs depends upon one's experience, then the contribution of these women to the future Latin American society should be a most positive and humanizing one, for their vision of the vow of poverty emphasizes a liberating dimension which enriches rather than impoverishes the human spirit.

Their style of life gives concrete evidence of the importance given not only to the vow, but also to the consequences of their identification with the poor. For this reason we asked them if the vow could be lived with sincerity in a different type of social context, in a less demanding style of life. Their responses reveal considerable ambiguity. Almost 40% denied the possibility of living the vow with sincerity in a more comfortable style of life. Those who showed more tolerance were from rural areas. It would appear that the tensions of a life of extreme simplicity, amidst the general misery of urban marginal sectors, influence the relative strength of opinions originating there. A danger is inherent in this intransigent attitude with respect to the vow of poverty. The great majority of religious women in Chile do not live in urban or rural marginal sectors. For this reason a judgment with respect to the "sincerity" of their mode of life, and particularly their living out of the vow of poverty, is questionable and, moreover, is symptomatic of an attitude of "exclusiveness" with respect to a particular style of life. These are the false dichotomies which cause divisions among personnel and damage pastoral efforts.

Conclusions

The above data may or may not point to a "new spirituality," but the foregoing facts are indicative of the multiple changes experienced by these women since coming to live in marginal areas.

The responses of religious women living in marginal areas reveal attitudes and values which have only a secondary place in our society. They have developed a way of life (or spirituality) based on values, qualities, and attitudes which have been repeated over and over again in the analysis: "authenticity, liberation, solidarity, compassion, sensitivity, openness, sharing, confrontation, self-acceptance, respect for life." These are human as well as Christian values, humanizing factors which at least partially define Christian existence and should inform the action of the Church. Their "spirituality" reflects definite interests, motives and options—it takes sides with the oppressed, the marginal, the poor in general, and for that very reason is based on praxis, solidarity, and shared experience.

These women do not express themselves in terms of abstract analysis or in intellectual discussion, but in the use of a wide gamut of human expression—art, music, dialogue, solidarity, compassion, and openness. They do not separate the sacred from the profane, the religious dimension from daily living. On the contrary, the content of their liturgy, prayer, and meditation is a reflection of the reality of their life situation. Through these same activities they give expression to their fears, frustrations, and feelings of oppression, but, above all, to their hope for a new society where justice and humanity will prevail.

Just as experience has shaped their spirituality, so too it has altered their values and attitudes as witnessed in responses to structures at all levels and in all areas of their lives: relations with the institutional Church, vocational commitment, work, recreation, planning, prayer, even their doctrinal stance have all been deeply affected by the marginal experiment. The four dimensions of social change have thus come full circle in the fertile ground of the *población* environment. To the extent that the emergence of the individual, innovation, the power controversy, and secularization become prevalent in an environment, whether singly or in conjunction, tensions inevitably result. We have seen evidence that the situations of these women point to a high degree of tension, and that the data suggest the urgency of dealing with the problem and seeking creative solutions if the Church continues to avail itself of their dedication. The institutional Church appears, in many instances, to be cautious of these women, of their growing self-awareness and the resulting conflictual relationship between institution and personnel. It is an uneasy courtship and we might ask ourselves what, in fact, sustains them. To a great extent, it appears to be their spirituality which overrides their frustrations and tensions. It likewise offers a surety that, despite a possible (or probable) continued environment of frustration and tension, these women will, unlike so many disillusioned political ideologists, remain in marginal areas.

This identification with the "broken ones" of society which has engendered such unexpected purpose, strength, and creativity in these women, has the potential to enrich the religious life of the entire Chilean Church.

> "Being rich He became poor that He might enrich us."
> (II Cor. viii.9.)

REFERENCES

CELAM [Council of Latin American Bishops] (1969) "Poverty of the Church." Second General Conference of Latin American Bishops, Bogotá: General Secretariat of CELAM.

Centro Bellarmino (1962) Pastoral Plan of the Chilean Episcopate, 1961-1962. Santiago, Chile: Centro Bellarmino.

GALILEA, C., K. GILFEATHER and J. PUGA (1976) Las Mujeres que Trabajan en la Iglesia: La Experiencia Chilena. Santiago, Chile: Centro Bellarmino.

GILFEATHER, K. (1978) Religiosas en Apostolados Marginales. Santiago, Chile: Centro Bellarmino.

GUTIÉRREZ, G. (1973) Theology of Liberation. History: Politics and Salvation. Maryknoll, NY: Orbis.

HUNT, R. (1972) "Mythological-symbolic religious commitment: the LAM scales." J. for the Scientific Study of Religion 2 (March).

MARTY, M. (1960) "Sects and cults." Annals of the American Academy of Political and Social Science 332 (November): 125-134.

NISBET, R. (1970) The Social Bond. New York: Alfred A. Knopf.

SMITH, B. (1979) "The Catholic Church and political change in Chile, 1925-1978." Ph.D. dissertation. Yale University.

9

BASIC CHRISTIAN COMMUNITIES IN LATIN AMERICA
Their Nature and Significance (especially in Brazil)

THOMAS C. BRUNEAU

There is a little question of the portentous changes taking place in the Catholic Churches in Latin America. Probably the most significant change concerns the rapid spread of the "Comunidade Eclesial de Base" (Basic Christian Community or CEB) in at least one-half the countries. While the greatest concentration of these units is undoubtedly found in Brazil with some 50,000 such communities, there are at least 1,000 in Chile, several hundred in Paraguay, and others in most of the countries of Central America. What is more, there is every likelihood that these CEBs will continue to spread both within those countries where they are already located as well as in other countries in the region. Their importance, as we shall see, is due not only to their incipient growth but also to the implications they bear both for the national Churches and the larger societies. Their growth and development presage a fundamental reorientation of the Churches as they act as a seedbed for popular initiatives in organizing within largely authoritarian military regimes. Thus, while other changes in the Latin American Churches are noteworthy and possibly significant, in comparison with the growth of the CEBs they become somewhat less important. This is the case for the following reasons.

The ideological positions defined by the bishops gathered at Medellín in 1968, Puebla in 1979, and nationally as well as locally in many countries are indicative of their changing orientations concerning a whole series of internal and sociopolitical issues. However, the nagging question remains regarding the implementation of these new orientations. Clearly the new positions are important in contrast with past positions, but, given the decentralized nature of the Church with the diocese as primary unit, it is ultimately up to each individual bishop to implement the new positions. Even with the best of good will, the bishop often finds

that he lacks the human and material resources to implement new policies in situations of intractable concrete reality. These statements, then
are easily understood as statements of intentions with significance in
terms of comparisons, and not as accurate descriptions of real implementation.

There have been significant innovations in some dioceses as well as
the creation of movements, groups, and institutes at the national level
in Churches such as Brazil, Chile, El Salvador, and Paraguay. This, of
course, is the nature of most of my research and publication on Brazil
during the past decade. However, in scrutinizing these innovations we
find that they normally result from very particular conjunctures of
ideological and process variables that are likely to hold only as long as
the conjunctures continue. What I have in mind here as typical is the
Church as surrogate opposition party when repression is too high to
allow other parties to survive. In this case, and in others, the innovations
are likely to disappear when the particular combination of factors
changes and the Church more precisely defines its role in "pastoral"
terms. Certainly both these innovations and the new ideological orientations are important, but they may not be lasting. The CEBs, however,
arise from the atmosphere created by these new orientations and as such
promise to continue regardless of particular conjunctures.

It must be emphasized that CEBs are not all of one piece; they vary
tremendously from one country or even one diocese to another, and
what is being presented here is a general statement representing the
higher or more defined level of the CEBs. What follows will rely heavily
on the case of Brazil but the evidence from the countries mentioned
above indicates that although the Brazilian case is somewhat more defined and maybe more advanced the general points hold elsewhere. I
deal with Brazil because the CEBs are more common and developed
there, because there is an abundance of primary and secondary literature, and because I have conducted extensive field research in which the
CEBs figured in a predominant way.[1] As a general introduction, we can
say that the CEBs constitute the perfect response to very concrete problems facing the Churches in Latin America. The lack of personnel
(clergy, male and female religious), the archaic and inappropriate
micro-structures such as parishes and devotional groups, and the
growing ideological commitment to work with the masses all find a solution in the CEBs. What is more, they are legitimated by the primitive
Church, from the catacombs, which could be argued to give them primacy as *the* Church. The CEBs are the single most important change in

the Latin American Churches both for their present implications, as we shall see, and for their promise to continue growing and developing.

The most frequent statement in the primary documents on the CEBs runs as follows: "The people get together once a week in groups of 20 or 30 in different parts of the neighborhood and reflect on the Bible." That is, they get together. On the basis of a local reality, a neighborhood or place of work, they get together in groups of the most varied kind. They get together and discuss this reality, and the problems arising from it for them, and they do this in light of the Bible, most frequently the Gospel. The form of the groups is varied. They would include at least the following: groups for preparation of the Mass, Bible groups, groups for the preparation of the sacraments, groups for human promotion, adult groups, mothers' groups, married groups, street groups, cooperative groups, and so forth, depending on the structure of the local Church and the environment. What distinguishes them from other possible groups in Latin America (although there is a low level of group formation) is the ecclesial dimension which indicates how they come together in the first instance and the basis of their reflection. At this point it might be well to examine in turn each aspect of the comunidade eclesial de base (for a similar analysis of the constituent elements of the CEB, see SEDOC, 1979: 797-810).

Community implies primary groups associated because of territorial and class proximity to one another. Instead of being but the lowest level in the hierarchy of the Church, the people come together in a community and in a sense *are* the Church. In these groups the people meet, get to know one another, exchange ideas and experiences, and support one another. The CEBs offer their members the possibility to group, grow, and conduct dialogues and therefore become communities—hitherto rare in Latin America and which de Tocqueville considered crucial in the development of North American democracy. The members are encouraged to speak in their own words, using their own terms, and express their own interests and ideas. By so doing they remove the need for "spokesmen" with the paternalistic connotation they carry in these societies. Following from this, and because of the focus on the members' own interests expressed in their own words, the possibility for critical reflection on themselves and their environment is created. This in turn gives rise to comprehension of the deeper causes of poverty, inequality, and misery. At some stage a collective consciousness may well develop with implications for action. The community, in short, implies interaction, equality, and opportunity for its members to speak and grow in a collective consciousness that has been previously missing in these Churches and is very rare in Latin American societies.

Ecclesial means the relationship with Church and religion. The themes of the first two national meetings in Brazil on the CEBs are indicative of the ecclesial dimension. The first in 1975 was termed "CEBs: A Church Born of the People" and the second in 1976 was "CEBs: A Church Born of the People by the Spirit of God" (SEDOC, 1975, 1976). Most of the CEBs have been formed through the initiative of elements in the Church and at the present time most are still linked with the institution. The link is also maintained by the instrument for reflection which is the Bible and, most frequently, the Gospel. The word of God is tied to the concrete concerns of the people, and one reflects the other. The use of the Bible and religion in general is particularly significant and powerful, since so much of Latin American "popular culture" is infused with religious elements of a "popular" or "folk" Catholicism that the symbolism is already familiar to most adherents. In contrast with the recent past, when the Protestants held almost a monopoly of the Bible, elements in the Church have now popularized it, made it readily available, and it is being used to reflect on concrete reality rather than held up as justification of a long (or not so long) wait for the next life. Bringing the Bible into the hands and finally control of the people is particularly important because they can grasp the meaning of the religion, as stated in this Bible, rather than being obliged to rely on the potentially paternalistic role of the clergy or pastoral animators. In this situation the pastoral animators are no longer people from without and above but rather find themselves more or less on the same level as the masses. There is, then, a fusion of these elements and the people and thus a democratic or participatory push for the community as a whole. What is more, as the Church becomes increasingly permeated and identified with these CEBs, it too must continue to change since its link with the international dimension of the state decreases since the justification for its policies must look more and more to the communities as the base. These people, once mobilized, will demand further involvement and control, as the Church is based on its members and not immutable hierarchical structures.

Base means both the basis of the Church, as just noted, but even more that the basis is found in the people (understood here as the masses— o Povo). Continually emerging is the vast majority of people involved in the CEBs from the poor: from the rural areas, the periphery of the large cities, and generally marginalized—those who are not benefitting from the modernizing society. Since the poor have historically been largely ignored by the Churches, this is a significant reorientation and as the poor in these societies are either actively or passively repressed, the implications noted above on the community aspect are serious. It is in the context of the CEBs that the lower classes are realizing their potential —both for the Church and the society—as they come to appreciate that they indeed do count and do matter.

In summary, the CEBs are groups of people from the same area and same class who come together to discuss concrete problems in light of the Bible. The overwhelming majority are poor, and the initial stimulus is normally found in concrete problems which are common for people "on the margins." These include lack of services (water, transport), particular cases of injustice (forcing from land and illegal housing), and natural disasters or recurring shortages which are so common for the lower classes. They meet in groups of 10 and 30, reflect on the implications of the Bible for their situations, and draw conclusions. After briefly describing their formation, we can then analyze further their implications for the Church and society.

The origins of the CEBs in each country and throughout Latin America can be traced (and have been; see LADOC, 1976: 1-7) to any number of particular events, processes, and statements. Their inception and rapid growth is due to at least three concrete reasons and one ideological point of support arising from the results of the Second Vatican Council (1962-1965).

(1) It has long been recognized in Brazil and is increasingly the case elsewhere in Latin America that the traditional structures or groups for relating to the laity are not viable or effective (if indeed they ever were). The system of parishes is correctly perceived as inappropriate and cumbersome in these societies: too large for contact, generally encompassing very disparate sections of society, and overly bureaucratic for very complex needs (Gregory, 1967a, 1976b). The traditional pietistic groups such as the Apostolate of Prayer, Legion of Mary, and so on are archaic and involve only a very small proportion of any given parish; generally the same individuals belong to a variety of these associations, rarely can any of them be called dynamic. the more modern groups such as the Christian Family Movement and the "cursilhos," with some notable exceptions, appeal to the middle and upper classes and de-emphasize a critical sociopolitical function. The more active and important movement in Brazil and Chile from the mid-1950s for relating the Church to sectors of the laity and the changing environment was

Catholic Action, but this association became impossible in Brazil in 1964 and faded in Chile with the rise of the Christian Democratic party. In effect, the institutional Church has lacked, and is perceived to lack, effective intermediary groups for relating its changing ideological orientations to a changing environment.

(2) The continuing crisis in priestly vocations is another reason for the emergence of the CEBs. The priest-to-population ratio in Brazil is worse than some other countries, better than still others, and is fairly typical in that it has never been high and is on the decrease. In 1970 the ratio was 7,081 people to priests, and by 1975 this was 8,528 people per priest. There is an absolute drop in the number of secular priests on the average of roughly 0.20% per year and the number of religious priests is falling at a faster rate—0.60% per year. Even if the institution were willing, as in the case of some dioceses, to allow nuns extensive new roles, this in itself is not a long-term solution, as they are decreasing at approximately 1% per year (CERIS, 1978). The historical shortage of clergy continues, if anything, at a greater degree. It is absurd to discuss contact with the Church when one priest serves more than 10,000 people (as is the case in much of the country); obviously some new mechanism has to be employed to relate the institution to the people.

(3) The Brazilian Church and about half the Churches in Latin America have increasingly opted at least in ideology for the poor and oppressed. In the context of authoritarian military regimes and extremely unjust societies, the more traditional structures of the Church are inappropriate to relate it to the people and thus a smaller, more flexible entity had to be found. The CEB fulfills this function by bringing together people from the same class, thereby avoiding a traditional problem of effectively silencing and excluding the lower class by mixing them in groups run by the middle classes. What is more, since work with the lower classes is often considered subversion, smaller and more flexible groups are required since large structures are obvious and easily intervened.

(4) The Council emphasized openness to the world, community, involvement of the laity, and diversity in ministries (among other things). These themes provide legitimation to the CEBs and with further ideological elaboration since the Council there is more support for the CEBs. Pope Paul VI in his apostolic exhortation of December 8, 1975, "Evangelii nuntiandi," supported the CEBs, as did the Roman synod of 1975 and the bishops assembled at Medellín in 1968 (Pro Mundi Vita,

1976: 2-4). In the conclusions of the Medellín document, the CEBs were frequently mentioned; one statement describes them thus:

> It is the first and fundamental ecclesiastical nucleus, which down on that grass-roots level brings richness and expansion to the faith—and to religious worship, which is its expression. This community, which is the initial cell of the Church and the radiating center for its evangelizing efforts, is today a most potent factor for human advancement and development [CELAM, 1970: 201].

Specifically in Brazil the CEBs have been encouraged and promoted at least since the Emergency Plan (which was inspired by a letter of Pope John XXIII) of 1962 and subsequently in the Joint Pastoral Plan of 1966-1970. In the National Conference of Brazilian Bishops'—CNBB— biennial plans of 1975-1977 and 1977-1979, the CEBs remain among the four highest priorities and this is also the case in a great many dioceses. It is particularly significant that Sáo Paulo, the largest archdiocese in the world, has opted clearly in this direction. The CEBs, then, have been promoted internationally and nationally and in all respects would appear to be an entity whose time has come as they seek to fulfill precisely those lacunae left in the face of archaic and inflexible structures of a Church traditionally weak and now seeking to change and become more relevant for society.

The legitimation is important. All the primary and secondary studies show that the CEBs emerge and flourish only with direct support of the Church. They do not spring forth spontaneously, but are rather the result of official Church strategies and actions. Mesters, for example, summarized dozens of reports on the CEBs and observes,

> Almost all the experiences described exist in dioceses where the bishop or the priests and nuns aid the creation of these communities. . . . It is known, on the other hand, that where the bishop or priest is against this type of renovation the process does not begin and remains blocked. This is evidence of the almost strategic importance of the ecclesiastical institution: when it aids the process, it works; when it is contrary, the process is aborted and has no future.

Furthermore, the initiative for the CEBs begins with religious activities and structures such as chapels, visits, the parish system, old associations, and the like, and:

In almost all the experiences described, the renovation is helped in its inception by the ecclesiastical institution. The institution takes the initiative; from the "center" the movement spreads to the bases. Using their uncommon gifts the priest, nun, layman, or even bishop stimulates and unleashes the process. But, to a degree in which this process takes form and begins to awaken the people so it also begins to dismantle the traditional organization of the same institution which promoted it, and the particular priest, bishop, or religious enters an unlimited identity crisis [SEDOC, 1975: 1137].

In effect, the formation of these entities is legitimated nationally and internationally and when promoted specifically in a diocese can give rise to active units. However, since there are so many diverse reasons for their formation and such extensive justification exists for their presence, it is obviously impossible for all the CEBs to be alike. Since they arise from concrete needs, the views on the part of the institution of their utility can be quite varied. Furthermore, since at the initial stages the institution plays an important role, the CEBs can evolve in very different ways. In the primary and secondary studies, and in my own field research, a general pattern emerged indicating that in the richer areas of Brazil, where the Church is generally more affluent and structured, the CEBs tended to remain as mini-parishes in which the laymen did the work of the priest. In poorer areas, either in rural sections or on the periphery of the large cities, the CEBs tended to extend this role and assume their own dynamic. Of course, the original intentions of the Church personnel may have varied but it seems that the concrete situations in which the CEBs are found and in which problems are defined prove most important in explaining their development. It is in these poorer areas that most of the CEBs are emerging, and while in 1976 there were some 40,000 there are today over 50,000 with some 1.2 million participating members (SEDOC, 1979: 807).

In 1974-1975 we did a survey research project consisting of some 2,000 questionnaires in eight dioceses of Brazil. The project was specifically concerned with religiosity and politicization, but we did gather some material on groups—both religious and civil—and on what can be termed CEBs. All the dioceses contained a variety of groups but those selected for their clear line of innovation had more CEBs. And, in the two most innovative dioceses, all the groups were CEBs. It seems, then, that data on the CEBs does exist, and this is no simple task given their characteristics of flexibility, religious definition, and location on the margins of society.

By means of the questionnaire we gathered information on the internal dynamics of the CEBs and found them much less clerical in terms of control. They function quite democratically in that the members do participate and control them (Bruneau, 1979: ch. 7). In the analysis of the information on religious beliefs and practices, we defined four main patterns of being a Catholic. By relating the membership of the various groups, traditional and the CEBs, we found that the more traditional groups were much more likely to involve people following more cult or orthodox patterns of religion. Among these more traditional groups there was no relationship with a progressive or social Catholicism pattern. In looking at the CEBs, however, we found just the opposite. There was a slight relationship with the orthodox pattern and a much stronger relationship with the social Catholicism pattern. And, in further dividing the CEBs into those that were most clearly of this pattern, we found much stronger relationship with the social Catholicism pattern. In short, then, our data were relevant to the general topic of the CEBs, and we found in general that it supports the view based upon the analysis of primary and secondary documentation. Those in the CEBs are more progressive in religious and socio-political terms and the groups themselves function more democratically. My own participant observation in at least a dozen dioceses supports these conclusions as well. Thus, while there may be much fanfare about the CEBs, and while they are not easy to analyze in large numbers, they do in fact seem to operate as stated above and to have the functions assigned to them by their members and those in the Church promoting them.

Encouraged by these supporting data, we can now draw out some of the implications or likely results from the experience of the CEBs. First of all, the CEBs emerge from religious functions and structures and are firmly based on religious activities. They are not civil societies but rather religious associations. However, by their very form as decentralized communities and by their purpose which is to relate the Gospel to reality they hold great implications for both the Church as institution and the pattern of religion it promotes. Once the process of decentralization is initiated and the people at the grass-roots are defined as the Church, then the whole system of authority is inverted and the laity no longer has to wait for word from above but can assume responsibilities on its own. The diagram below contrasts the authority system of the CEB with the traditional pattern. It can be seen that there is now a direct and unmediated link between the people (in the CEBs) and Jesus Christ without all the formal structure. Thus in this new system of involvement and decision-making the archaic groups and structures of the Church

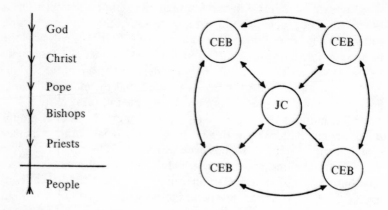

are superseded. If the Church is based on the laity united in the CEBs, then there is little justification for the rest of the institutional paraphernalia which is increasingly viewed as superfluous. This is further encouraged by the emphasis in the CEBs on reading and reflecting on the Bible and relating its passages to everyday life. The layman need not wait for the priest but can, as in the practice of Protestantism, interpret God's message for himself. These CEBs tend to reverse the matter of ecclesiastical authority and structure and by bringing the Church into close contact with the reality of the vast majority of its members force a redefinition of religious goals and attitudes.

The result in terms of redefinition of the goals and structure is perhaps best expressed in the following quote from Leonardo Boff, one of the theologians most deeply involved in the CEBs: "Slowly but surely there has been developing in significant sectors of the Church a clear option: option for the people, for the poor, for liberation. The basic Christian community is the place where the theological essence of the Church is realized and at the same time the practice of liberation of the poor by the poor themselves" (SEDOC, 1979: 705). The theme of the third national meeting on the CEBs in 1978 was "CEB: Church, a People Liberating Itself." The implications for the Church could not be more all-encompassing. The fundamental goal, nature, and structure is put into question and as the CEBs develop a momentum the very nature of the Church as institution is no longer what it was once thought to be.

Clearly this is important, and perhaps not fully appreciated by those at various levels promoting the CEBs, but given the history of the Church as community and the concrete problems facing the Church in Latin America there is some chance of the CEB becoming in fact *the* Church.

Even though the CEBs are primarily religious groups, they have obvious sociopolitical implications. First, they offer an opportunity to participate in a society which has never encouraged participation and has failed to provide channels for this process. There is undoubtedly a carryover of demands from participation in the religious realm to the civil. Second, the various reports on the formation of the CEBs indicate that they are usually founded on concrete issues such as land tenure problems and lack of essential services and resources. Thus from the beginning at least one of their functions has been the resolution of certain practical problems, and if they are successful on one there is every likelihood that they will go on to take up other issues. And, third, by the mere fact of relating reality to the Bible there is a tendency to radicalization as, depending on the selections, the Bible has been and can still be a very utopian document indeed. Generally the more utopian texts are selected in the work with the CEBs, and these need little exaggeration to relate to the present situation in Brazil. A general and increasingly widely appreciated sense emerges from discussions with members of these groups, their documents, and the survey research project, and it is that they are politically significant in the present Brazilian context and are potentially radicalizing. As Demo (1974: 37) emphasized after indicating the implications for the Church, "In the case of the CEB this contestation strikes not only the dimension of the ecclesiastical hierarchy, here called to take a background role, but also affects, to a certain degree, the political activity of the traditional leaders who are then considered somewhat alien from the basic necessities of the members." This is recognized by the traditional politicians as well as newer anti-regime candidates who are very actively seeking the support of the CEBs. In the legislative elections in 1978 the politicians of all parties (and parties in formation) attempted to approach the CEBs. They realized that after 14 years of military dictatorship that there were few grass-roots organizations of any vitality, and these CEBs represented an obvious resource for their campaigns. Generally, the CEBs were able to maintain their independence from these attractions and have gone on to further develop their critical roles for further organization and future strategies. They offer, then, the seedbed of future popularly inspired and popularly based initiatives rather than easy votes for politicians in the present regime. It is widely recognized that the current "Union Opposition" in the São Paulo area had its origins in CEBs, a situation which is increasingly apparent in the efforts at rural organization. The CEBs are not necessarily large, well organized, or dynamic, but rather exist in a terrain which has been thoroughly cleared by the military regime. In this context the CEBs assume a larger role in generating popular initiatives.

The CEBs represent the single most important change in the Latin American Churches. Because of historical legitimacy (from the Church as community in ancient times), the current commitment to work with the poor, and the concrete lacks in these Churches, the CEBs have begun and are spreading quickly. They hold tremendous implications for the Church and, in the current types of regimes and extremely unjust societies, also for the societies. They vary tremendously from country to country and diocese to diocese, and the very difficulty in identifying them is the source of much of their strength. Not all the CEBs hold, or will hold, the implications I have drawn, but once this process is initiated there may well be other forms that emerge with even greater vitality. There are obvious problems involved, not the least of which is continued legitimation from Rome and the national Churches. Assuming that this continues, and if it does not there may well be tremendous tensions as indicated in the statements emerging from some CEBs in preparation for the Puebla meeting, there are still other problems. In a sense the CEBs are sects but to this point linked to the institution. The loss of this link would probably spell the creation of real sects. What has happened so far has been rather the specialization of some CEBs into other forms of organizations for work in the sociopolitical situations. This is crucial but extremely tricky and those in the Church who are promoters of the CEBs are prepared to see much of their work of encouragement and stimulation go on to another level. If and when the regimes open, then there will be another question as to the future of the CEBs since many of the concrete problems will presumably have other solutions. One wonders if they will have such a dynamic and spread when the sociopolitical dimension is less important. Be that as it may, at present they are important and fully justified if only in providing the basis for further popular initiatives in the society and a questioning of the authority structure of the Church.

NOTE

1. A general review of the CEBs can be found in Pro Mundi Vita (1976); some statements from Latin America, LADOC (1976); SEDOC (1975, 1976, 1978, 1979) has the most complete assortment of texts and analyses from Brazil. The nature of my field work and the description of the survey can be found in Bruneau (1979).

REFERENCES

BARREIRO, A. (1977) Comunidades Eclesiais de Base e Evangelização do Pobres. Sao Paulo: Ediçõés Loyola.

BOFF. C (1978) Comunidade Eclesial/Comunidade Politica. Petrópolis: Editora Vozes.

BRUNEAU, T. (1979) Religiosity and Politicization in Brazil: The Church in an Authoritarian Regime. São Paulo: Edições Loyola.

———— (1974) The Political Transformation of the Brazilian Catholic Church. Cambridge: Cambridge Univ. Press.

CELAM [Council of Latin American Bishops] (1970) The Church in the Present Day Transformation of Latin America in the Light of the Council; Conclusions. Bogotá: Author.

CARAMURU DE BARROS, R. (1967) Comunidade Eclesial de Base: Uma Opcáo Pastoral Decisiva. Petrópolis: Editora Vozes.

CERIS [Centro de Estatística Religiosa e Investigações Sociais] (1978) Assorted Statistics on the Structure of the Church. Rio de Janeiro: Author.

DEMO, P. (1974) Comunidade: Igreja na Base. São Paulo: Edições Paulinas.

GREGORY, A. et al. (1973) Comunidades Eclesiais de Base: Utopia ou Realidade. Petrópolis: Editora Vozes.

————(1967a) Pastoral de Grandes Cidades. Petrópolis: Editora Vozes.

————(1967b) A Paroqui a Ontem, Hoje e Amanhã. Petrópolis: Editora Vozes.

LADOC [Latin America Documentation] (1976) Basic Christian Communities. Washington, DC: U. S. Catholic Conference.

PASTOR F. A. (1977) "Paroquia e Comunidade de Base." Síntese (Rio de Janeiro) 4 (May-August): 21-45.

Pro Mundi Vita (1976) Basic Communities in the Church. Brussels: Author.

RAMALHO, J. (1977) "Algumas Notas sobre duas Perspectivas de Pastoral Popular." Cadernos do ISER (Rio de Janeiro) 6 (March): 31-39.

SEDOC (1975, 1976, 1978, 1979) Comunidades Eclesiais de Base. Petrópolis: Editora Vozes.

10

SALVATION THROUGH CHRIST OR MARX
Religion in Revolutionary Cuba

MARGARET CRAHAN

Unlike churches in the rest of Latin America, those in Cuba did not embark at the outset of the 1960s on a period of liberalization and innovation in theology, pastoral forms, lay participation and political strategies. Rather, the coming to power in 1959 of a revolutionary government and the initiation of substantial societal restructuring reinforced conservatism within the churches. Strong challenges to the legitimacy of the government by the churches from 1959 through 1961 were not effective due largely to institutional limitations and their identification as bulwarks of prerevolutionary structures. Hence, in spite of a marked increase in participation and contributions, the churches' counterrevolutionary stance had limited impact. Contributing to this was the exodus of many religious activists to the United States and Spain, and a turning in upon themselves by the churches which came to serve as refuges from change. During a period of religious ferment in the rest of Latin America, the Cuban churches entered a period of stasis from which they only began emerging in the late 1960s, challenged by the consolidation of the revolution and by international developments.

The crisis which the Cuban churches underwent was the result primarily of institutional and theological conservatism which sprang largely from the nature of their own and Cuba's historical development. While the churches were weak, Christianity was a pervasive cultural presence which encouraged negative reactions to the introduction of socialism. This helps explain why resistance to the revolution based on religious motives was greater than the low levels of participation in church services and activities in prerevolutionary Cuba would suggest.

After a period of retreat and quiescence from 1963 to 1968, the Catholic and Protestant churches began exploring the possibilities of rapprochement with the government and experimentation with new theological definitions and pastoral programs better adapted to the reality of Christians living in a socialist society. This process has proceeded slowly and with more caution than comparable activities in other areas of Latin America, partly the result of the fact that, rather than having the opportunity to react and adapt gradually to rapid change, the Cuban churches were swept up in a period of turbulence in which many of their basic premises were directly challenged. Hence, it was only in the early 1970s that Cuban churchpeople really began exploring the implications of such developments as liberation theology, increased lay participation in ecclesiastical decision-making, and other innovations. To a considerable extent, the Cuban revolution, rather than transforming the Cuban churches, reinforced traditional policies and behavior, making the churches today less open and innovative than those in most other Latin American countries.

In order to better understand the distinct nature of the Cuban churches as compared to those in other Latin American countries, this essay will analyze religious affiliation, practice, and attitudes in Cuba through an examination of the evolution of the protestant and Catholic churches principally since 1959. Institutionalized rather than Afro-Cuban religion (santería) will be emphasized, as the former appears to have been more directly affected by the revolution, and more empirical studies have been undertaken concerning it. Due to the absence of survey data regarding Cuban Judaism, it will not be included. The data available consists of some dozen studies dating from 1940 to the present dealing with both national and subnational samples (Cepeda, 1966; Davis, 1942; de la Huerta Aguiar, 1960; Echevarría Salvat, 1971; El Equipo Diocesano de Jovenes de Camagüey, 1967; Noguiera Rivero, 1962; Rochon, 1967; Universidad Central "Marta Abreu" de las Villas, 1959; Torroella, 1963). These include the results of a survey of some forty Cuban church leaders, both clerical and lay, resident in Cuba, Europe, and the United States, whom I interviewed in 1973, 1974, and 1976. The interviews were in-depth explorations of both prerevolutionary and postrevolutionary conditions designed to elicit not only individual attitudes, but also evaluations of general trends within institutions.[1] Since the surveys are not generally fully comparable, the data available are suggestive rather than definitive and are most revealing in the context of other sources. In addition, given the high degree of ideological permeation of both Catholic and Protestant belief systems, no attempt has been made to isolate religious from ideological factors. Indeed, the presence or absence of change in Cuban religious attitudes is more comprehensible if one regards them in the context of ideological developments.

I. Prerevolutionary Background

It is widely held that religion in general and the Catholic Church in particular were relatively weak in prerevolutionary Cuba (Aguilar, 1974: 21-22; Davis, 1942: 49; Dewart, 1963: 93-99; Nelson, 1970: 268; Houtart and Rousseau, 1971: 113-114; and Ruiz, 1968: 162). This opinion is based primarily on the nominal nature of many Cubans' commitment to Catholicism, the numerical weakness of Protestants and Jews, and the noninstitutional nature of the Afro-Cuban sects. Other factors include the urban concentration of Catholic and Protestant personnel and institutions and their consequent scarcity in rural areas, emphasis on institution-building and elite education rather than pastoral duties, higher percentage of female over male formal participation, limited number of Cuban vocations, and the image of the churches as foreign institutions—the Catholic Church being tied to Spain and the Protestant churches to the United States.

While all this is true, certain cautions should be kept in mind. Although throughout Latin America the frequency of attendance at services traditionally has been low and the institutional churches often the object of considerable hostility, Christianity exerts a predominant influence which in moments of crisis can result in a reassertion of loyalty to the churches. The Cuban case is an apt demonstration of this, for while the vast majority of Catholics in the prerevolutionary period rarely practiced their religion according to standard indicators, many Cubans rejected the revolution, in part, because of the strong animosity toward Marxism which socialization in a predominantly Christian society encouraged. The appearance of weakness on the part of the Catholic Church was stimulated, in part, by the fact that Cuba was the object of the most intense proselytizing efforts by U.S. Protestants in all Latin America. In addition, the importation of substantial numbers of Africans as slaves up through the mid-nineteenth century resulted in the proliferation of spiritist beliefs which became mingled with Christian ones. The presence of Protestant, Jewish, and Afro-Cuban religions not only provided competition for the Catholic Church, but also gave Cuba perhaps the most diverse religious scene in all Latin

America, particularly in the post-World War II period.

The presence of a multitude of denominations and sects contributed to a degree of flexibility and casualness toward religion that was reinforced by the increasing secularization of Cuban society. Nevertheless, even in rural areas most Cubans identified themselves as Christians, though they may never have had any contact with a church. Such individuals can be found among those who adduce religious motives for leaving Cuba after 1959. The so-called weakness of religion in pre-revolutionary Cuba was primarily institutional rather than cultural and, to a degree, due to the nature of the historical evolution of the Catholic Church in the island.

Catholicism was introduced into Cuba with the arrival of Columbus. The transformation of the island into a way-station or staging area for expeditions to the more heavily populated mainland colonies meant that it became of secondary, or even tertiary, importance to colonial authorities both civil and ecclesiastical. By the nineteenth century decay in the Catholic Church was pronounced. Increasingly the island was populated by miscreant peninsular clerics exiled to Cuba for punishment or conservative priests and religious fleeing from the newly independent mainland Spanish colonies. This combination contributed to the development of reactionary attitudes within the Church and lax observance of clerical duties. The conservatism of the Catholic Church was demonstrated by the hierarchy's strong opposition to Cuba's breaking away from Spain. Yet even after independence, when the Catholic Church's prestige was very low, the influence of the values it encouraged was evident. In 1900, for example, 80 of 107 Cuban municipalities, three of six provincial governors, and all but one judge of the first instance opposed the legalization of civil marriage (Ruiz, 1968: 161). This reflected the fact that the religious values of Cubans and the opinions and actions of church personnel were not necessarily identified as one by the general populace. Generalized religious belief and esteem for religion continued in spite of unpopular political and social positions taken by the churches.

The temporal and spiritual poverty of the Catholic Church in Cuba at the outset of the twentieth century provided opportunities for more liberal and populist competitors, such as the U.S. Protestants, as well as political movements, such as the socialists. This stimulated an internal reevaluation of Catholic strategies and by the 1920s the Church had recouped somewhat and was beginning to reassert its political clout. Part of its strategy derived from a belief in the desirability of maintaining an alliance with secular power and extracting from it financial benefits and a guarantee of a religious monopoly. The Cuban Catholic Church became aware of pressures for modernization, particularly among the urban bourgeoisie—the prime source of its vocations and local financial support. In an effort to cultivate the loyalty of this group, lay organizations were expanded and given a more activist orientation. In the late 1920s Catholic Action, aimed at keeping the bourgeoisie active in the Church , hile helping Catholics adapt to changing times, was introduced from Spain. This organization opened up decision-making to limited lay input and tended to focus energies on the creation of an idealistic new Christendom which bore little relevance to the Cuban reality.

The challenge of socioeconomic injustice in Cuba, as well as competition from secular groups such as political parties and labor unions, was also felt by the Protestant churches in the 1920s and 1930s resulting in increased emphasis on social welfare activities, particularly in the unevangelized rural areas. There was also a rise in interest in *santería* and pentecostalism, which provided a more direct sense of participation and a supportive community wherein problems of daily life were dealt with. Increased resources and the appearance of greater relevance resulted in more widespread religious activity in Cuba in the 1940s and 1950s. This encouraged a sense of optimism within the churches (Crahan, 1977, 1978). There was an upsurge of involvement not only in nontraditional organizations, but also in traditional ones such as Hijas de María and Caballeros Católicos. These groups reduced the possibilities of integrating churchpeople into secular movements, a factor which contributed to the churches' marginalization during the 1950s conflict between the forces of Fulgenico Batista and Fidel Castro.

Prior to 1959 the Catholic Church, and to a degree the Protestant denominations, largely adhered to a policy which Levine (1973) has defined as "traditional interventionism," which emphasized the cultivation and manipulation of elite secular ties. Such tactics are characteristic of highly stratified societies in which power is concentrated in the hands of a few who hold sway over a relatively noncomplex institutional order. In such situations the Church benefits as a result of the strength of allied structures more than from its own actions or those of its membership. Given the weakness of secular institutions in Cuba, due primarily to the heavy influence of the United States in the prerevolutionary period, the civil-ecclesiastical linkages which existed did not provide the churches with the degree of influence resulting from this strategy in other Latin American countries. The dependency of Cuban political and economic structures on the United States and the fact that the Catholics and Protestants received most of their funding and personnel from abroad caused the churches to suffer from a double dependency. Dominance first by Spain and later by the United States undercut the development of strong national institutions. This encouraged political instability and contributed to the turning to strongmen, such as Gerardo Machado and Fulgencio Batista. Most churches attempted to build links with these regimes even in the face of corruption, repression, and maintenance of acute socioeconomic injustices. This further contributed to the low esteem Cubans held for the institutional churches.

The strategy recommended by Vallier (1970) that Latin American churches build an independent base for themselves as articulators of universal values would have been unworkable in Cuba given the substantial gap between social classes. This meant that goals would have to be, and were, defined in terms so general as to have little possibility of implementation. This helps explain the difficulty clerics encountered in proselytizing among the urban and rural poor, who tended to identify the churches as bulwarks of the status quo. Notable is the degree to which religious values did permeate Cuban society. Such penetration of Christian beliefs, including Afro-Cuban versions, has been repeatedly attested to in the anthropological and other literature (Barnet, 1968: 56-57, 84-86).[2] The depth of the roots of generalized religious belief helps explain the negative reaction of many ostensibly nonreligious Cubans as the revolution became increasingly Marxist.

Within six months of the establishment of the Castro government, many churches, particularly the Catholic, experienced growth in membership and activities as they became the prime institutional opponents of the revolution. Attendance at Mass and other services increased and there was an influx of new members and contributions to such groups as Agrupación Católica, while 1,000,000 Cubans turned out in Havana for the National Catholic Congress in November 1959, a gathering which previously had attracted about 10,000. In this period the traditionally low levels of formal participation were reversed and the churches became highly politicized (Crahan, 1976). Growth was not sustained to a considerable extent as a result of the emigration of a substantial proportion of the faithful, as well as 70% of the Catholic priests and 90% of Catholic religious, together with 50% or better of

Protestant clerical and lay leaders.[3] It was this exodus more than any other single factor which threw the Cuban churches into crisis.

II. Religious Affiliation

Church estimates of the number of nominal Catholics in pre-revolutionary Cuba cluster around 70-75% of the total population (@7,500,000), while estimates for the 1970s range from 60-65% of 9-10,000,000 people. In the pre-1959 period there was approximately one priest for every 10,000 Cubans, and since the mid-1960s one for every 40,000. In 1970 it was reported that two-thirds of the population were still being baptized and buried in Catholic ceremonies, as compared with 95% for the rest of Latin America (Hageman and Wheaton, 1971: 30-31; López Oliva, 1970: 180). The number of currently practicing Catholics is well under a million (IH 4731191).

In a 1957 survey of 4,000 agricultural workers throughout Cuba, 52.1% claimed to be Catholic, while 96.5% expressed belief in God. More than half (53.5%) claimed never to have seen a parish priest and only 7.8% admitted having any dealings with one. A substantial proportion (41.4%) of rural workers insisted they had no religion whatever (Echevarría Salvat, 1971: 14-15; Domínguez, 1975: 16-17). A 1958 survey of rual youths in Las Villas province, where there was a relatively high concentration of clerics, revealed a far smaller percentage professing no religion—13% of the males and 11.3% of the females, 84.8% of the men and 83.3% of the women asserting they were Catholics (Universidad Central, 1959: 29-30). Two years later, in 1960, a survey of 4,000 Cubans in all six provinces revealed that 72.5% claimed to be Catholic and 19% professed no religion. The same investigation reported that in Bayamo in rural Oriente only 48% were Catholic, while 30% had no religion (de la Huerta Aguiar, 1960: 45-47). These figures highlight the concentration of Catholics in urban areas and the resultant weakness of the Church in the countryside. Nevertheless, the vast majority identified themselves as Christians.

In both prerevolutionary and revolutionary Cuba not only was there a scarcity of pastors, but they were distributed very unequally throughout the island. In 1972 there were 211 priests in Cuba: 102 in Havana Province, 36 in Oriente, 25 in Las Villas, 18 in Camagüey, 17 in Matanzas, and 13 in Pinar del Río. An equal number of nuns was distributed with like disproportion—176 located in Havana Province, while 32 of 37 male religious were there (Wallace, 1973: 5). This compares with 232 priests in urban Havana in 1953, 200 of whom were teaching in private schools (Houtart and Rousseau, 1971: 115). There were also approximately 3,000 Catholic religious in Cuba at that time, mainly in the cities engaged in nonpastoral work. As a consequence, there were rural areas and even some urban neighborhoods which were virtually unevangelized or, at most, superficially so. This helps explain the loose hold of the institutional church over the bulk of the population, as well as its identification with the urban bourgeoisie.

In 1958 Protestant officials claimed from 150,000 to 250,000 adherents. This was substantial growth from a 1940 estimate of 40,000 to 50,000 by U.S. sociologist Davis, who surveyed Cuba's 440 organized Protestant churches. Davis believed there were 35,000 Protestants in ten main groups (Northern Baptist, Church of God, Society of Friends, Protestant Episcopal Church, The Methodist Church, Presbyterian Church, Salvation Army, West Indies Mission, Southern Baptist, and Seventh Day Adventist), with 5,000 more in small independent congregations. Active membership constituted one percent of the total Cuban population of 4,200,000. Annual Protestant growth was 10.5 new members per church (Davis, 1942: 52, 62-63), which if maintained would have added 83,160 to the Protestant rolls by 1959 for a total of 123,160. Given the repeated references to membership increases and expansion of the number of churches in the late 1940s and 1950s, an estimate of 150,000 Protestants in Cuba by the time of the revolution does not seem exaggerated.[4] Data from the 1950s, however, indicate more substantial increases. A 1957 survey of 4,000 agricultural workers reported 3.3% of the respondents were Protestant, while a 1958 survey of Las Villas reported 3.1%. A 1960 study claimed the somewhat inflated figure of 6% (Echevarría Salvat, 1971: 14; Universidad Central, 1959: 29-30; de la Huerta Aguiar, 1960: 45).

Recent estimates of Protestant strength range from 25,000 to 65,000.[5] Evidence from most Protestant churches supports substantial declines as exemplified by the Methodists, who constituted the largest non-Catholic denomination in 1960.

CHANGES IN METHODIST MEMBERSHIP, 1957-1974*

1957	1960	1972	1974
7,847	10,347	2,629	2,478

*(Lewis, 1960; United Methodist Information, 1972: 1; Ordoñez, 1974).

Losses resulted primarily from migration abroad, particularly prior to 1970. A 1969 survey of Catholic parishes in urban Havana projected that by 1972, 50% to 70% of their prerevolutionary membership would have left the island (Jover, 1974: 27). A small Baptist church in Oriente lost 49 of its 80 members from 1960 to 1969, nine of them in the period 1961 to 1964 because the pastor was not sympathetic to the revolution. Some of these became members of the Communist party, although most did not (García Franco, 1970: 6-8).

Other congregations reflected such declines. The Reformed Presbyterian Church of Luyano reported a drop from 266 members in 1959 to 94 in 1970, in spite of 142 new members having been received during that period. The prime reasons were departure from Cuba of 105 members or loss of commitment by 129. The average age of Luyano members or aspirants in 1970 was 45.5 years, with 60.6% over 50 and 48% having six years of education or less. Thirty-eight percent were housewives, 28% workers, 14% retired males, with an equal percentage of students, while the remainder was unclassified (Wallace, 1973: 6). These and other data confirm that churchgoers in contemporary Cuba are often individuals who reached their majority before the revolution, with a continued heavy proportion of females, children and older persons, rather than adult males. There are exceptions, such as the Catholic parish of San Juan del Monte in a working-class neighborhood in Havana. In the prerevolutionary period it was quite active and has suffered fewer losses than, for example, the wealthier parishes of Vedado. Baptist congregations in Oriente have also held firm, aided by the fact that almost none of their pastors migrated abroad.

Davis' 1940 data concerning the occupations of Protestants identified approximately 29% as housewives, 20% as workers, 1% as retired, and 23% as students. A comparision with Luyano thirty years later reveals some changes precipitated by the revolution. The drop in student membership suggests that the ideological transformation prompted by revolutionary education was having its impact on Cuban youth. Proportionally more housewives and retirees participated in 1970, indicating less integration into revolutionary society, as well as more leisure time for these groups. Such comparisons can only be hypothetical without further data and consideration of other variables.

Overall, the Catholic Church and the less populist Protestant denomiations (Methodist, Presbyterians, and Episcopalians) suffered the greatest losses of membership and pastors. Groups whose appeal

TABLE 1
Occupations of Protestant Faithful in 1940 and 1970

	PERCENTAGES	
OCCUPATIONS	NATIONWIDE 1940*	LUYANO 1970**
Housewives	29	38
Workers	20	28
Students	23	14
Unemployed	13	0
Retired	1	14... (males only)
Unclassified	14	6

* Davis, 1942: 74
** Wallace, 1973: 6

was traditionally to the poor and which were more adaptable were better able to weather the ferment of the 1960s in Cuba. The Baptist Convention of Western Cuba, for example, reported in 1971 that the denomination was "alive and growing" with 7,000 members, 319 having joined in 1970 and 22 students enrolled in a four-year seminary course. They also claimed that there were 9,000 Baptists in the Eastern Convention (Religious News Service, 1971: 7; Ordoñez, 1974: 11). This would make them, together with the Jehovah's Witnesses, the most rapidly growing denomination in Cuba. Statistics on the Jehovah's Witnesses and Seventh Day Adventists are difficult to obtain. Estimates by officials of the Cuban Council of Evangelical Churches place their strength at 20,000 to 35,000 with an increasing number in Havana, although prior to the revolution they were concentrated in the rural areas (IH 47413; IH 471119; IH 3703212). Such groups, as well as other fundalmentalist sects, provide alternative communities for those who resist integration into the socialist society being built in Cuba. Individuals, for example, who oppose universal military service, public education, and the collectivization of small privately held farms, find reinforcement among the Jehovah's Witnesses. For those who wish to publicly express their disaffection from the present government, membership in such groups is an obvious means.

The limited evidence available suggests that there has been less of a decline in adherence to Afro-Cuban beliefs than to institutional religion. Prior to 1959 *santería* was identified primarily with the rural lower class and did not exclude formal affiliation with an institutional church. While only one percent claimed spiritism as their religion in a 1957 survey of agricultural workers and in a 1960 national sample, other evidence indicates that one-quarter of the Cuban people engaged in spiritist practices (Echevarría Salvat, 1971: 14; de la Huerta Aguiar, 1960: 45, 48). Given the syncretic nature of Afro-Cuban beliefs, their adaptability to changing conditions in Cuba appears greater than that of the more institutionalized religions.

III. Religious Practice

Afro-Cuban religious services, as well as Catholic and Protestant ones, have remained substantially unchanged since 1959. Those adaptations which have occurred are as much the result of international factors, including Vatican II and new theological formulations, as Cuban circumstances. This is not to say that the revolution has not stimulated attempts to make religion responsive to the challenges posed by contemporary Cuba. The tremendous membership losses most churches suffered, however, encouraged passivity and left many congregations without a critical mass to generate new programs and strategies. Only in the late 1960s, and more especially the 1970s, have serious efforts been undertaken to make the churches consonant with their existential situation.

Nonetheless, a frequently expressed opinion of current church leaders in Cuba is that their congregations are stronger, having been purified of members whose commitments were superficial. As one patriarch of the Presbyterian Church expressed it:

Before, many became members of the church precisely to take advantage of the benefits of the primary schools and of the colleges, to be a candidate for a scholarship in the United States, to receive help—social and economic—from the church. There were 600,000 unemployed in Cuba before the triumph of the Revolution—it was a society of crisis, no? You can imagine how a pastor could be of influence, can't you? But people come to church now because of a profound religious conviction; we have members of greater quality [Wallace, 1973: 7].

Consequently, the decline in membership does not upset some pastors and, as in the prerevolutionary period, there is considerable variation in the level of activity almost always related to the vitality of a particular congregation's leadership, as well as the services rendered.

According to a 1966 survey of agricultural workers, only 0.7% of the 4,000 Catholic and non-Catholic respondents had attended church four or more times a year; 93.5% had not attended at all. Of professed Catholics, 88.8% reported not having attended Mass in a year, with 4.3% attending three or more times (Echevarría Salvat, 1971: 15-16). A 1958 study of Las Villas Province revealed that only 3.8% of 201 male Catholic respondents had attended Mass in the previous month, while 5.1% of the females had. Close to 90% of the females and 92.6% of the males had not attended any sort of church service (Universidad Central, 1959: 32). Nine years later, a 1967 survey of the diocese of Camagüey revealed that 3,597 of the province's residents, some 0.6% of its population, were attending Mass regularly.[6] This included 1,618 children, and with the exception of the city of Camagüey, most of those attending were children. For the entire diocese, 49% of those frequenting Mass were 24 or younger. A comparison of these results with 1965 diocesan statistics reveals that the socioeconomic status of those who attended Mass remained essentially the same, with housewives constituting one-half and students one-fifth. Workers and professionals amounted to 3% and 9% respectively. Of those who attended Mass, 12% never received communion, while 10% received only once a year. Forty-seven percent received communion occasionally. The most frequent communicants were in Camagüey, Ciego de Avila and Morón—urban centers with 100,000 populations. This implies that the greater availability of church facilities and personnel in cities continued to influence the level of religious activity (El Equipo Diocesano, 1967: 12-14).

In 1940 Davis reported that only 25% of Cuban Protestants were active in their respective churches, with the remainder neither attending services nor contributing financially (Davis, 1942: 56, 63). Close to two decades later Protestant attendance in Las Villas was 82% of those males claiming to be Protestants and 88% of the females, a substantial increase. This confirmed frequent reports in the 1950s of increasing fervor on the part of congregations (Universidad Central, 1959: 32). In the Luyano Presbyterian Church in 1970, 48% of the 130 members interviewed regularly attended services, 33% irregularly, and 19% never. It was also reported that a good number of young people were beginning to attend services (Wallace, 1973: 6). In the same year a 33-member Baptist Church in Oriente claimed 42% of the congregation were regular attendees, 33% rarely, and 25% never (García Franco, 1970: 5-6, 10). The growth of Protestantism in Cuba begun in the 1950s was obviously shortcircuited by the turmoil precipitated by the revolution, as was the level of participation in church activities of all denominations.

Attendance at religious instructions in the Catholic diocese of Camagüey in 1967, for example, was 1.1%, or 1,641 of all elementary school age children. Fifty-five percent of the Catholic children were receiving instruction at home. Religious instruction for adults was emphasized beginning in 1962, with 50% of the Catholic faithful having some type of formal instruction between 1962 and 1967. This would seem to have been partly an effort to counteract the ideological inroads of Marxism-Leninism. Nine percent of the Catholic adults who were active in the diocese served as catechists, while 7% helped prepare liturgies, and 6% participated in discussion groups. Such activities were concentrated in Camagüey city where the greatest number of trained leaders were, as well as the strongest tradition of church involvement (El Equipo Diocesano, 1967: 10-21).

The continued urban concentration of militant Catholics and church activitists in Havana, Santa Clara, Santiago and Camagüey, in the face of difficulties with the government in the 1960s, was ascribed by the former Catholic Action leader, Mateo Jover (1974: 23), to the more flexible attitudes of civil officials in urban areas. No doubt the relatively greater strength of church people in these areas also helped. This is linked to greater access to means of religious formation, including more contact with clerics.

Reforms stimulated by both domestic Cuban conditions and international factors such as Vatican II were implemented slowly and with some tension between those who regarded the church as a refuge from change and those who looked to reform as a means of making the church more relevant to the existing situation. The pattern is similar in the Protestant churches, which shared a preoccupation with encouraging and maintaining religious loyalty, particularly among young people, in order to guarantee the churches' institutional futures.

Prior to the revolution, lay activists and priests, ministers, and other religious were frequently recruited through the church schools. The nationalization of private schools in 1961 elminated that source. With one exception, the present and former church leaders I interviewed had all attended such schools. This was in spite of the fact that approximately 60% of them came from families which were not formally religious, illustrating the phenomenon that the chief appeal of church schools was their reputation for quality education. The departure from Cuba of a high proportion of the teachers in such schools meant a vacuum was created in the early 1960s with respect to the religious formation of youth. Traditional groups, such as Catholic Action and the Protestant Student Christian Movement, also suffered.

By 1962 the churches were counteracting or responding to Marxism with catechetical instruction and discussion groups which met to explore the relevance of Christian faith to their daily lives (El Equipo Diocesano, 1967: 10; IH 5771112). Such groups would later raise basic questions concerning the goals and functions of the churches, and served in some instances as stimuli for internal reforms and liberalization of church attitudes toward the revolution. Perhaps the most basic was whether or not church people should continue to oppose the government, since it was making some headway in remedying such chronic socioeconomic ills as unemployment and poverty, particularly in rural areas. This prompted explorations of whether a Christian might at times support a political system traditionally condemned by the churches. As such discussions progressed, a liberal minority began to argue that one achieved salvation not simply through rectitude in one's own life, but also through struggle to achieve socioeconomic justice in one's community. These conclusions combined with the development of liberation theology in the rest of Latin America to stimulate increased questioning of traditional theological formulations, hierarchical authority, and pastoral strategies by a minority of Cuban Christians.

IV. The Churches in Prerevolutionary and Revolutionary Cuba as seen by Cuban Christians

In spite of continuing traditionalism among most church people in contemporary Cuba, all 40 of the clerical and lay Catholic and

Protestant church leaders I interviewed residing both within and without the island were critical of their institutions in the prerevolutionary period. Some held that radical changes were and still are needed, while others supported more limited measures which were essentially adaptive, not just to changing conditions in Cuba, but also to trends within the international ecclesial community. Progressivism was stronger among Protestants than Catholics, but in both cases reformers have recently captured high positions within their institutions. The result is that church leadership is sometimes more liberal than the faithful. The trauma of the radical changes initiated by the revolution and the political and economic isolation of Cuba instigated by the United States helped insulate Cuban Christians from liberalizing currents which were present in the rest of Latin America in the 1960s. Receptivity to the policies of the progressive leadership has consequently been somewhat limited. Beyond this, an almost exclusive dependence on theologies developed in response to European and North American circumstances left the churches with few resources to bring to bear on their actual situation.

Major criticisms of the churches in pre-1959 Cuba were elitism, lack of concern with socioeconomic justice, autocracy, over-preoccupation with financial matters, using charitable gestures to avoid confronting the structural bases of poverty and exploitation, cowardice in the face of political repression and corruption, overdependency on foreign and domestic political and economic elites, and failure to assume a prophetic role in a highly inegalitarian society. In addition, the churches were scorned for racism, pietism, pacifism, triumphalism, enclavism, puritanism, paternalism, individualism, and escapism.[7]

The charge of racism sprang from the fact that some church schools and organizations were unwilling to admit blacks. In addition, the predominantly Spanish Catholic clergy harbored attitudes of superiorty which, at times, depreciated Cuban culture as well as Cuban capacity to administer church institutions. Something akin to this existed in most of the U.S.-dominated Protestant churches. Among both Catholics and Protestants there was a pietistic emphasis on devotional aspects of religion and individual regeneration as the means to salvation. This permitted Christians to limit their responsibility for those less fortunate to occasional acts of charity. Given the widespread emphasis on misfortune as the "will of God," religion in prerevolutionary Cuba served to encourage acceptance of the status quo. For the poor the churches alleviated some of the pain of everyday existence by promising a reward in the hereafter. As the conflict between the forces of Batista and Castro escalated in the 1950s most churches maintained themselves aloof from the struggle, although some individual churchpeople assumed partisan roles. It is illuminating to note that one cleric who distinguished himself for his social activism in the 1950s and who subsequently left Cuba as a result of fear of communism, estimated that only 1.5% of Cuban churchpeople were seriously engaged in attacking endemic socioeconomic problems in the prerevolutionary period (IT 57311). He and other churchpeople concede that they did little to transform Cuba in pre-1959 period to conform more closely with Christian ideals. This would appear to be supported by the opinion of several thousand agricultural workers in a 1957 survey in which only 3.4% of them expressed any belief that the Catholic Church would be of any assistance in improving their lot (Echevarría Salvat, 1971: 25).

Belief by religious leaders that to change society it was necessary simply to change the individual and his or her values has changed somewhat since the revolution, with progressive and liberal sectors accepting the necessity of structural change and rejecting the notion of the churches as neutral or apolitical. There has also been a move away from the position that one can separate a church from the political, social, and economic contexts in which it exists. This has resulted in a push to abandon the role of the Church as primarily a consoler of the suffering and protector from divine wrath. In its place is offered the concept of a Christian community totally compromised in the struggle for socioeconomic justice.

While a prime impetus for this has been the revolution, the majority of Cuba's Christians did not conceive of the possibility of far-reaching changes resulting from the triumph of the 26th of July Movement. In reality the support of churchpeople for Castro's movement prior to 1959 sprang largely from opposition to Batista.[8] Hence the widespread reaction, both within and without the churches as radical changes began to be introduced, that the revolution was being betrayed. Such feeling was particularly strong within reformist groups such as Catholic Action and the Young Christian Workers, together with the Student Christian Movement. Castro's declaration of his Marxism-Leninism strengthened the sense of having been duped, an opinion which continues to hold sway among some Cuban churchpeople.[9]

This was reinforced by the loss of church personnel through emigration, the marginalization that retreat into religion as a refuge from change caused, and divisions within the churches. Further, the Catholic Church had no long-range strategy of response, nor did it appear to comprehend the realities of the situation (Jover, 1974: 20-21). The Protestant churches, less obviously counterrevolutionary than the Catholic, followed a policy of neither supporting nor opposing the revolution, but rather placing emphasis on Christian witness and opposition to atheism. They were also concerned with dissociating themselves from the counterrevolutionary image of Catholicism. Yet their greater identification with the United States presented its own problems given the anti-American turn of the revolution (United Methodist Information, 1972: 3; IH 471191; ISM 472115).

A 1964-1965 survey of Protestant youth found that the turn toward socialism was generally considered a betrayal which resulted in replacing one dictatorship with another. Some said they had expected it and that it was the fault of U.S. policy which drove Castro into the arms of the Soviet Union. A minority held it was a natural and logical step and in reality the only option. Pietism came into play with those who felt that, since God had permitted it, then it was all for the best. Some believed it was a challenge to proselytize the communists (Cepeda, 1966: 25-26). Reactions among Catholics were generally negative, with a good proportion feeling that opposition to the revolution was a moral responsibility.

Even prior to Castro's declaration of his Marxism-Leninism, disaffection had been growing over agrarian reform, nationalization of businesses, and executions of Batistianos and active counterrevolutionaries. For many Christians the agrarian reform law of 1959 was a violation of what they regarded as the Christian principle of the sanctity of private property (Dewart, 1963: 147-148; Rivas, 1971: 6). However, by 1965 a majority of Christian youth surveyed felt that it had been a pressing necessity and an unavoidable step, although some objected to what they regarded as injustices resulting from it. Support for the government's nationwide literacy campaign in the early 1960s was also strong, although 6% regretted what they felt was its ultimate objective—communist indoctrination. The reaction to the 1961 closing of the church schools was very negative—87.2% still opposing it in 1964 and 1965, although 81% approved of the nationalization of industries and businesses. This latter was a far more liberal stance than that of older churchpeople. Finally, 100% of the Protestant youths surveyed opposed the official executions which occurred in the early years of the revolution (Cepeda, 1966: 25). These youths must be regarded as atypical, as a national survey in the early 1960s revealed that only 3.5% of Cuban young people wanted to emulate Jesus Christ, and most regarded piety as an indication of a weak individual (Tor-roella, 1963: 21-22, 38-39, 45).

Church youth in the mid-1960s essentially contented themselves with being Christian witnesses, while minorities were either fervently prorevolutionary or antirevolutionary (Cepeda, 1966: 22). More recently there has been a small number of young people from non-religious backgrounds who have been attracted to the churches in the hopes of finding solutions to some of the transcendental questions which they do not find satisfactorily answered by Marxism-Leninism (Jover, 1974: 29; Wallace, 1973: 6-7). Most Cuban youths, however, continue to be relatively unattracted to religion.

Overall, the reaction of the Cuban churches was more direct and less complex than that of the Chilean churches to Salvador Allende's attempted introduction of parliamentary socialism from 1970 to 1973. Religious, political, and economic changes throughout Latin America in the 1960s reduced the traditional hostility toward Marxist options, and there was within Chile a vocal minority of Christians who strongly supported this development. The very correct relations between the Chilean episcopacy and Allende's government are in contrast to the early responses of most Cuban church leaders. The differences between the Cuban and Chilean reactions highlight the diminishing of cold war tensions in the 1960s and the growing diversity of political analysis within the churches, although the leadership continues by and large to emphasize institutional preservation via traditional strategies.

V. The Churches in Revolutionary Cuba

The revolution precipitated crises within the churches not simply as a result of the official adoption of Marxism-Leninism, but also because of tremendous losses in the ranks of the laity and the emigration or expulsion of priests, ministers, and other religious. Voluntary departures caused sometimes acrimonious debate within the churches and served to emphasize the differences between those who supported the revolution, those who argued it was the responsibility of the individual to stay and bear Christian witness, and those who felt their only recourse was to leave Cuba.[10] The reaction of Protestant youth to pastors and lay leaders who left ranged from acceptance to criticism of what they considered the abandonment of the flock in the face of the wolf (Cepeda, 1966: 27-28).

In the mid-1960s some clerics and laypersons were drafted into the Military Units to Aid Production (UMAP), a short-lived manual labor program for tramps, pimps, homosexuals, common criminals, and others regarded as deviants. A few pastors were jailed for counter-revolutionary activities and some 30 Baptist ministers for dealing with blackmarket currency. The reaction of Protestant youths to this was unanimous: if the pastors or lay leaders were imprisoned for counter-revolutionary activities and no other reason, then it was justified. However, if the actions considered counterrevolutionary were simply the preaching of the Gospel or the free exercise of their beliefs, then prison was deemed unjust (Cepeda, 1966: 28). Of significance is the fact that those of my informants who had been in jail or in UMAP all made the point that the most painful thing had been their sense of having been abandoned by their churches. The shock of doing manual labor alongside individuals they normally would not have come into contact with occasioned for some a reevaluation of the meaning of religion in their lives, while for others it resulted in a further retreat into traditional views. Furthermore, all resumed their church activities upon their release, some being greeted warmly as martyrs, while others were regarded with some disconfort (García Franco, 1966; IM 5771112; IH 4701181; IH 377221).

The loss of substantial proportions of their staffs resulted in opening the way for increased lay participation in the churches, which combined with international currents to stimulate reform. Pressure for change resulted in some liberalization, most notably in the Presbyterian, Methodist and Baptist churches and less so among the Catholics, Episcopalians, Seventh Day Adventists, and Jehovah's Witnesses. Within the Catholic Church it precipitated a crisis which came to a head in the late 1960s just prior to the issuing of the conciliatory pastoral letters of 1969 which broke the silence maintained since the early 1960s. In a 1972 article, "Cuban Catholics and Castro," the Cuban emigrée political scientist, Jorge Domínguez, ascribes the issuance of the conciliatory April 10, 1969 document to four factors: a desire for "political reinsertion or breathing space in the prevailing system"; "doctrinal reintegration into the post-conciliar church"; "transnational interaction within the Church"; and "ecumenical dialogue" (Domínguez, 1972: 25). A fifth factor was the struggle within the Church over internal liberalization.

Prior to this time the reforms envisioned by Vatican II had been ignored and unrealized in Cuba, due in large measure to the resistance to change which a sense of being beleaguered encouraged. Catholic theology and seminary training adhered to prerevolutionary forms and the theology of liberation made only slight inroads. This was in spite of strong lay support for reforms in the manner of saying Mass—94% in the diocese of Camagüey in 1965 and again in 1967; reception of communion—72% in 1965 and 75% in 1967; and reduction of the number of statues in churches—65% in 1965 and 58% in 1967 (El Equipo, 1967: 17).

By the late 1960s three main groups emerged among Catholic activists: conservatives who were not enthusiastic about liturgical and other reforms promoted by Vatican II and the 1968 Latin American bishops meeting at Medellín, Colombia, and who in general supported a passive witnessing church; the pragmatists who favored tight episcopal control of any move toward rapprochement with the government and were lukewarm toward substantial increases in lay participation; and the reformers, who included some of the most militant advocates of lay participation and who felt that dialogue with the government should proceed only if the Church recognized its obligation not only to support the government for its positive accomplishments, but also to criticize it. The episcopacy's argument that relatively uncritical support was first necessary to win the confidence of the government in view of past difficulties was rejected by both conservatives and reformers. The precise nature of the Catholic Church as critic was detailed by the ex-president of Cuban Catholic Action Youth, Mateo Jover, in a 1969 seminar in New York. Jover suggested the initiating of dialogue between Christians and Marxists at the grass-roots level. The feedback to government cadres which would result from this, he felt, would help open them up to Christian opinions to a greater extent than if the dialogue was limited to the upper echelons of church and state (Jover, 1974). Clearly, the presumption was that both institutions would better reflect the attitudes of the bulk of their adherents if this path was followed.

The Cuban bishops rejected both the reformist and conservative positions, publishing on August 10 and September 3, 1969, pastoral letters appealing for the lifting of the U.S. trade embargo of Cuba and emphasizing support for national developmental goals and the need to respect the atheistic position. These letters precipitated internal crises. The reformers objected to what they regarded as the episcopacy's failure to balance support for the government with the raising of critical issues, and the conservative majority regarded the declarations as evidence of the treason or cowardice of the bishops. A good number of Catholic activists left the Church at this point, and a papal emissary was sent from Rome in an effort to ameliorate some of the divisions.

One hundred lay leaders and an equal number of priests met in Havana in October 1969 to discuss Church-State relations and reform within the Church. An alliance of clerics and lay conservatives held sway against the calls for substantial lay participation in decision-making relating not only to internal Church matters, but also to relations with the government. In the aftermath of this meeting, some new Christian communities were formed by the disaffected, a few of which emphasized charismatic practices (IM 5771112). While relations with the government did improve after 1969, in some respects the divisions within the Church became more pronounced. Rapprochement with the government was favored, however, by the positive impression Castro obtained when he met with progressive Christians in Chile in 1971 and increased contacts of Cuban churchpeople with such progressives throughout Latin America. Episcopal strategy since the late 1960s has been marked by caution. Current emphasis is on pastoral renewal and spiritual regeneration.

Comparable but less severe struggles occurred within some of the Protestant churches. Here, too rapprochement with the government was actively pursued by most churches beginning in the late 1960s. This reflected the increasing consolidation of the progovernment left in positions of leadership, in spite of the fact that many Protestants continued to oppose the revolution. As late as the mid-1960s many Protestant youths who were generally more liberal than their elders continued to be against their churches taking a public stance for or against the revolution—44% against; 17% in favor; 39% no opinion (Cepeda, 1966: 27). Most local churches regarded political involvements as taboo, although the national leadership of such denominations as the Presbyterians and Methodists and the Cuban Council of Evangelical Churches increasingly took stands on national and international issues in favor of government policies. This was the result of a desire to insert themselves into revolutionary society not only as the most pragmatic course, but also as the most prophetic.

The majority of Cuban church people, however, continued into the 1970s to be negatively disposed toward the revolution, a fact which one minister noted condemned the churches to be constituted largely of social outcasts. Those changes which had occurred within the churches he deemed inadequate.[11] A World Council of Churches official, a frequent visitor to Cuba, estimated in 1971 that 95% of Cuba's Protestants seemed ill-at-ease in their own society. In addition, he found a tendency in them to idealize the past and to look to emigration as the solution to their discomfort (Tschuy, 1971: 4). This was especially true of the more middle-class congregations, whereas the rural, lower-class churches were less inclined toward inner or exterior migration and more open to the possibilities offered by the revolution. Overall, the churches attracted a fairly high proportion of the disaffected, with indications that those groups least integrated into contemporary Cuba, such as the Jehovah's Witnesses, were the fastest growing (IH 47413; IH 471191). Today the churches as institutions provide some shelter for those who do not accept the revolution, while within the marginal-ized religious community those churches which are most conservative provide reinforcement and justification for dissatisfaction with the current system.

Those who desire to substantially change the values and opinions of churchpeople look to the conscientization of the Cuban Christian through new pastoral programs, revised educational materials, and more prophetic theological formulations. As Cuba's leading theologian, Dr. Sergio Arce Martínez, phrases it, the future of the churches in Cuba "will depend greatly on the way we are able to get a wide biblical-theo-logical education and create serious Cuban theology that is adequate to our specific situation.[12] This attitude is shared by the former papal nuncio in Cuba, Archbishop Cesare Zacchi, who was instrumental in the period between 1963 and 1975 in bettering relations with Castro's government. Zacchi holds that Catholics should integrate themselves into the revolution through the mass organizations. Such action, the nuncio feels, would produce a beneficial interchange between Christians and Marxists which could result in the introduction of Catholic ideals into the revolution (López Oliva, 1970: 63; IH 4714111). Such positions run into opposition from those who feel, as does Jover, that at the level of systems legitimation and values an absolute impermeability exists between the Catholic Church and the revolutionary government. Unlike Arce and Zacchi, Jover feels that Marxist-Christian agreement over national virtues and objectives does not imply any fundamental agreement over values. Hence, he and others continue to urge the Catholic Church to work toward a situation where "there will be a pluralism of systems of legitimacy and permeability on the level of both values and norms" (Jover, 1974: 28). Given the manifold weak-nesses of the churches in Cuba, such a strategy has limited viability.

Resistance to change within the Cuban churches can be explained, in part, by the fact that the impulse for renewal has come primarily from the leadership rather than the base resulting in limited involvement of the laity. The outcome has been a degree of resentment on their part towards church officials. In the early 1970s this resulted in the defeat of some progressives in Protestant church elections, as well as a period of quiescence and reassessment within the Catholic Church. By 1974 the progressives were again gaining strength and consolidating their position. There was also some movement toward the formation of fundamentalist and charismatic groups within and without the church. Thus, in terms of religious beliefs and resultant actions, the strongest tendency is toward the continuance of prerevolutionary patterns, although some are expressed in new forms. What is new is the slow increase in progressive leaders and the theological conceptualizations they promote.

The most essential of these is a new definition of salvation which deemphasizes other-worldly elements in favor of the responsibility of the Christian to seek the kingdom of God on earth. Influenced by liberation theology, the emphasis is on the obligation to struggle for socioeconomic justice and collaborate with those movements which appear most likely to achieve it. Stress is laid on the integration of one's Christian commitment and one's socioeconomic contribution to an equitable society, even if it involves the overthrow of existing secular as well as ecclesial structures. This position conflicts with the division many Cuban Christians continue to make between the spiritual and the secular. In 1967 forty percent of the Catholics in the diocese of Camagüey felt that one's religious life and secular life are independent entities. In addition, the notion of divine intervention remained strong, with 37% regarding God as the one to turn to for solutions to problems (El Equipo, 1967: 18-21). These attitudes set them apart from the majority of Cubans who were strongly imbued with secularism well before the revolution (Torroella, 1963: 14-28). New theological definitions to date have failed to transform the world view of most Cuban Christians.

VI. Conclusion

Religion in prerevolutionary Cuba appeared to be weaker than in the rest of Latin America due to the institutional limitations of the churches and their reliance on a dependent national bourgeoisie and foreign sources of funding and personnel. This, combined with a relatively high degree of secularism in Cuban society, tended to relegate the churches to a marginalized position. These weaknesses resulted in the churches' power being less feared than in some other Latin American countries, which may, in part, explain the revolutionary government's apparent lack of deep concern even in the tense early years of 1960. Yet Cuba was a strongly Christian country which had been evangelized not only by Spanish Catholics, but also by U.S. Protestants, which resulted in the widespread dissemination of certain cultural values and norms even among those Cubans who never had any contact with formal religion.

The generalized Christian orientation of Cuban society contributed to a negative reaction to the revolution as it became more socialist. The situation was compounded by strong anticommunism among elements of the Spanish Catholic clergy and the U.S.-linked Protestant churches. While involvement in the churches was greater on the part of the urban bourgeoisie, the nature of religious certitude resulted in counterrevolutionary reactions on the part of strong believers from all classes, even when they were not frequent practitioners. Hence, even among the rural poor who were, by and large, the prime beneficiaries of such revolutionary programs as the expansion of public health and educational facilities, upgrading of housing, and elimination of unemployment, there were those who believed that support of the Castro government was totally inimical to their duties as Christians. Since the Church proclaimed itself the center of value and source of all meaning in life, the government's attempt in the early 1960s to capture the ultimate loyalty of all Cubans was regarded as antireligious. Under threats to its existence both from within and without Cuba, the government was suspicious of churches whose ultimate allegiance was to a source of meaning and values which had temporal links to western capitalism. As mutual hostility receded, in part as a result of the migration of the more negatively disposed church personnel and laity abroad, the churches turned in upon themselves in response to a desire for refuge from turmoil.

For some the revolution reinforced commitment to traditional religious practices, and there was a general tendency to escape into pietism. However, government mobilization of the population, particularly in programs aimed at dealing with traditional societal ills, prompted some positive response by a minority of churchpeople. In instances where there was enough latitude within the individual's church to allow for the operation of a dual commitment, there was the possibility of remaining one of the faithful. This was not the case with many churches, and between 1962 and 1968 there was considerable attrition in church membership beyond that caused by emigration. Increasingly in the late 1960s and early 1970s, losses appear to have resulted from conflicts within the churches. The possibility of the disintegration of the churches as constituted stimulated reflection aimed at rooting the churches firmly in their existential context, a task which required major theological reformulations and structural modifications. This process is more advanced in some Protestant churches than in the Catholic, in part because of the more flexible authority structures of the former.

As the churches were exposed to foreign explorations of Marxist-Christian dialogue and cooperation, they became more open. Church leadership was stimulated to join with the government in identifying problems of mutual concern and cooperating in such areas as education, health care, and the establishment of ethical goals. The churches were, in fact, challenged by the government's successes in eliminating such chronic problems as gambling, prostitution, and begging. Individuals began to voice their feelings that the churches' only means of survival was to integrate into the revolution. The definition of this process resulted in tensions between those who urged the churches to establish themselves as both supporters *and* critics of the government. Since the revolutionaries feel the only valid criticism is that which comes from within the process, such a strategy requires greater integration into the revolutionary process than that desired by many churchpeople.

A continuing problem has been doubts within the churches that they have the spiritual, intellectual, and emotional resources to assume a prophetic role in society. A majority of Protestant youth surveyed in the mid-1960s did not think their institutions possessed such abilities (Cepeda, 1966: 26). The attitude within the Catholic Church is pessimistic too; only six of 100 young activists from Santa Clara in 1970 were still with the church in 1975 (IM 5771112). Some Christians hope for a change in the government's ideological stance, but the increasing institutionalization of the revolution and the orthodoxy of the Party Congress in December 1975 does not encourage this. The Constitution adopted at that gathering provides for freedom to practice one's religion, although the government officially supports atheistic materialism. There is also some possibility that the greater democratization mandated by this document, particularly the establishment of nationwide representative assemblies under a program known as Popular Power, may result in more diversity within the revolution which could encourage increased integration of Christians.

The consolidation and institutionalization of the revolution, how-ever, will probably result in increased ideological pressure on Christians, as well as on those who harbor Afro-Cuban beliefs. Given the small minority of Cubans presently affiliated with churches, such pressure over the long term could have substantial impact on the churches as institutions. Furthermore, changes outside Cuba may very well reduce the ability or willingness of international ecclesial structures to support them.

The beliefs of Cuban churchpeople are not changing rapidly enough to cause them to incorporate themselves into the revolution in any number, nor would this necessarily secure the future of the churches given the ideological distance between Marxism and Christianity. Even those who are most positively disposed toward the revolution and who accept Marxist economic analysis do not accept the materialist explanation of life. This is the most profoundly disturbing dilemma for those progressives I interviewed. If they maintain a belief in a transcen-dental explanation of life, there will always be the possibility of conflict of goals with the government. Revolutionary change in Cuba has al-ready had a tremendous effect on the churches as temporal institutions. Only if substantial numbers of Cubans feel a strong need for an other-worldly explanation of life is there a likelihood that the churches will recuperate. Even then, it is probable that believers will seek to change their churches substantially to meet their specific needs in a socialist society. This portends even greater upheavals for the Cuban churches in the future than those already experienced.

NOTES

1. These interviews are subsequently identified throughout the paper by a series of numbers beginning with IH, IT, ISM and IM. Since they are privileged in nature, further information is not available. Therefore, they are not listed in the reference section.

2. Pertinent studies not listed in the references include the works of Fernando Ortiz, Lydia Cabrera, and John Dumoulin.

3. Approximately 550 of 800 Catholic priests left and 2,700 of some 3,000 religious. Of these, approximately 8% were expelled by the Cuban government for alleged counter-revolutionary activities. Beginning in 1963 some Cuban and Spanish priests returned, joined by a few French and Belgian clerics. In the late 1960s the government indicated its willingness to grant residence permits to some 100 foreign religious if they could be recruited. This process has been slow (Houtart and Rousseau, 1971: 124; IH 4714111). The mainline Protestant denominations were hit particularly hard, losing as much as 50%

or more of their congregations and 80% to 90% of their ministers. More populist groups, such as the Baptists and Pentecostals, were less severely affected (United Methodist Board of Missions, 1971b: 3; Tschuy, 1971; Rivas, 1971: 7).

4. This is the sum claimed by Cepeda (1966: 11) and Hageman and Wheaton (1971: 31), while the Libro de Cuba (Anonymous, 1954: 747) reports 400,000 active Protestants.

5. Hageman and Wheaton (1971: 31) estimated 50,000 in 1970, when membership appeared to be stabilizing. Wallace reiterates that number two years later (Wallace, 1973: 10).

6. The study included parishes in Camagüey, Ciego de Avila, Morón, Florida, Nuevitas, Guaimaro, Santa Cruz del Sur, Jatibónico, Amancio Rodríguez, Vertientes, and Esmerelda.

7. Such criticisms have been reiterated by Tschuy, former Latin American Secretary of the World Council of Churches, and in evaluations by some U.S. churches of their prerevolutionary operations in Cuba (Rivas, 1971: 4; United Methodist Board of Missions, 1971a).

8. Of 50 Christian youths interviewed in the mid-1960s, 24% claimed to have been members of anti-Batista clandestine organizations. Only 2% claimed to have been pro-Batista (Cepeda, 1966: 25). Of the 33 Methodist ministers in Cuba in the 1950s, 15% were nonviolent anti-Batista activists; 60% passive opponents, and 25% claimed neutrality (Rivas, 1971: 5).

9. For a perceptive analysis of the impact of Castro's declaration, see Dewart (1963).

10. For the impact of the Cuban emigrées on the U.S. churches, see Cuban Research Center newsletters, 2 and 4. More recently there has been some liberalization among these individuals as attested to by the formation of progressive groups such as the Florida-based Cuban Christians for Justice and Freedom, which supports the end to the U.S. embargo of Cuba and encourages the resumption of diplomatic relations.

11. Reverend Israel Batista as quoted in Hageman and Wheaton (1971: 53).

12. Arce as quoted in Hageman and Wheaton (1971: 171).

REFERENCES

AGUILAR, L. (1974) Cuba, 1933: Prologue to Revolution. New York: W. W. Norton.

Anonymous (1954) Libro de Cuba. Habana: no publisher.

BARNET, M. [ed.] (1968) The Autobiography of a Runaway Slave: Esteban Montejo. New York: Pantheon.

CEPEDA, R. (1966) "La juventud evangélica y la iglesia: estudio sobre Cuba." (unpublished).

CRAHAN, M. E. (1978) "Protestantism in Cuba," forthcoming in R. Millett, [ed.] Protestantism in Latin America. Grand Rapids: Eerdmans.

——— (1977) "Penetracao religiosa e nacionalismo em Cuba: atividades metodistas norte-americanas, 1898-1958." Religiao e Sociedale 1, 1 (Maio): 81-103.

——— (1976) "Testimony." Hearings before the Subcommittee on International Organizations of the Committee on International Relations, House of Representatives, Ninety-Fourth Congress, First Session, H.R. 6382. Washington: U.S. Government Printing Office: 274-288.

DAVIS, J. M. (1942) The Cuban Church in a Sugar Economy. New York: International Missonary Council.

DE LA HUERTA AGUIAR, R. F. (1960) "Espiritismo y otras supersticiones en la ponlación cubana." Revista del Hospital Psiquiátrico de la Habana 2, 1 (Enero-Marzo): 44-48.

DEWART, L. (1963) Christianity and Revolution: The Lesson of Cuba. New York: Herder & Herder.

DOMÍNGUEZ, J. (1975) Unpublished manuscript excerpts.

——— (1972) "Cuban Catholics and Castro." Worldview 15 (February): 24-29.

ECHEVARRA SALVAT, O. A. (1971) La Agricultura Cubana, 1934-1966: Régimen Social, Productividad y Nivel de Vida del Sector Agrícola. Miami: Ediciones Universal.

EL EQUIPO DIOCESANO DE JOVENES DE CAMAGÜEY (1967) "Estadistica socio-religiosa de la Diocesis de Camagüey." (unpublished).

GARCÍA FRANCO, R. (1970) "Estudio socio-religioso de una iglesia pequeña." (unpublished).

——— (1966) "Pastores en la U.M.A.P.: diálogo en la U.M.A.P." October 2. (unpublished)

HAGEMAN, A. L. and P. E. WHEATON [eds.] (1971) Religion in Cuba Today: A New Church in a New Society. New York: Association Press.

HOUTART, F. and A. ROUSSEAU (1971) The Church and Revolution. Maryknoll, NY: Orbis.

JOVER, M. (1974) "The Cuban church in a revolutionary society." LADOC 4, 32 (April): 17-36.

LEVINE, D. H. (1973) "The meaning of politics to Catholic elites in Latin America." Paper presented at IX World Congress of the International Political Science Association, August 19-25, 1973, Montreal.

LEWIS, B. H. [ed.] (1960) Methodist Overseas Mission, 1960: Gazetteer and Statistics. New York: Board of Missions of the United Methodist Church.

LÓPEZ OLIVA, E. (1970) Los Catolicos y la Revolucion Latinoaméricana. Habana: Instituto del Libro.

NELSON, L (1970) Rural Cuba. New York: Octagon.

NOGUEIRA RIVERO, G. (1962) "El sincretismo religioso como causa desencadenante y lo determinante de sindromes neuróticos y pseudo-psicóticos en el niño cubano." Revista del Hospital Psiquiátrico de la Habana 3, 1 (Enero-Marzo): 37-46.

ORDOÑEZ, J. (1974) "Informe sobre una visita a Cuba, 20 a 28 de junio 1974." Panamá. (unpublished)

Religious News Service (1971) Press release. March 18.

RIVAS, G. (1971) Minutes of the Cuba Sub-Group, Latin American Methodist Task Force. March 1.

ROCHON, L. (1967) "La sociedad agropecuaria 'Jesús Feliú': un caso de cambio en el medio rural bajo un régimen socialista de transición." Etnología y Folklore 4 (Julio-Diciembre): 23-37.

RUIZ, R. E. (1968) Cuba: The Making of a Revolution. Amherst: Univ. of Massachusetts Press.

TORROELLA, G. (1963) Estudio de la Juventud Cubana. La Habana: Comisión Nacional Cubana de la UNESCO.

TSCHUY, T. (1971) "Responses to questions in Mr. Davis' letter of February 11, 1971, Tannay, Switzerland." (unpublished)

UNITED METHODIST BOARD OF MISSIONS (1971a) Minutes of May 14 meeting. Cuba Sub Group, Latin American Task Force.

——— (1971b) Minutes of March 1 meeting. Cuba Sub Group, Latin American Task Force.

UNITED METHODIST INFORMATION (1972) News Release. July 25.

UNIVERSIDAD CENTRAL "MARTA ABREU" DE LAS VILLAS (1959) La Educación Rural en Las Villas: Bases para la Redacción de Unos Cursos de Estudios. Santa Clara: Universidad Central.

VALLIER, I. (1970) Catholicism, Social Control, and Modernization in Latin America. Englewood Cliffs, NJ: Prentice-Hall.

WALLACE, J. (1973) "Christians in Cuba." Cuba Resource Center Newsletter 3, 1 (April): 3-11.

11

TEN YEARS OF CHANGE IN THE CHURCH
Puebla and the Future

ALEXANDER W. WILDE

The meeting of the Latin American bishops at Puebla in early 1979 was a historic benchmark for the Church, but its significance has been debated. Observers who have looked at Puebla as a dramatic event have interpreted it essentially as a conservative reaction to Medellín. John Paul II and Alfonso López Trujillo, the Secretary-General of CELAM, are attributed crucial roles. The Pope's visit, in this view, was meant to reassert traditional ecclesiastical authority and to redirect the Church away from a politicizing kind of social involvement. López Trujillo is seen as a New World variant of the traditional Curial conservative, managing policy behind the scenes from his post in the bishops' regional administrative apparatus.

Puebla takes on quite a different significance, however, if one steps back from the short-run manuevering and tries to judge the larger process of change since Medellín. Those ten years produced extraordinary activity and conflict in the Latin American Church. Looking back, however, it is possible to discern clear directions in the overall change.

Since Medellín, the Church has achieved unprecedented integration as an institution nationally and regionally, in Latin America as a whole. New local-level units—the Christian "base communities"—have begun to give the Church a vitality in society not known for centuries. An unexpected historical dynamic has impelled it into an increasing commitment to the poor in deed as well as word. And throughout the region, it has been thrust into politics and confrontation with state authority.

Puebla capped that decade of change, and to a notable degree, faithfully reflected both the state and the direction of the Church.[1] The text

AUTHOR'S NOTE: The author gratefully acknowledges comments on earlier versions of this essay from Penney Lernoux, Daniel Levine, Abraham Lowenthal, Laurie Lucey, Tommie Sue Montgomery, and Thomas Sanders.

of the final document, and the process by which it was produced, showed clearly the coexistence within the Church of divergent and at times directly opposed points of view. At the same time, however, the meeting demonstrated a surprising consensus in the Church—remarkable in view of the rapid changes it has undergone—about its past experience, its present context, and its future direction.

The bishops sought unity around their central religious purpose, evangelization. Their meditations and debates all focused on the meaning of that task in the concrete, historical setting in which the Church finds itself. Their final document endorsed the fundamental lines set out at Medellín in 1968, which marked such an innovative departure at the time:[2] an identification with the poor and oppressed, a sociological analysis of "structural sin," of "institutionalized injustice," and of "mechanisms of oppression" which produced poverty. Where Puebla departed from Medellín, it sometimes went beyond earlier positions. This was particularly true of its political analysis, which was clearer and more specific in its condemnation of dictatorial regimes (CELAM, 1979: 40-50).

Puebla, much more than Medellín, was a product of the collective experience of the Latin American Church, Medellín was a kind of manifesto for the Church produced by its more progressive sectors (although the radical Catholic Left was disappointed with it at the time). But Puebla, despite efforts to manage the outcome, turned into an encounter quite representative of different forces found in the Church today. The final document records their efforts to make sense of their experience in the last decade. It is significant for both the consensus and the divisions it reports.

This chapter is an analysis of the ten years of change that preceded and produced Puebla. It is an interpretation of the conditions and forces —outside as well as within the Church—that brought the Church to the state reflected there. And it offers a way of thinking about what this broad process of change signifies for the future.

What was it, first, that gave the ideas of Medellín such deep resonance in the Church? Why have they so significantly oriented what it has actually done, rather than remaining, as so many other Church documents have, statements of good intentions? Second, how much does a socially progressive posture really characterize the Church as a whole? Will this stance be a source of growing consensus in the future, or of increasing division? Third, very much related to the previous question, what kind of role is the Church likely to play in the future in society and politics as a whole? What are the factors that will shape its direction and influence?

I

The new theological directions marked out by Medellín had the impact on Church action they did because of their congruence with the particular historical setting in which they emerged. In a longer line of theological change, these new directions extended Vatican II and anticipated the Theology of Liberation. At Medellín the bishops were attempting to adapt the ideas and insights of the Council to Latin American reality. But they built better than they knew. Dynamic forces in Latin American societies and within the Church itself reinforced new theology to push change toward consequences they did not foresee.

Although students of the Church frequently see new theology at the root of institutional change, doctrinal positions are hardly ever fully implemented merely because they are directives from recognized authority. If they resonate with the institution the way that Medellín did, there must be other factors at work. The Church's new commitment to the poor, for example, or its confrontation with the state, would not have taken place in the way they did without the texts of Medellín. But the depth of the change that has occurred is due also to the context of authoritarian military regimes, within which the meaning of new theological formulations (of, for example, "institutionalized violence") has been defined by experience and struggle. The depth of the Church's new social commitments in different countries closely parallels the harshness of their regimes. Where there have not been institutional military governments (e.g., in Colombia, Venezuela, and Mexico), the Church has changed its social stance much less, in spite of exposure to the same progressive theology.

On the other hand, however, authoritarian conditions alone were not sufficient to have "forced" the Church into the social and political roles it has assumed. When other associations in society have been repressed, some of their functions have undoubtedly been displaced onto the Church (about which, more below). But there is nothing automatic about this process. The Church certainly could have chosen to fight much less than it has; it often so chose in the past, and in some countries today (notably Argentina) the balance of forces within it has not led the Church to resistance. That it has begun to put itself on the line in the last decade is the result of courage and leadership—sometimes from the hierarchy, often from priests, nuns, and lay people at local levels (Smith, this volume; compare Vallier, 1970). Their courage has been fortified and enlightened by the new theology of the last ten years. Under conditions of the authoritarian regimes, concepts such as "structural sin," Christian "liberation," *concientización*, and "human rights" have helped them make sense of their environment and their responsibilities in it.

Without important organizational changes, however, the Church would have lacked the institutional resources to resist authoritarian regimes. At the grass roots, it has created a variety of structures—many of them called *communidades de base*—that are smaller, more informal, and more personal than the traditional parish. It has tried through these groupings to engender more authentic religious commitment among its faithful by speaking to their real human problems. Thus it has taken up its fundamental pastoral task in just the way signalled by Medellín, rooting its religious purposes in concrete social situations. The Church is an unquestionably more vital presence in society where these new units have taken hold at the local level (Bruneau, 1978: Dela Cava, 1978). At Puebla the bishops gave them a ringing endorsement, recognizing them as a key to the Church's most basic task (e.g., CELAM, 1979: 96-97, 239, 629, 640-643).

The base communities have been sustained under repressive conditions by a complementary strengthening of Church structures at higher levels. National episcopal conferences have made each country's bishops aware of a common agenda of national and international issues, and CELAM and CLAR (for the Religious Orders) have gone a long way toward accomplishing that for Latin America as a whole.[3] The new specialized commissions, such as those for peace and justice, have used new permanent staff to monitor and respond to situations (such as human rights violations) in an ongoing way, within individual nations and across the region. The Church's institutional capacity to know what is going on, and to utilize its linkages abroad for support, has become a critical resource for protecting its social and pastoral initiatives at the local level (see Smith, this volume).

II

A "Latin American Church" exists today in several senses it did not a decade ago. As the previous section makes clear, political environments are more similar, theological understandings more shared, institutional integration more established. To close observers 10 years ago, the differences between various national Churches seemed more important than their similarities; change in them suggested a variety of distinctive "profiles" of Church development (Vallier, 1970: 121-147). Today Churches formerly as disparate as those of Brazil and Paraguay, Bolivia and Chile, Ecuador and El Salvador, are using the same arguments to fight similar battles and are comparably committed, in their pastoral missions, to social change (compare Smith, this volume).

The great degree to which a truly regional Church has developed, despite important internal divisions, was established by Puebla. With greater confidence than its Medellín counterpart, Puebla's final document plunged into analysis of different facets of the general regional context—cultural, economic, political—that shapes the Church's mission despite local variations. The document is also willing, with some specificity, to characterize the broad—and as the Church sees them, frequently deteriorating—trends of the region's recent history (e.g., CELAM, 1979: 27-50). Even among bishops who evaluated the situation differently, there was widespread acceptance of a regional perspective and sociological method. The Pope, too—symbol of universality in the Church—seemed pleased rather than threatened by regional solidarities. After he expressed cautions in his opening statement at Puebla, his subsequent behavior suggested that he was confident of the Latin American bishops' fidelity in adapting universal truths to regional realities. They, for their part, supported their position with abundant references to his messages and those of his predecessors (notably Paul VI and his "Evangelii Nuntiandi").

The Church's overall position represents a relative triumph for the Catholic Left of a decade ago (Dodson, this volume). Although different from what those on the Left would have wished, the Church has become more socially committed than they believed possible.) But this position is the outcome of an interplay of forces within the institution. It is a point of balance for a complex coalition more than a uniform conversion to a point of view. To maintain a religious institution encompassing divergent perspectives, the hierarchy of the Church seeks the position that engenders greatest unity. That position has shifted over the course of the last ten years toward a "structural" understanding of social problems and a widening "pastoral" commitment to the poor and suffering. The dynamic of the Church's historical situation since 1968 has pulled the institution as a whole in the direction of its socially most progressive sectors.

The presence of authoritarian military governments has been crucial. As the bishops reemphasized with great clarity at Puebla, the Church has come increasingly to view these regimes in regional terms. Where formally it might have distinguished between national cases as different as Paraguay, Chile, and Brazil, it now looks on them all as manifestations of a common economic model (CELAM, 1979: 47) and common national security ideology (Calvo, this volume; CELAM, 1979: 547, 549). The recent political situation of the region has "fit" the new theological directions of the Church with particular aptness. That congruence has effectively moved the point of unity which the Church seeks (e.g., CELAM, 1979: 520, 526, 688) to the left during this period.

In the future, that political environment could become less uniform. There may be openings in some regimes which allow some degree of political participation and open partisan activity. Even where such openings do not develop into the full political democracy the Church endorses (e.g., CELAM, 1979: 1263), the changed situation will create difficulties, within particular national Churches and between them. To the extent that regimes in the region become more different from one another, the Latin American Church will find it more difficult to interpret them within a common framework.

Politics—political developments in the region and the Church's involvement in them—is likely to be the central issue challenging the consensus that existed at Puebla. The position reached there (which is analyzed in the next section) distinguishes partisan political activity, which is not appropriate for the Church, from prophetic and pastoral social activism, which is fundamental to its purposes. The difficulties of making this distinction in practice may well prove as great for the Church in "decompressing" systems in the future as they did in populist situations in the past (most strikingly in Chile, in the late 1960s and early 1970s). Brazil, whose bishops played such an important part in achieving the progressive consensus at Puebla, is likely to be the key test of Church unity in this regard in the years to come.

The most surprising element of the bishops' consensus at Puebla— their enthusiastic support for ecclesial base communities (CEBs)[4]— will also be tested in the future (and very likely in Brazil, where more base communities have been created than anywhere else). The bishops

were clearly impressed with the promise of the CEBs for religious renewal at the grass roots. The Puebla document designates them as a
major instrument for the Church in its fundamental task of evangelization. But the proliferation of CEBs also poses real problems of authority for the Church. The bishops made clear their concerns (CELAM,
1979: 98, 261-263, 630, 648) that these small groupings be linked institutionally with clerical authority (hence their description as "ecclesial
base communities," and not "base communities" alone, as they have
frequently been called in practice). Balancing clerical authority over
the base communities with those qualities that give them such promise
for evangelization—their responsiveness to personal concerns, their
authenticity, their spontaneity—will be a significant challenge to the
Church in the future, as the next section analyzes in more detail.

III

Puebla made it obvious that the Church will be deeply involved in
politics in the future. Its broad understanding of its prophetic and pastoral responsibilities will draw it into basic issues of freedom, equality,
justice, participation, and power (Levine and Wilde, 1977). Whether its
involvement will be a source of unity and consensus—and will have
significant effects on society as a whole—will depend on the nature of
its political context, which will change over time and will differ for the
various national Churches. It will also depend on the Church's success
in evangelization, the kindling of a genuine religious renewal among
Latin America's people.

The Church's involvement in politics is both a paradox and a problem. It is a paradox because that involvement exists in the face of a sincere desire to stay out of politics. The Puebla document was explicit
and adamant that the institution must avoid any partisan activity
(CELAM, 1979: 523-530). It echoed the opening message of Pope John
Paul II in asserting that the Church is a mystery and not a political
party, a position that seems in particular to reflect the experience of the
Chilean Church. The Church has a problem, as Daniel Levine writes
in this volume, with politics. It would be torn apart from within if it
allowed partisan factions to claim its universal truths for their particular
programs and politics (CELAM, 1979: 523, 526).

Authoritarian regimes, however, make it almost inevitable for the Latin American Church, as it now understands its purposes, to become politically involved. This involvement occurs in several ways, with implications which vary in different *coyunturas* of these regimes.

The efforts of dictatorships, first, to repress or strictly control manifestly political activity have the effect of displacing pressures and participation into structures which the Church defends as "religious" and its own. To the extent that competition among manifestly political groups is not legitimate, social activists in the Church are freed from easy identification with particular parties or programs. Church unity can more easily be maintained and a pastoral commitment to "the poor" become more significant when it does not operate among different partisan movements claiming to represent them.

The repressive extremes of authoritarian regimes, second, have moved the Church to explicit political statements about the desirability of democracy. The Puebla document is eloquent about the qualities that should characterize the good polity—equal protection under the law, an independent judiciary, more equitable distribution of wealth and opportunity, a guaranteed right for workers and peasants to organize themselves, and repeatedly widespread popular participation (CELAM, 1979: 44, 1159-1165, 1238-1247). The bishops see all this as falling within the Church's larger pastoral mission, as "Mother and Teacher of all" (CELAM, 1979: 160). They expect resistance but express confidence that the Church will accept the "consequences" of its mission (CELAM, 1979: 160-161, 515, 519).

Particularly in an authoritarian setting, third, the Church has become an advocate of political pluralism and social "space" for institutional as well as theological reasons (CELAM, 1979: 1206-1253). In a society of demobilized organizations and intervened institutions, the Church is determined to insist on autonomy in its own religious sphere (CELAM, 1979: 144, 519, 558, 1238). As the Chilean bishops said in 1976, "To define the limits of our pastoral competence, we recognize the authority only of the Roman Pontiff" (Roncagliolo and Reyes Matta, 1978: 177.[5] In condemning the "totalitarian" implications of National Security Doctrine, the Church both rejects many of the policies that the ideology is used to justify and affirms its own Social Doctrine, which stresses the importance of intermediary bodies between the individual and the state (CELAM, 1979: 49, 549, 1214). But even more fundamentally, the Church rejects the presumption of National Security Doctrine that its values have some overriding primacy in society (Roncagliolo and Reyes Matta, 1978: 45-62; CELAM, 1979: 549). The Church, "expert in humanity" (CELAM, 1979: 511, 1268), asserts a right to articulate social values and goals autonomous of the state, any state.[6]

As Puebla made clear, the Church sees this mission as quite distinct from politics and does not intend to be deterred from pursuing it, in both its pastoral and prophetic faces. But beyond its possible confusion with politics, there is a further difficulty the Church will face with its broad sense of its pastoral responsibilities. The basic image of the shepherd, the *pastor*, and his flock evokes a relationship of leader and followers of a more traditional kind than seems to be evolving in the contemporary Church. *Lo pastoral* involves clerical solidarity with the poor and suffering ("compartir las angustias"; CELAM, 1979: 27-39) as well as their "formation" under clerical tutelage, and pastors as well as their flocks seem to undergo concientización. Both sides of pastoral action are reflected in the Puebla document. Although individual bishops will undoubtedly draw different lines about what is legitimately pastoral, observers at Puebla were impressed by their sincerity about pastoral concerns. The fact that they made them as central as they did and accepted the basic direction of change since Medellín suggests that the Church will become still more active socially in the future.

Whether that activity will have significant effect depends on how firmly the Church's role is rooted in religious commitment at the local level. Ultimately its impact will turn on the efficacy and the extent of initiatives such as the new "base communities."[7] Although they have proliferated rapidly in some areas (Della Cava, 1978; Bruneau, 1978), we do not really know yet how widespread these communities are or may become (estimates run to 100,000 and more for Latin America as a whole). But we can already make some preliminary observations about the effects of those that do exist.

As a fundamental unit of the Church, the base communities differ from the parish in several ways. They are smaller and typically involve much more active lay participation, both in liturgical ceremonies and in religious study. Characteristically, they have much more uniform social membership than the parish, permitting greater face-to-face communication. As a more informal kind of grouping, they have made most progress where the previous institutional existence of the Church was least established—that is to say, among the poor (Bruneau, 1978). They have tried to reach new social groups by addressing the concrete realities of their social situations in religious terms: This is the ground to the Church's pastoral commitment to authentic "liberation."

In cases such as Chile and Brazil, these local communities—sheltered under the Church's institutional shield—have provided a "surrogate" for otherwise repressed associational life (Smith, this volume; Della Cava, 1978). Where there had previously been political polarization, they have played a specific role in bringing Marxists and Catholics together. They have provided the sites for shared experience, which have given new meaning to their old concepts of "dialogue" and "praxis." It has been a process not so much of one side convincing the other as of both old antagonists realizing they had much to learn from the other (e.g., Smith, this volume).

It is interesting in this connection to see how the authoritarian setting changes the implications of the Church's role. A fundamental element of its position on social change since 1968 has been the insistence of its centrist hierarchy on consensus rather than coercion. The Puebla document systematically balanced its denunciation of dictatorial repression with condemnation of revolutionary violence (e.g., CELAM, 1979: 42-43, 531-532). In the more open environment of polarized populist politics, this emphasis on consensus was viewed by both Left and Right as deceptive and divisive. In the authoritarian regime, where the decisive balance of violence lies with the state, to foster consensus among popular forces may be a contribution that progressive forces view much more positively (but see Krischke in Della Cava, 1978). In a transition away from authoritarianism, however, the focus of the Church's efforts may shift more toward creating consensus between the regime and its opponents. Such a transition will clearly activate tensions in the Church over the primacy of its "option" for the poor.

It is difficult to know yet whether the Church's new base communities will affect social consciousness on a large scale or, by giving their members experience in participation in one setting, facilitate a participatory society more broadly.[8] In a significant case of political "opening" recently, in Brazil, one observer attributed great importance to the Church's grass-roots initiatives among the working class of Sao Paulo, a "vast mobilization . . . in silence, without fanfare, and with all deliberation required for schooling men in a way of life" (Della Cava, 1978: 10). Whether the Church will play that sort of role more generally remains to be seen.

It is difficult, also, to know how well the CEBs will be able to balance their two sides, as "centers of evangelization" on the one hand and "engines of liberation and development " on the other (CELAM, 1979:

96, cf. 261-263); or to put it differently, how well they can reconcile loyalty to the ecclesiastical institution with commitment to their particular small community. We do know that the bishops see them as the "hope of the Church" (CELAM, 1979: 629) and will attempt to create more of them, impelled by falling clerical vocations and a genuine "option" for the poor. On the basis of the authoritarian experience of the last ten years, we also know, as Levine (this volume) puts it so well, that these communities will at least be "keeping alive hope for a different kind of future."

Puebla was one frame in a film ten years long. Seen as a still photograph, it captured a highly dynamic collectivity at a particular point in time. Its final document, shot through with compromises and even contradictions, accurately recorded the current state of the Church. But to judge its larger significance, one must see it in a longer unfolding process. The decade from Medellín to Puebla had quite specific historical characteristics which produced new solidarities for the Church both within and between nations. The focus of unity within the institution was moved in a socially progressive direction.

At Puebla the bishops sought to consolidate this past as the foundation for the future. Their document demonstrates that the changes of the last ten years are real—that they have been written into the lives of those who are the Church and cannot be reversed by the intentions of some ecclesiastical elites. But what Puebla will come to mean in the future cannot be extrapolated from the words of the document or from past experience. The future will quite likely erode the old bases for solidarity and consensus. New circumstances will test in experience the distinctions drawn at Puebla. What they will mean for the Church will be shaped above all by the political contexts of particular national Churches, and by the degree to which unity and momentum can be maintained around the central purpose of evangelization. Much of that will depend on the leadership of the bishops, and their ability to foster a pastoral authority for new times, within the Church and for society as a whole.

NOTES

1. For a contrasting interpretation, see Berryman (this volume). Bouvy (1978) and IDOC (1978), both provide useful collections of articles on the background to Puebla.

2. See the chapters by Poblete and Levine in this volume. This chapter will draw particularly upon all the chapters in this volume which originated in the special issue of the *Journal of Inter-American Studies and World Affairs* edited by Levine, and on papers given originally at a Workshop on the Church and Politics in Latin America, at the Woodrow Wilson Center in Washington, D.C., in May 1978.

3. One should not overemphasize the degree to which continental consensus could be produced by these newly institutionalized regional organizations. The secretariats of the bishops' CELAM and the Orders' CLAR have had significant differences for several years, a conflict which came into the open just before the CELAM meeting in Puebla.

4. The Spanish "eclesial" has been translated by "ecclesial," a word now returning to English usage, rather than "ecclesiastical," because the latter would imply inclusion in the canonical structures of the Church.

5. The statement by the Permanent Committee of the Chilean Episcopate was made in reaction to the Riobamba incident in Ecuador in August 1976. A meeting in Riobamba to "exchange pastoral experiences" was denounced as "subversive" and forcibly broken up by dozens of heavily armed police. The priests and bishops involved, from throughout the hemisphere, were summarily deported by the Ecuadorian authorities. Roncagliolo and Reyes Matta (1978) provide a useful documentation.

6. Those who would assert the autonomy of Christian values fight, in effect, for political pluralism in any authoritarian setting. The situation of reformist elements of the Catholic Church in Cuba, who would like to support the Revolution but on their own Christian grounds, is an interesting parallel (see Crahan, this volume).

7. See the Smith and Bruneau articles, this volume. It is worth noting that the term "base community" is a broad one, applied to a variety of local-level structures. The Puebla document, following *Evangelii Nuntiandi*, attempted to distinguish the *ecclesial* base community within the broad range.

8. It is worth noting, as Crahan (this volume) does for the Cuban case, that active participation by lay people in a religious setting by no means precludes their holding conservative social views. Whether such experience has "progressive" implications for a wider environment depends very much on the character of that setting.

REFERENCES

BOUVY, J. [ed.] (1978) "Latin America: approaching the Puebla Conference." Lumen Vitae 33: 3.

BRUNEAU, T. (1978) "Notes toward the study of popular religiosity and strategies of change in Church: evidence from eight Brazilian dioceses." Presented at the Workshop on Religion and Politics in Latin America, Woodrow Wilson International Center for Scholars, Washington, D.C.

CELAM [Consejo Episcopal Latinoamericano] (1979) "La Evangelización en el presente y en el futuro de América Latina." III Conferencia General del Episcopado Latinoamericano, Bogotá, D.E., Colombia.

DELLA CAVA, R. (1978) "Short-term politics and long-term religion in Brazil" (with a critique by Paulo Krischke). Latin American Program Working Paper 12. Washington, DC: Woodrow Wilson International Center for Scholars.

IDOC International (1978) The Church at the Crossroads: Christians in Latin America from Medellín to Puebla (1968-1978). Rome: Author.

LEVINE, D. and A. WILDE (1977) "The Catholic Church, 'politics,' and violence: the Colombian case." Rev. of Politics 39 (April): 220-239.

RONCAGLIOLO, R. and F. REYES MATTA (1978) Iglesia, Prensa y Militares: El Caso Riobamba y los Obispos Latinoamericanos. Mexico: Instituto Latinoamericano de Estudios Transnacionales.

VALLIER, I. (1970) Catholicism, Social Control, and Modernization in Latin America. Englewood Cliffs, NJ: Prentice-Hall.

BIBLIOGRAPHY

Books and Articles

ANTOINE, C. (1973) Church and Power in Brazil. Maryknoll: Orbis.

ASSMANN, H. (1976) Theology for a Nomad Church. Maryknoll: Orbis.

———(1971) Opresión-Liveración Desalfío a los Cristianos. Montevideo: Tierra Nueva.

BAILEY, D. (1974) ¡Viva Cristo Rey! The Cristero Rebellion and the Church-State Conflict in Mexico. Austin: University of Texas Press.

BERRYMAN, P. (1973) "Latin American liberation theology." Theological Studies 34 (September): 357-395.

BRODERICK, W. J. (1975) Camilo Torres. Garden City, NY: Doubleday.

BRUNEAU, T. C. (forthcoming) Religiosity and Politicization in Brazil: The Church in an Authoritarian Regime.

——— (1974) The Political Transformation of the Brazilian Catholic Church. New York: Cambridge University Press.

——— (1973) "Power and influence: an analysis of the Church in Latin America and the case of Brazil." Latin American Research Review 8 (Summer): 25-52.

BUEHLMANN, W. (1976) The Coming of the Third Church. Maryknoll: Orbis.

CAMARA, H. (1972) Revolution Through Peace. New York: Harper & Row.

——— (1969) The Church and Colonialism: The Betrayal of the Third World. Denville, NJ: Dimension books.

CARDENAL, E. (1978) The Gospel in Solentiname II. Maryknoll: Orbis.

——— (1976) The Gospel in Solentiname. Maryknoll: Orbis.

COMBLIN, J. (1977) "The Church in Latin America after Vatican II." LADOC 7 (January/February): 1-18.

COURLANDER, H. and R. BASTIEN (1966) Religion and Politics in Haiti, Washington: Institute for Cross-Cultural Research.

COX, H. (1973) The Seduction of the Spirit: The Use and Misuse of People's Religion. New York: Simon & Schuster.

DAVIES, J. G. (1978) Christians, Politics, and Violent Revolution. Maryknoll: Orbis.

DELLA CAVA, R. (1976) "Catholicism and society in twentieth century Brazil." Latin American Research Review 11 (Summer): 7-50.

——— (1970) Miracle at Joaseiro. New York: Columbia University Press.

DE KADT, E. (1971) "Church, society, and development in Latin America." Journal of Development Studies 8 (October): 23-43.

——— (1970) Catholic Radicals in Brazil. New York: Oxford University Press.

——— (1967) "Paternalism and populism: Catholicism in Latin America." Journal of Contemporary History 2 (October): 89-106.

DODSON, M. (1974) "Religious innovation and the politics of Argentina: a study of the movement of priests for the Third World." Ph.D. dissertation, Indiana University.

――――― (1974) "Priests and Peronism: radical clergy in Argentine politics." Latin American Perspectives 1: 63-67.

―――――(1972) "The Catholic Church in contemporary Argentina," pp. 57-67 in A. Ciria (ed.) New Perspectives on Modern Argentina. Bloomington: Indiana University Latin American Studies Program.

DUSSEL, E. (1978) Ethics and the Theology of Liberation. Maryknoll: Orbis.

――――― (1976) History and the Theology of Liberation. Maryknoll: Orbis.

ECKSTEIN, S. (1978) The Poverty of Revolution: The State and the Urban Poor in Mexico. Princeton: Princeton University Press. "Politicos and Priests: Oligarchy and Interorganizational Relations." (chap. 4)

EINADUI, L., R. MAULLIN, A. STEPAN, and M. FLEET (1969) Latin American Institutional Development: The Changing Catholic Church. Santa Monica: RAND.

FLORA, C. B. (1976) Pentecostalism in Colombia: Baptism by Fire and Spirit. Rutherford, NJ: Fairleigh Dickinson University Press.

FLORIDI, A. and F. STIEFBOLD (1973) The Uncertain Alliance: The Catholic Church and Organized Labor in Latin America. Miami: Center for Advanced International Studies.

FREIRE, P. (1974) Education for Critical Consciousness. New York: Seabury.

――――― (1968) Pedagogy of the Oppressed. New York: Seabury.

GALILEA, S. (1974) "Liberation as an encounter with politics and contemplation," pp. 19-33 in C. Geffré and G. Gutierrez (eds.) The Mystical and Political Dimensions of the Christian Faith. New York: Herder & Herder.

――――― (1972) ¿A los Pobres se les Anuncia el Evangelio? Bogotá: CELAM.

GALLET, P. (1972) Freedom to Starve. Baltimore: Pelican.

GEFFRE, C. and G. GUTIERREZ [eds.] (1974) The Mystical and Political Dimensions of the Christian Faith. New York: Herder & Herder.

GIBELLINI, R. (1979) Frontiers of Theology in Latin America. Maryknoll: Orbis.

GUTIERREZ, G. (1974) "Liberation, theology, and proclamation," pp. 57-77 in C. Geffré and G. Gutierrez (eds.) The Mystical and Political Dimensions of the Christian Faith. New York: Herder & Herder.

――――― (1973) A Theology of Liberation History, Politics, and Salvation. Maryknoll: Orbis.

HEBBLETHWAITE, P. (1975) The Runaway Church Post-Conciliar Growth or Decline. New York: Seabury.

HINKELAMMERT, F. J. (1977) Las Armas Ideologicas de la Muerte. El Discernimiento de los Fetiches: Capitalism y Cristianismo. San José, Costa Rica: EDUCA.

HOUTART, F. and A. ROUSSEAU (1971) The Church and Revolution. Maryknoll: Orbis.

HOUTART, F. and E. PIN (1965) The Church and the Latin American Revolution. New York: Sheed & Ward.

ILLICH, I. (1970) Celebration of Awareness. Garden City, NY: Doubleday.

LANDSBERGER, H. [ed.] (1970) The Church and Social Change in Latin America. Notre Dame: University of Notre Dame Press.

LENERO OTERO, L. (1970) Población, Iglesia, y Cultura: Sistemas en Conflicto. Mexico, D.F.: IMES-FERES.

LEVINE, D. H. (forthcoming) Religion and Politics in Latin America: The Catholic Church in Venezuela and Columbia. Princeton: Princeton University Press.

—— (1979) "Church elites in Venezuela and Colombia: context, background, and beliefs." Latin American Research Review 14 (Spring): 51-79.

—— (1978) "Authority in Church and society: Latin American Models." Comparative Studies in Society and History 20 (October): 517-544.

—— (1976) "Democracy and the Church in Venezuela." Journal of Interamerican Studies & World Affairs, 18 (February): 3-22.

—— (1974) "Religion and politics: recent works." Journal of Interamerican Studies & World Affairs 16 (November): 497-507.

—— and A. WILDE (1977) "The Catholic Church, 'Politics', and violence: the Colombian case" Review of Politics 39 (April): 220-239.

LEWY, G. (1974) Religion and Revolution. New York: Oxford University Press.

LOPEZ TRUJILLO, A. (1977) "A los 10 Años de la Populorum Progressio." Tierra Nueva 22 (July): 81-96.

—— (1975) "El Compromiso Político del Sacerdote." Tierra Nueva 14 (July): 17-53.

—— (1973) "Analisis Marxista y Liberación Cristiana." Tierra Nueva 4 (January): 5-43.

—— (1972) "La liberación y las liberaciones." Tierra Nueva 1 (April): 5-26.

MACAULEY, M. (1972) "Ideological change and internal cleavages in the Peruvian Church: change, status quo, and the priest. The case of ONIS." Ph.D. dissertation, University of Notre Dame.

MECHAM, J. L. (1966) Church and State in Latin America. Chapel Hill: University of North Carolina Press.

MIGUEZ BONINO, J. (1976) Christians and Marxists: The Mutual Challenge to Revolution. Grand Rapids, MI: Eerdmans.

MIRANDA, J. (1974) Marx and the Bible: A Critique of the Philosophy of Repression. Maryknoll: Orbis.

MUTCHLER, D. (1971) The Church as a Political Factor in Latin America. New York: Praeger.

O'DEA, T. (1968) The Catholic Crisis. Boston: Beacon.

OLIVEROS MAQUEO, R. (1977) Liberación y Teologia: Genesis y Crecimiento de una Reflexión (1966-1977). Lima: Centro de estudios y publicaciones.

PAZ, N. (1975) My Life for My Friends: The Guerrilla Journal of Nestor Paz, Christian. Maryknoll: Orbis.

READ, W., V. MONTERROSO, and H. JOHNSON (1969) Latin American Church Growth. Grand Rapids, MI: Eerdmans.

REUTHER, R. (1970) The Radical Kingdom: The Western Experience of Messianic Hope. New York: Paulist Press.

RIDING, A. (1979) "Latin Church in siege." The New York Times Magazine (May 6).

SANDERS, T. G. (1974) "The new Latin American Catholicism," pp. 282-302 in D. E. Smith (ed.) Religion and Political Modernization. New Haven, CT: Yale University Press.

—— (1968) Catholic Innovation in a Changing Latin America. Cuernavaca: CIDOC.

—— (1968) "The Chilean Episcopate: an institution in transition." West Coast South America Series 15, 3. New York: American Universities Field Staff.

—— and B. H. SMITH (1976) "The Chilean Catholic Church during the Allende and Pinochet regimes." West Coast South America Series 23, 1. New York: American Universities Field Staff.

SCHWAN, H. and A. UGALDE (1974) "Orientations of the Bishops of Colombia toward social development, 1930-1970." Journal of Church and State 16 (Autumn): 473-492.

SEGUNDO, J. L. (1976) The Liberation of Theology. Maryknoll: Orbis.
————— (1974) Our Idea of God, Volume Three: A Theology for Artisans of a New Humanity. Maryknoll: Orbis.
————— (1974) The Sacraments Today, Volume Four: A Theology for Artisans of a New Humanity. Maryknoll: Orbis.
————— (1974) Evolution and Guilt, Volume Five: A Theology for Artisans of a New Humanity. Maryknoll: Orbis.
————— (1973) The Community Called Church, Volume One: A Theology for Artisans of a New Humanity. Maryknoll: Orbis.
————— (1973) Grace and the Human Condition, Volume Two: A Theology for Artisans of a New Humanity. Maryknoll: Orbis.
SMITH, B. H. (forthcoming) The Catholic Church and Political Change in Chile, 1920-1978. Princeton. Princeton University Press.
————— (1975) "Religion and social change: classical theories and new formulations in the context of recent developments in Latin America." Latin American Research Review 10 (Summer): 3-34.
————— and T. H. SANKS (1977) "Liberation ecclesiology: praxis, theory, praxis." Theological Studies 38 (March): 3-38.
SMITH, D. E. (1970) Religion and Political Development. Boston: Little, Brown.
TORRES, C. (1972) Father Camilo Torres, Revolutionary Writings. New York: Harper & Row.
————— (1970) Cristianismo y Revolución. Mexico: Ediciones Era.
TORRES, S. and V. FABELLA [eds.] (1978) The Emergent Gospel Theology from the Underside of History. Maryknoll: Orbis.
TORRES, S. and J. EAGLESON [eds.] (1976) Theology in the Americas. Maryknoll: Orbis.
TURNER, F. (1971) Catholicism and Political Development in Latin America. Chapel Hill: University of North Carolina Press.
VALLIER, I. (1972) "Radical priests and the revolution," pp. 15-26 in D. Chalmers (ed.) Changing Latin America: New Interpretations of Its Politics and Society. New York: Academy of Political Science.
————— (1970) Catholicism, Social Control, and Modernization in Latin America. Englewood Cliffs, NJ: Prentice-Hall.
————— (1967) "Religious elites: differentiations and developments in Roman Catholicism," pp. 190-232 in S. Lipset and A. Solari (eds.) Elites in Latin America. New York: Oxford University Press.
VEKEMANS, R. (1976) "La Iglesia en el Proceso de Liberación." Tierra Nueva 19 (September): 80-86.
————— (1974) "Iglesia y cambio social en America Latina." Tierra Nueva 11 (October): 36-64.
————— (1972) Caesar and God: The Priesthood and Politics. Maryknoll: Orbis.
————— (1972) ¿Agonía o Resurgimiento? Reflexiones Teologicas Acerca de la "Contestación" en la Iglesia. Barcelona: Editorial Herder.
WARREN, K. (1978) The Symbolism of Subordination: Indian Identity in a Guatemalan Town. Austin: University of Texas Press.
WAYLAND-SMITH, G. (1978) The Catholic Church and Social Change: A Research Note and Some Preliminary Findings on the Archdiocese of Yucatán. Erie, PA: Institute of Latin American Studies of Northwestern Pennsylvania.

WILLEMS, E. (1967) Followers of the New Faith. Nashville: Vanderbilt University Press.
WILSON, B. R. (1973) Magic and the Millenium: A Sociological Study of Religious Movements of Protest Among Tribal and Third World Peoples. London: Heinemann.

Documents and Journals

ABBOTT, W. (1966) The Documents of Vatican II. New York: America Press.
CELAM (1979) III Conferencia General del Episcopado Latinoamericano Puebla La Evangelización en el Presente y en el Futuro de America Latina. Bogotá: Author.
——— (1978) III Conferencia General del Episcopado Latinoamericano Puebla Documento de Trabajo. Bogotá: Author.
——— (1978) La Evangelización en el presente y en el futuro de America Latina Puebla Mexico, 1978 Preparación Documento de Consulta a las Conferencias Episcopales. Bogotá: Author.
——— (1970) The Church in the Present Day Transformation of Latin America in the Light of the Council. Bogotá: Author.
EAGLESON, J. and P. SHARPER [eds.] (1979) Puebla and Beyond. Maryknoll: Orbis (official texts of Puebla documents plus commentaries).
EAGLESON, J. [ed.] (1975) Christians and Socialism Documentation of the Christians for Socialism Movement in Latin America. Maryknoll: Orbis.
EPICA (1978) Reflections and Problems of a Church Being Born Among the People. Washington, DC: Ecumenical Program for Interamerican Communication and Action.
GHEERBRANT, A. [ed.] (1974) The Rebel Church in Latin America. Baltimore: Penguin.
GREMILLION, J. [ed.] (1976) The Gospel of Peace and Justice: Catholic Social Teaching Since Pope John XXIII. Maryknoll: Orbis.
Peruvian Bishops' Commission for Social Action (1970) Between Honesty and Hope: Documents from and About the Church in Latin America. Maryknoll: Orbis.
Pro Mundi Vita (1976) "Basic Communities in the Church." Pro Mundi Vita Bulletin 62, September.
RONCAGLIOLO, R. and F. REYES MATTA (1978) Iglesia, Prensa, y Militares: El Caso Riobamba y los Obispos Latinoamericanos. Mexico: Instituto Latinoamericano de Estudios Transnacionales.
ROSSI, J. [ed.] (1969) Iglesia Latinoamericana ¿Protesta o Profecía?. Avellaneda, Argentina: Ediciones Búsqueda.
U.S. Catholic Conference (n.d.) Social Activist Priests: Chile. LADOC Keyhole Series 5, Division for Latin America, Washington, D.C.
——— (n.d.) Social Activist Priests: Colombia, Argentina. LADOC Keyhole Series 6. Division for Latin America, Washington, D.C.
——— (1978) Latin American Bishops Discuss Human Rights. LADOC Keyhole Series 15-16. Latin America Documentation, Washington, D.C.
——— (1976) Basic Christian Communities. LADOC Keyhole Series 14, Latin America Documentation, Washington D.C.
——— (1975) Women in Latin America. LADOC Keyhole Series 10, Latin America Documentation, Washington, D.C.

LADOC (1970-present) Monthly Publication of Latin American Church Documents in English. Prepared by the U.S. Catholic Conference.

Tierra Nueva (1972-present). Published regularly in Bogotá, with focus on issues related to the Church in Latin America.

NOTES ON THE CONTRIBUTORS

PHILLIP BERRYMAN has worked in a barrio in Panama City. He is currently Central American representative for the American Friends Service Committee, and has published articles on liberation theology and on political events in Latin America.

THOMAS C. BRUNEAU is Associate Professor of Political Science and Director of the Centre for Developing Area Studies at McGill University. He is the author of *The Political Transformation of the Brazilian Catholic Church* and of a forthcoming study of religiosity and politicization in Brazil.

ROBERTO CALVO is the pen name of a sociologist, university professor, and specialist in Latin American affairs. He is the author of several scientific monographs and articles.

MARGARET CRAHAN is currently Associate Professor of History at Herbert H. Lehman College, City University of New York, and John Courtney Murray Fellow at the Woodstock Theological Center. She has published on colonial administrative history, on religion and politics, and on twentieth-century Cuba. Presently she is writing a study of U.S. missionaries in Cuba and has recently completed editing, with Franklin W. Knight, *Africa and the Caribbean: Legacies of a Link*, to be published by Johns Hopkins Press. Research for the present essay took her to Cuba in 1973-1974, 1976, and 1977.

MICHAEL DODSON is Associate Professor and Chairman of the Department of Political Science at Texas Christian University. He is now working on the contributions of Christian thought to the development of democratic and constitutional ideas. His current interests are in Latin American politics, with a focus on the relationship of religion and social change. He has published in *Latin American Perspectives* and the *Journal of Latin American Studies.*

KATHERINE ANNE GILFEATHER, Maryknoll sister and sociologist, is a member of staff of the Bellarmino Center for Research and Social Action in Santiago, Chile. She has lived and worked in Chile for almost 25 years.

T. S. MONTGOMERY holds a Ph.D. in political science from New York University. During 1978-1979 she was a Visiting Scholar at the Union Theological Seminary in New York City. Research for this chapter was begun in Mexico in 1978 under the auspices of a City University of New York Research Foundation Faculty Grant to study the Church as an agent of social change in Latin America.

DANIEL H. LEVINE is Associate Professor of Political Science at the University of Michigan. He is the author of *Conflict and Political Change in Venezuela,* and of *Religion and Politics in Latin America: The Catholic Church in Venezuela and Columbia. (forthcoming)*

RENATO POBLETE is a Jesuit priest and sociologist affiliated with the Centro Bellarmino in Chile. The author of numerous works on Latin American society, he is also Executive Secretary for the Social Action Department of CELAM.

BRIAN H. SMITH is Research Associate at the Woodstock Theological Center, Georgetown University. He has published articles on the contemporary Church in Latin America and has recently completed a study of the Chilean Catholic Church and political change from 1925 to 1978.

ALEXANDER W. WILDE is Research Associate in the Latin American Program at the Woodrow Wilson International Center for Scholars in Washington, D.C. He is the author of a forthcoming book on politics and the Church in Colombia, and has written on the Latin American Church for general as well as scholarly audiences.